Teachers investigate their work

Action rese essional development fo it provides a practical w teachers to uncover some of the complexities of the teaching process and thereby to improve the quality of their pupils' learning.

Teachers Investigate their Work introduces the methods and concepts of action research through examples drawn from studies carried out by teachers. The book is arranged as a handbook with numerous sub-headings for easy reference and 41 practical methods and strategies to put into action, some of them flagged as suitable 'starters'. Throughout the book, the authors draw on their international practical experience of action research, working in close collaboration with teachers.

Teachers Investigate their Work is an essential guide for teachers, senior staff and co-ordinators of teacher professional development who are interested in investigating their own practice in order to improve it.

Herbert Altrichter is Professor of Business Education and Personal Development at the University of Innsbruck. **Peter Posch** is Professor of Curriculum Studies at the University of Klagenfurt. **Bridget Somekh** is Lecturer at the Centre for Applied Research in Education at the University of East Anglia and Co-ordinator of the Classroom Action Research Network.

Routledge series in investigating schooling

Emerging as a Teacher
Robert V. Bullough Jnr., J. Gary Knowles and Nedra A. Crow

Studying Teachers' Lives
Edited by Ivor F. Goodson

Teachers' Voices for School Change
A. Gitlin, K. Bringhurst, M. Burns, V. Cooley, B. Myers, K. Price,
R. Russell, P. Tiess

Teachers investigate their work

An introduction to the methods of action research

Herbert Altrichter, Peter Posch and Bridget Somekh

 Routledge
Taylor & Francis Group

LONDON AND NEW YORK

First published in 1993
by Routledge
2 Park Square, Milton Park, Abingdon, Oxon OX14 4RN

Simultaneously published in the USA and Canada
by Routledge
270 Madison Ave, New York NY 10016

Reprinted 1995, 1996, 1998, 1999, 2003

Transferred to Digital Printing 2004

Routledge is an imprint of the Taylor & Francis Group

© 1993 Herbert Altrichter, Peter Posch and Bridget Somekh

Typeset in 10 on 12 point Palatino by LaserScript Limited, Mitcham, Surrey
Printed and bound in Great Britain by
TJI Digital, Padstow, Cornwall

British Library Cataloguing in Publication Data

A catalogue record for this book is available from the British Library.

Library of Congress Cataloging in Publication Data

Altrichter, Herbert.
  Teachers investigate their work: an introduction to the methods of action
  research/Herbert Altrichter, Peter Posch, and Bridget Somekh.
  p. cm. – (Investigating schooling series)
  Includes bibliographical references and index.
  ISBN 0-415-09356-2 – ISBN 0-415-09357-0 (pbk.)
  1. Action research in education. I. Posch, Peter, 1938-
II. Somekh, Bridget. III. Title. IV. Series.
LB1028.24.A46 1993
370'.78–dc20   92-45851
                                                                              CIP

ISBN 0-415-09356-2
ISBN 0-415-09357-0 (pbk)

Contents

Methods and strategies

Figures

Acknowledgements

A considerable portion of this book was first published in German: Herbert Altrichter and Peter Posch (1990) *Lehrer erforschen ihren Unterricht*, Bad Heilbrunn/OBB: Klinkhardt. Chapters 1 and 9 have been substantially rewritten and throughout the book many examples have been changed from Austrian schools to British schools. The authors and publisher thank Oxford University Press for permission to reproduce the poem *My Old Cat* by Hal Summers on page 94.

Chapter 1

Introduction:
What will you find in this book?

The reader is just opening this book, slowly reading the first lines and starting to build up an impression of what may be contained in the following pages. How can we give this reader an idea of the book's importance for us, and what has driven us to devote energy to writing it over a long period of time (which we could easily have spent on easier jobs)? These are the wistful thoughts of many authors sitting in front of a manuscript which has achieved a certain status – or at least size – through being written, rewritten and finally polished. It is now to be given the last finishing touch: the introduction, which will introduce some key ideas and whet the reader's appetite to read on.

We have decided to tackle the introduction in a particular way. We want to recount some personal experiences that convinced us of the importance of this approach to research: specifically, research conducted by teachers in order to develop their own practice. Maybe, like us at the time, you will wish to learn more. If so, it is the purpose of this book to satisfy your curiosity.

In the early 1980s we were all three strongly influenced by the work of the Teacher–Pupil Interaction and the Quality of Learning Project (TIQL) in which teacher-researchers investigated what it means to understand a subject or a topic and how pupils' understanding can best be developed through classroom work (see Ebbutt and Elliott 1985). They investigated this question in their own classrooms, shared their experiences, tried to identify and explain common and contradictory findings, developed and experimented with new teaching strategies, and wrote case studies of their work. Although we had different connections with the project – as a project teacher (Bridget Somekh) and as interested observers (Herbert Altrichter and Peter Posch) – for all three of us it was an important landmark in our professional development. The teachers' research provided us with new insights into the process of teaching and learning: it paid much closer attention to details and practicalities than other kinds of research; and it probed the differences between stated aims and actual practice in a way that integrated teaching with research. To show you what we mean, there follow some examples.

The first example focuses on Carol Jones (1986), teacher of a mixed-age class of 7 to 9 year olds. She investigated her pupils' understanding of their school work. She kept notes of what the children did each day, the tasks she set, and anything special about the way in which they carried them out. She soon realised that the children understood the tasks in terms of their previous expectations, and had developed an idea of the sort of work she, as their teacher, would be expecting. Her research then focused on, 'the extent to which children operate according to criteria of their own, rather than according to the intention of the teacher'. She enlisted the help of an outsider who visited her classroom and interviewed the children. By transcribing and analysing these interviews, she found that the children's criteria for judging the value and importance of their work were, indeed, different from hers. For example, when they were asked to observe puss moth caterpillars, and make drawings and notes of what they saw, they made a clear distinction between writing and drawing, 'holding writing to be a more "worthwhile", or higher status task, than drawing'. In addition, because they were used to being given cards to help with spelling, one child had not understood that the work card gave instructions about how to observe the caterpillars, and instead said, 'it just tells you the spellings'. These data suggested that the children were not engaging in the kind of observation and interpretation that Carol had intended, but instead had turned the work into 'a routine writing task'. She also found that the children did not value working in collaboration as she did, but instead used the criterion of 'liking to have your own ideas' and rejected sharing ideas, calling this 'copying'.

Another teacher, Nell Marshall (1986), carried out research into the way in which 13–16 year old pupils in her school prepared for written examinations. She chose this topic because she had begun to suspect that examinations were an important incentive for the pupils' learning, but also had an impact upon the nature of their learning. She began by administering a questionnaire during the week before the examinations. She found that over two-thirds of the pupils had not begun 'revising' until the last two or three weeks. In part this seemed to be because they had not completed the course and were still being given 'new' work and no specified homework time for revision, but in part it seemed to be because they saw revision as a rote learning exercise and felt it was best left to the last minute – as one pupil put it: 'it is impossible to revise three weeks in advance and be expected to remember it'. On the basis of these preliminary data, Nell began to focus her research on the quality of pupils' understanding when they were 'revising'. She found that most pupils had very little idea about how to revise effectively. They tended to 'read through the notes' without any planned structure. If they had found difficulty understanding the work when it was originally taught, many pupils were unable to understand it any better at revision time, when they had nowhere to turn for help. In some cases this made revising, 'so daunting that many do not begin'.

In addition to developing their own teaching, some of the TIQL teachers worked in schools where a number of other colleagues were also engaging in research. Thus, it was possible to discuss what they were doing and to begin to develop new shared understandings. This kind of work can be a valuable professional development experience for many individual teachers, but in some schools, with the support of a member of senior management, teachers undertaking research can also make a significant impact on the development of the curriculum as a whole. For example, in a large secondary school, Brian Wakeman, one of the deputy heads, co-ordinated a group of teachers who all carried out research into aspects of their pupils' understanding and in this way built up a picture of the kind of changes which it might be helpful for the staff as a whole to implement (Wakeman *et al.* 1985).

Looking back after a number of years, it is easy to explain the deep impression the TIQL Project made on us from our different points of view.

For Herbert and Peter, as visitors from Austria with experience in educational research and teacher education, it was important and unusual that these teachers not only saw themselves as 'users of knowledge produced by professional researchers' but also did research themselves – producing knowledge about their professional problems and substantially improving their practice. In their developmental work, the teachers sometimes made use of external support (for example, in-service training courses and external consultancy from the project team) but, on the whole, retained the initiative in the work themselves.

For Bridget, it was an opportunity to stand back after ten years' experience as a teacher and analyse the complexities of teacher–pupil interactions and their impact on children's learning. For the first time she described, and theorised about, her professional practice and found that others were interested. She realised that as a teacher she had insights into classroom processes which were of value in developing educational knowledge.

It was impressive that the TIQL teachers were reflecting on their experiences and self-confidently discussing them in public, thus successfully overcoming the notorious disregard for teachers' knowledge and the tradition of teacher 'privatism'.

These practitioners understood themselves as 'teacher-researchers' and they are not alone. Through the Classroom Action Research Network,[1] and contacts with a large number of schools, in-service institutions and universities, we have met enough individuals and teams working in a comparable way to understand why some people talk about an action research 'movement'. This book is rooted in the British tradition of action research and in recent developments in Austria that build on this tradition. (For an account of the German tradition of action research, and suggested reasons why recent work in Austria links more closely with the English tradition, see Altrichter and Gstettner 1992.) This book attempts to collect and present in concise form the various ideas, methods and strategies for research that have been developed by British and Austrian action-researchers in recent years – in particular, in the fields of in-service training of teachers (Posch 1986b; Somekh 1991a), initial teacher education (Altrichter 1988), staff development in higher education (Altrichter 1986b), curriculum innovation (Somekh 1991b; Somekh and Davies 1991) and environmental education (Posch 1990; OECD 1991).

In this book we draw exclusively upon examples of action research carried out by teachers because this is the field of our personal experience. However, a number of individuals and groups from other professional fields are also actively involved. For example, there is a tradition of action research in industrial and social settings, police training and nursing. We are therefore confident that many of the methodological and strategic considerations presented in this book are relevant for research carried out by practitioners from fields other than schools.

THE PURPOSES OF ACTION RESEARCH

The shortest and most straightforward definition of action research is given by John Elliott (1991: 69), whose work has been influential in this 'movement': action research is 'the study of a social situation with a view to improving the quality of action within it'. This simple definition directs attention to one of the most essential motives for doing action research. It lies in the will to improve the quality of teaching and learning as well as the conditions under which teachers and students work in schools. Action research is intended to support teachers, and groups of teachers, in coping with the challenges and problems of practice and carrying through innovations in a reflective way. Experience with action research,

---

1 CARN is an international network linking all those interested in action research through regular conferences and publications. For information, write to The CARN co-ordinator, Bridget Somekh, Centre for Applied Research in Education, University of East Anglia, Norwich NR4 7TJ, UK. At the time of going to press, discussions are in train to extend the teacher research network in the US (details will be available through CARN).

so far, has shown that teachers are able to do this successfully and can achieve remarkable results when given opportunities and support.

These teachers have not only carried out development work for their schools but have also broadened their knowledge and their professional competency. They have passed on this knowledge to colleagues, students, parents and, in written form, also to the wider public. They have shown that teachers can make an important contribution to the knowledge base of their profession. And they have demonstrated that they can engage successfully with professional problems without recourse to external direction. They did not restrict their work to adopting a set of practical routines, but acted as professionals precisely in developing new theories about their practice, including a critique of its educational and social contexts.

These teachers are 'normal' teachers, who reflect on their practice to strengthen and develop its positive features. They are not prepared to accept blindly the problems they face from day to day, but instead they reflect upon them and search for solutions and improvements. They are committed to building on their strengths and to overcoming their weaknesses. They wish to experiment with new ideas and strategies, rather than letting their practice petrify.

Through our book we aim to encourage teachers to investigate those aspects of their practice that they want to improve and develop in their classroom work, and to investigate also their relationships with students, colleagues, parents, external groups and managers/administrators. We want to provide a range of methods which can help them to gain a more comprehensive view of their situation, to develop action strategies to bring about improvement, and to evaluate the outcomes of their efforts. We want to encourage teachers to share their experiences and, by this means, to give a degree of publicity to the professional thinking that informs practice. The book contains some simple suggestions to make this possible. We believe that sharing ideas with colleagues, and keeping the public well informed about professional concerns and endeavours, may contribute to raising the self-confidence of teachers as a professional group and, thereby, to improving both performance and professional satisfaction.

Finally, the book is intended to stimulate teachers as a group to professionalise their concept of work, in particular by taking control of the development of schools, and of the identification and resolution of crucial professional problems. The current period of rapid social change (while challenging stability) offers exciting possibilities for the educational system to build a more dynamic culture of teaching and learning in schools. This implies a need, however, for teachers and heads individually and collaboratively to reflect upon their practice, analyse the functioning of their institution and its strengths and weaknesses, develop perspectives for the future, translate them into actions and structures, and monitor their impact on real situations.

FEATURES THAT DISTINGUISH ACTION RESEARCH

What are the characteristic features of this kind of research?

1 Action research is carried out by people directly concerned with the social situation that is being researched. In the case of the social situation of a classroom, this means in the first place teachers who take professional responsibility for what goes on there. While action research will usually be initiated by teachers, sustainable improvements in classroom situations will rarely be possible if other concerned persons are not won over to its purposes. According to the problem being investigated, these might include students, parents, LEA advisers, governors or representatives of the local community. Thus, the long-term aspiration of action research is always a collaborative one. In cases where action research begins as a more private and isolated concern, external consultants are often involved (for example, from higher education institutions). However, in these cases, the role of the outsider is to provide support and not to take responsibility and control over the direction and duration of the project.

2 Action research starts from practical questions arising from everyday educational work (and not from those which might be 'in fashion' in some learned discipline). It aims to develop both the practical situation and the knowledge about the practice of the participants.

3 Action research must be compatible with the educational values of the school and with the work conditions of teachers (see Chapter 5, pp.74f. for a more extensive discussion of this point). However, it also contributes to the further development of these values and to the improvement of working conditions in the educational system.

4 Action research offers a repertoire of simple methods and strategies for researching and developing practice, which are characterised by a sensible ratio of costs to results. Methods are tailored to what is achievable without overly disrupting practice.

5 However, specific methods or techniques are not what distinguish action research. Instead, it is characterised by a continuing effort to closely interlink, relate and confront action and reflection, to reflect upon one's conscious and unconscious doings in order to develop one's actions, and to act reflectively in order to develop one's knowledge. Both sides will gain thereby: reflection opens up new options for action and is examined by being realised in action.

6 Each action research project – whatever its scale – has a character of its own, and so we hesitate to provide an elaborate step-by-step model

which might limit the variety of different paths to be pursued. Nevertheless, some typical broad stages can be found in any action research process (see Figure 1).

```
┌────────────────────────────────────────────────────────┐
│                                                        │
│   A    Finding a starting point                        │
│                                                        │
└────────────────────────────────────────────────────────┘

┌────────────────────────────────────────────────────────┐
│                                                        │◄───┐
│   B    Clarifying the situation                        │    │
│                                                        │    │
└────────────────────────────────────────────────────────┘    │
                                                               │
┌────────────────────────────────────────────────────────┐    │
│                                                        │    │
│   C    Developing action strategies and putting them into practice │───┘
│                                                        │
└────────────────────────────────────────────────────────┘

┌────────────────────────────────────────────────────────┐
│                                                        │
│   D    Making teachers' knowledge public               │
│                                                        │
└────────────────────────────────────────────────────────┘
```

Figure 1 Stages of action research processes

STAGES OF ACTION RESEARCH

Action research begins with the finding of a starting point for development within one's practice and having the will to invest energy in pursuing it (see stage A in Figure 1). Then, through conversations, interviews and other methods of collecting evidence, and through analysis of the information gained, the situation is clarified (stage B). As a consequence of this clarification, action strategies are developed and put into practice (stage C).

As a rule, it is not expected that new action strategies will solve a problem immediately. Therefore, their effects and side-effects need to be monitored in order to learn from experience and further improve the action strategies. Thus, the research process enters a new stage of clarification of the situation which will lead to the development and putting into practice of further action strategies (see the circular process between Stages B and C in Figure 1).

Teacher-researchers finish their projects by making their professional knowledge accessible to others, for example by oral presentations to the group in in-service courses or by the production of written case studies. By these means, their insights are opened up for critical discussion (see stage D in Figure 1).

STRUCTURE AND USE OF THIS BOOK

The intention of writing this book was to introduce readers to action research. We present this research approach on two levels:

1 On the one hand, we have collected a variety of practical suggestions that have been developed by action researchers for investigating, and introducing innovation into, classrooms and schools. To do this we use many examples drawn from studies by practitioners. The book does not contain a full case study written by a teacher, but if you are interested in reading this kind of outcome of action research, you will find examples in Elliott and Ebbutt (1986), Hustler *et al.* (1986), or PALM (1990/1).

2 On the other hand, we also want to explain the theoretical background of action research which underpins the methodological suggestions and gives them meaning. We do this from time to time as part of the process of clarifying the various research strategies, as well as in Chapter 9, which offers a view behind the scenes. However, for a more systematic and detailed analysis of the theoretical concepts of action research, readers who are interested might turn to Elliott (1991), Winter (1989), or Carr and Kemmis (1986).

This book is primarily written for teachers and head teachers who want to engage in classroom innovation and school development. It also addresses people working in institutions concerned with the in-service education of teachers, who attempt to promote classroom innovation and school development by their courses and consultancy work. The most rewarding use of this book will be for those who are prepared to engage in an action research process alongside their reading. They can make immediate use of the suggestions and proposed strategies while, at the same time, critically examining and further developing them. In this way, the book is intended as a source of practical support for those engaging in research, without in any sense being prescriptive.

The structure of the book has been planned as follows: After this introduction in Chapter 1, the main part of the book follows in Chapters 2–8. This offers suggestions, examples and exercises to facilitate the way into action research. The arrangement of chapters follows the sequence of phases of an action research process outlined above (see Figure 2).

Chapter 2 provides suggestions on how to start, and focuses on the use of a diary which, in our experience, is a good way into an action research process. Chapter 3 explains some ways of identifying issues for investigation through action research. Chapter 4 introduces suggestions to help to clarify the issue, once a productive starting point has been chosen. The two following chapters present a wealth of methods which can be used to clarify the issues further: the understanding of the situation

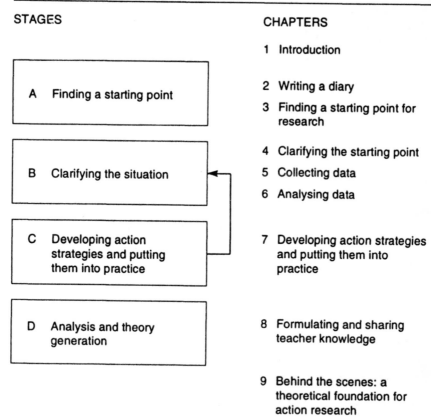

STAGES	CHAPTERS
	1 Introduction
A Finding a starting point	2 Writing a diary 3 Finding a starting point for research
B Clarifying the situation	4 Clarifying the starting point 5 Collecting data 6 Analysing data
C Developing action strategies and putting them into practice	7 Developing action strategies and putting them into practice
D Analysis and theory generation	8 Formulating and sharing teacher knowledge
	9 Behind the scenes: a theoretical foundation for action research

Figure 2 Structure of the book

may be deepened by the collection of additional data (Chapter 5) and by the analysis of these data (Chapter 6). Chapter 7 discusses how action can be planned in response to clarification and analysis of the situation. Chapter 8 argues that it is a primary concern of action research to promote the sharing of knowledge and experiences of the teacher-researchers who engage in it, in order to develop classrooms and schools. Chapter 9 finally poses some of the theoretical arguments which have been important in the evolution of a practitioner-driven approach to research. In this way the structure of the book mirrors our belief that theory arises from practice, and is valuable primarily as a means of reflecting upon practice, subjecting it to critical appraisal and stimulating its further development.

We have attempted to make the descriptions of methods and strategies sufficiently concise and self-explanatory to be used as handouts in courses and projects. For easy reference, they are displayed in boxes, numbered M1–M41, and are listed on p. vii.

Chapter 2

The research diary:
companion to the research process

The research diary is one of the most important research methods and is very commonly used by teachers doing research. It also makes a good way into research. We want to suggest that you regard it as a companion to the whole research process, rather than simply as a means of collecting data or of recording analysis. Our suggestions for writing and using research diaries are based on personal experience as well as on our experience of working with others who keep similar diaries. At the end of the chapter we provide some exercises which should make it easier to start a diary.

WHY DIARIES ARE USEFUL FOR RESEARCH

We believe that the following characteristics make diaries particularly useful.

1 Writing a diary builds on an everyday skill of many teachers. In this sense, writing a diary is simpler and more familiar than other research methods, such as interviewing. In addition, diary writing is easier to organise than most other research methods. It is always possible to make a diary entry if paper and time are available, whereas to carry out an interview you need a partner who is willing to answer some questions, which may or may not have been prepared in advance.

2 A diary can also contain data collected by other research methods. For example, it is a good place to record notes from unstructured classroom observations or to record the description of the context and conditions of an interview just carried out. Zamorski (1987) used a diary in this way in a study of the sensitive issues surrounding the 'invisibility' of an Asian boy with poor self-esteem in a predominantly white rural English classroom, as did Prymak (1989) in her account of working as a teacher mentor with a colleague.

3 Short memos or ideas about the research issues can be recorded frequently, if necessary daily, in a diary. Because of this continuity, a

diary can develop a quality which makes it more valuable than other research methods: it becomes a companion of your own personal development through research; it links investigative and innovative activities; it documents the development of perceptions and insights across the different stages of the research process. In this way, it makes visible both the successful and (apparently) unsuccessful routes of learning and discovery so that they can be revisited and subjected to analysis.

4 Research diaries draw on a tradition. 'From the very beginning of European culture, texts have been written with the aim of increasing self-understanding, becoming aware of self-delusions, and articulating and reducing pain' (Werder 1986: 4).[2] Diaries in which the self and its surrounding conditions were investigated have ranged from Saint Augustine's *Confessions* to Handke's *Weight of the World*. Such texts published with philosophical or literary intentions are rare islands in a sea of anonymous diaries by writers whose reflections on themselves and on their everyday lives remained unpublished. At first sight, such diaries appear as self-reflective or introspective texts or as 'literature', but only rarely as research. This does not mean, however, that introspective diaries cannot lead to important insights or that they are necessarily self-indulgent: Elias Canetti (1981) regards conversation with oneself in a diary as a dialogue with a 'cruel partner'. One of the main points of this chapter is to show how action research can learn from these literary and self-reflective diaries. Holly (1989: xi) presents a similar point of view in describing, 'how keeping a journal can facilitate observation, documentation, and reflection on current and past experiences, including one's life history and the social, historical, and educational conditions that usher in the present'.

5 Diaries in which researchers recall the fruits of their daily observation in the research field hold a central position in many disciplines: for example, in zoological field research, DeVore's (1970) diary containing his observations on the behaviour of apes; or in ethnographical research, Malinowski's (1982) use of a diary to record his detailed observations. Qualitative sociological research makes intensive use of research diaries in building up thorough insights into the functioning of institutions through participant observation and through conversations with key informants (for example, the famous studies of the Chicago School: Whyte 1955; Cressey 1932). Whether they are called diaries, log books, field notes or lab books, these records are important companions to the research process.

---

2 Quotations from German sources have been translated by the authors.

To sum up, on the one hand diaries can contain *data* which are obtained by participatory observation and by conversations and interviews in the field, sometimes enriched by explanatory comments and photographs; on the other hand, they can contain written *reflections* on research methods and on your own role as researcher (perhaps similiar to the conversation of the ethnographer with him- or herself in a foreign culture). In addition, ideas and insights are noted, which can lead to the development of the theoretical constructs which, in turn, can be used to interpret the data. Keeping such a diary ensures that data collection is not artificially separated from reflection and analysis. Glaser and Strauss (1967) have emphasised that analysis accompanying such data collection should be actively used for the further development of research: preliminary results of an analysis show which data are still necessary to fill in the gaps in a theoretical framework and to evaluate intermediate results through further investigation.

Inspired by sociological field research, qualitative educational research has developed using similar methods. Action research therefore has a rich tradition of educational research diary-writing to draw upon. An early and today still highly readable example of this qualitative school research is Philip Jackson's (1968) *Life in Classrooms*. In this book the author tried to 'move up close to the phenomena of the teacher's world' (ibid.: 159). As a participant observer, he had to use a mixture of methods and perspectives since 'classroom life . . . is too complex an affair to be viewed or talked about from any single perspective.' (ibid.: vii). Interestingly, the author argued in the concluding sections of his book that 'in addition to participant observers it might be wise to foster the growth of observant participators in our schools.' (ibid.: 175). A step in this direction is taken by another landmark book of qualitative educational research, *The Complexities of an Urban Classroom* (Smith and Geoffrey 1968), which was written collaboratively by a participant observer and an observant teacher. In Britain, Armstrong's (1980) well-known book, *Closely Observed Children*, used a diary as the basis for detailed description and analysis of a primary classroom, over a year, in a book, 'about intellectual growth and intellectual achievement; about understanding the understanding of children'. Research diaries containing observations, ideas, plans, etc. have been increasingly used during the past years by those interested in action research. For example, Fuller (1990) and Williams (1990), investigating ways of enabling children to become more autonomous learners, made a diary the basis of their data collection.

SOME SUGGESTIONS FOR WRITING RESEARCH DIARIES

In this section we present some ideas and suggestions for writing research diaries. These are based on our own experiences, some of which have been positive and others frustrating, but all of which have deepened our understanding of diary-writing as an instrument for action research.

1 Writing a diary is a personal matter. In due time, every diary writer develops a style and idiosyncrasies which are an important part of making diary-writing valuable as a research method. For this reason, the recommendations below are offered only as suggestions to be adopted or rejected after due consideration.

2 Diaries should be written regularly, at times that fit in with the kind of research question being investigated. For example, they might be written after each lesson in which a particular teaching strategy has been implemented, or after each meeting with a 'difficult class'. Some people find it is useful to reserve specific periods of time for this activity by writing them into their timetable, to prevent diary-writing from being drowned in the whirlpool of daily necessities. These 'diary times' can then be complemented and expanded by irregular recording of relevant scenes, experiences and ideas.

3 People who are not used to diary-writing often experience some barriers to establishing the habit. Sometimes it is necessary to go through a difficult period before diary-writing becomes personally satisfying. When deciding whether the exercise is worth the time and effort, it is worth considering its side-effects. For example, regular diary-writing generally increases the quality and speed of one's own written articulation. We found diary-writing easier if we collaborated with a research partner to whom we could read extracts from our text and talk about them. This, in turn, had spin-offs in terms of increased understanding, which enriched the whole research process (see point 14 below).

4 The above suggestion, however, does not take away from the private nature of a diary. The decision to make parts of it available to other people should always remain with the author. It is particularly important to stress this again and again in projects, courses and workshops, in order to prevent the recurring subtle, social pressure to go public, on the principle: 'I have said something, now it's your turn'.

5 The privacy of the diary makes it easier to disregard considerations of style, punctuation, etc. while writing it. Self-censorship often disturbs the free flow of thoughts; this can come later if the results of your research activities are to be published.

6 For our diary entries, we use thick notebooks (of more than 40 pages). We have found that these become more and more 'elegant' the more we enjoy diary-writing. They are highly personal artefacts. For us, the use of notebooks facilitates reflection on our own process of learning. Other researchers write their notes on loose leaves which they can file later under different categories. A primary school teacher, who focused on introducing innovative methods of teaching reading,

wrote her diary notes on pink sheets which she put between the white sheets of her lesson notes. In this way she obtained a good record of the relationship between plans and the experience of putting them into action. Find a form to suit yourself.

7 Leave a wide margin on each page (or buy a booklet with a ruled margin). This can be used to record changes, additions, or references to other parts of the diary or to other data, at a later date. Such a margin is especially helpful for the analysis of diary data (which we will return to in Chapter 6). Notes (from single words to sentences) can be entered here, indicating the meaning or interpretation of a diary sequence within the framework of your research aim. This process is illustrated in the diary extract that follows in the next section (see p. 16). For example, as preliminary analysis (and in preparation for a written report), the margin can be used for coding and for identifying examples to illustrate particular concepts (see M26). Generally, we use a pencil to record provisional codes or analytical commentaries on diary entries, because pencil contrasts with the ink of the normal text and catches the eye more easily. Apart from that, we find that a pencil's erasability is useful in keeping coding and analysis provisional.

8 Each entry should be accompanied by the following information:

- The date of the event (and date of the written record if it took place on a different day)
- Contextual information, such as time, location, participants, focus of study, and anything else (such as unusual weather or a fire drill) which seems important for the research.

If this is ordered in the same manner for all entries, it is likely to be easier to 'read oneself back in' to the data at a later date.

9 It is easier to orientate yourself quickly and to analyse the data if paragraphs, headings, subheadings and underlinings are used to structure the text. Some people like to number paragraphs and headings to make cross-referencing easier.

10 It is helpful to make a running list of contents on the first or last pages of the booklet to make it easy to go back to particular pieces of data.

11 As well as the factual account, all information that helps to develop a more profound understanding of a situation and to reconstruct it later can be included in the diary: 'Observations, feelings, reactions, interpretations, reflections, ideas, and explanations' (Kemmis and McTaggart 1982: 40). You can also stick items into the diary which seem relevant to the research process: ideas jotted down on a piece of paper, photographs, or copies of documents and of pupils' work, etc. If research activities and the data obtained by them (for example, a

transcript of a lesson or an interview) cannot be written directly into the diary because of lack of space or for other reasons, it is a good idea to make a cross-reference to them in the diary.

12 In this way, a research diary contains various kinds of records. This wide-ranging approach corresponds to our everyday form of tackling problems, but it is open to some pitfalls. For example, in general we expect research to go back and forth between description and interpretation. Because of their practical forward-looking interests, teachers doing research are often inclined to neglect detailed description. It is useful, therefore, with each diary entry to make clear whether it refers to description or to interpretation. One way of coping with the fuzzy borderline between description and interpretation is to use the 'ladder of inference' described in M12.

13 From time to time it is helpful to do a provisional analysis of the diary entries (see Chapter 6). This shows whether descriptions and interpretations are in a useful balance; which of the initial research questions can be answered from existing data; and which data are still necessary. Through this provisional analysis, it is often possible to reformulate the initial questions more clearly, to modify them, or to pose them in a new way. It also helps you to plan the next steps in research and action in a more rational way. Last but not least, it reduces the danger of being flooded by 'data overload' towards the end of an investigation.

14 It is often very helpful in extending the research process to read sequences from your diary to a colleague or research partner. The conversation about experiences can provide deeper insights into the fine texture of educational situations. Such conversations are especially fruitful if the researcher is rigorous in relating speculations to interpretations and descriptions recorded in the diary or other data – in other words, relating ideas to specific events and reflections rather than allowing the conversation to become diffuse and generalised.

15 Research diaries can also contain a great number of vivid descriptions of situations (sometimes called 'thick descriptions'). These provide a quarry of examples for in-depth discussion. They also provide vicarious experiences which are particularly useful as a means of helping other teachers to reflect on practice. We find that materials of this kind are very useful for in-service courses, as they enable teachers to learn more independently and still remain close to experience.

AN EXAMPLE TAKEN FROM A RESEARCH DIARY

It seems important at this stage to give an example from the kind of diary we have been describing. You may find it useful to cross-check the example with the suggestions outlined in the previous section – which ones have been adopted and which not, and why that might be. The example is not intended as a model of 'the right kind of diary', rather it demonstrates the personal and highly focused nature of diary-writing.

The extracts are taken from a diary kept by an English teacher in a secondary school who is introducing computer use in the teaching of writing. The diary was kept over a six-month period as a means of carrying out action research on the introduction of computers in English teaching. In the extract chosen, a visitor (who is hoping soon to train as a teacher) has been asked to make observation notes (some of which are quoted and commented upon in the diary). This is seen by the teacher as a good opportunity as none of her colleagues has been able to come into her lessons. There are eight groups of children writing stories colla-boratively: four groups have access to writing on one computer at the same time (using four alternative keyboard extensions called Quinkeys and software which divides the screen into four separate work areas) while four other groups are doing their writing on paper. As well as this story-writing, the groups are engaged in drawing maps, in making lists of necessary equipment, and other 'backup' activities. In practice, two pupils from each group are usually at the computer at the same time – one sitting at the Quinkey keyboard and the other standing behind and sharing in the process of composition; while the other two group members are working on the maps, equipment lists, etc.

On the left side of the diary, the teacher left a margin. After a first review (a provisional analysis) of the diary, she entered several catchwords and references which are explained in more detail later in this chapter, for example: MNs (methodological notes) and TNs (theoretical notes).

Extract from a secondary English teacher's diary.

Nov. 14: Notes and reflections after talking to Susan, a visitor who observed my lesson

Susan focused more than I expected on the high level of noise. Her expectations seemed a bit unrealistic – told myself that she must have gone to a very formal school, but I felt quite vulnerable although probably didn't show it. Is it worthwhile getting observation notes in this way

MN1
observation notes

from anyone who happens to come along? It would be nice to have a regular critical friend/partner, but as I don't, this seems the best compromise.

Susan said:

1 Group 1 seemed to be very reliant on Amnon – that at the beginning Billy was 'crawling all over the table . . . very disruptive'.

TN1 individual differences

☐?

Comment: Is this because Amnon is known as the computer expert? Billy misses some classes for help with reading. Can I give him extra time to make up?

2 Group 2 were working well – Robert and Tim mainly at the table and Quentin and Keith at the computer – periods of lapses, but on the whole working OK. Quentin and Keith were the motivating powers. Quentin wanted to ask Keith's advice. Keith felt he was in control. They had Carlo on their left – and his keeper, Edward. Carlo seemed OK for about half an hour and then got very aggressive.

3 Group 5, Carlo and Edward were talking about their work. Edward was making suggestions and Carlo writing them down – later having an argument about a sentence at the end. Carlo very reluctant to change it. Edward, in rather a nice way, pointing out they could improve it. Edward feeding spellings – sometimes Carlo getting it right himself. The time span was too great for him.

TN2 Collaboration – benefits and drawbacks

Comment: really worried about Carlo. This didn't sound too bad, but he's a disruptive force. Edward's role seems very helpful, but what does he gain from it? Looking forward to Carlo and Edward working on the computer – maybe a pity I have left them out of the first four groups.

4 Group 6, girls at the front, in their stride – wrote a lot, didn't put down their pens – a marked difference from the beginning of the lesson when Susan felt they weren't very interested. Really keen.

MN2 reliability of data?
TN3 effects of computer on my role

Comment: sounds good, but what were they writing? I neglected this group – problem when the computer is in the room is that I am concentrating my attention mainly on the children working on it. How can I guard against this? Maybe I can't until I am more used to it.

5 Didn't watch Group 3 because every time she had a look they were doing very nicely – they didn't move much – whereas other children moving round the room quite a bit. I suggested that movement was to do with groups using the computer – no need for Group 3 to move as they were all sitting near the computer anyway. Susan agreed – they could communicate with whoever was at the keyboard – yes.

TN4 movement related to computer use

Comment: using a computer for collaborative writing necessitates movement between those writing on the computer and other members of the group back at the table. Movement, discussion and noise are therefore consequences of collaboration. To reduce movement and noise it may be best to place the computer in the middle of the room and seat the groups at surrounding tables – would need an extension cable for the computer *December 10* ☑ – I think I'll try this.

6 Group 4 were working well too – though there was a difference of opinion. Fiona got really stroppy. She stormed back from the computer and said, 'That Caroline, she's been there for such a long time – she's messing about with commas that we can deal with when we get the printout. She should be getting the story into the computer.' She was very irritated – she lost her stride after that – near the end of the lesson so it didn't matter too much, but she was extremely put out.

TN5 collaboration – raising tension

Comment: Really worrying that there seem to be these rows. Billy's behaviour is part of the same pattern, I think (there's actually been some racial taunting between him and the others in his group – an Indian, a Chinese and an Israeli). Working with the computer seems to be raising greater tensions. Why? Is it the way I've set up the work or is it because they are all so highly motivated? If it's the latter, then maybe they are *all* trying much harder than usual to keep some ownership of the task – so they are *really* trying to collaborate instead of portioning out bits of the task with differential levels of ownership and responsibility. Co-operating in collaborative group work requires specific social skills – should these be taught? Heavens, I find collaborative writing difficult myself! Maybe tensions within groups are inevitable, but deliberate teaching might make them more aware of the need to work together and of tendencies of group members to *November 21* ☑ dominate or to withdraw. How can I do that? Perhaps it would be good to hold a class discussion about the way they are managing their group work.

I need to understand better the way the groups are organising themselves – I'll try to fix up 5-minute interviews with every child in Groups 1–4 at the end of this first two weeks of writing on the computer.

Diaries can be useful for recording unplanned events and conversations which may be important in understanding a situation. For example, a university teacher who was carrying out action research into his teaching of an in-service course recorded the following conversation with a teacher on the course.

Extract from a university teacher's diary

Accidental meeting with Martin, 7 May 1985 Cosmopolitan Café

Martin tells me that he has given his case study to his pupils. He had not said a word to them about his research. At first they were 'shocked' about having been observed by him behind their backs. Afterwards, however, they were 'enthusiastic'. (Why? I can't remember.) As a result, the passive pupils became noticeably more active and co-operative during the lessons for a while (this is the theme of his case study) but after a month their activity level is fading again.

TN6
compatibility of
research
TN7 ethical =
practical

Comment: How can research become an integral part of teaching?
I could interpret this as an example of the fact that disregarding ethical considerations (carrying out covert research on pupils) can lead to practical problems. More than that, it also reduces the possibility of practical outcomes (see 'noticeably more active and co-operative').

DIFFERENT KINDS OF DIARY ENTRIES

Drawing on the example in the previous section, we would now like to build on the general suggestions for diary-writing set out earlier (points 1–15 on pp. 13–15), by providing suggestions for different kinds of diary entry, such as *memos* and *in-depth reflections*.

Memos

Memos, such as the examples quoted above, are the most frequent kind of entries in research diaries. Memos are produced when trying to recall and write down experiences that occurred in a specific period of time (for example, during a lesson). The memo often provides the only possibility of collecting data on your own practical activities without too much investment of time and energy. Sometimes, teachers doing research fear that after teaching for an hour they will not be able to remember in enough detail, or with sufficient accuracy, to write useful memos. In our experience this is not too much of a problem, particularly if you follow procedures that help to improve the quality of your recall. For example, Bogdan and Biklen (1982) suggest:

- The earlier a memo is written after an event the better.
- Before writing down from memory, you should not talk about the events with anybody as this may modify your recollection in an uncontrolled way.
- The chronology of events is generally the best way to arrange written records. However, as it is important to make entries as 'complete' as possible, anything you remember later can be added to the end.
- Sometimes it is possible to jot down catchwords and phrases during the course of the activity you want to record: for example, when pupils are working independently, with partners, or in groups; when you are listening to pupils' reporting back to the class; or when you are not teaching but observing a colleague or a student teacher. Later on, when writing the diary, these catchwords and phrases jotted down during the lesson prove very useful as *aides-mémoire*.
- Memory improves if you can find time and leisure for recall. If lessons are to be documented in a memo, it is useful to reserve some time afterwards that can be kept free of interruptions. The time necessary is often underestimated. In general, it is easy to spend a full hour writing down observations and reflections on a lesson. You should plan to spend at least half an hour, particularly as you may find you get delayed in starting.
- Memos are written primarily to describe and document events after they have taken place. At the same time, these descriptions are usually frequently interspersed with interpretations. Within memos it is important to make a clear distinction between *descriptive sequences* and *interpretative sequences*.

Descriptive sequences

Descriptive sequences contain accounts of activities; descriptions of events; reconstructions of dialogues, gestures, intonation and facial expressions; portraits of individuals – their appearance, their style of talking and acting; description of a place, facilities, etc. Your own behaviour as the participant action-researcher is, of course, an important part of these descriptions.

In any descriptive passage, the detail is more important than the summary, the particular is more important than the general, and the account of an activity is more important than its evaluation. Whenever possible, speakers should be quoted exactly (marked by inverted commas) or in a paraphrase (some people indicate this in a diary by single as opposed to double inverted commas). Words and phrases that are typical of a person, group or institution should be recorded as exactly as possible.

Interpretative sequences

Memos should contain not only descriptive sequences but also interpretative sequences: interpretations, feelings, speculations, ideas, hunches, explanations of events, reflections on your own assumptions and prejudices, development of theories, etc. Interpretations will occur not only when writing down experiences but also at a later date, when diary entries such as observation notes are reflected upon.

In daily life, any writing will usually be reread afterwards: thereby mistakes are discovered and many things become clearer. On rereading, it is much easier to judge which things are important, and which are not so important, than it is at the time of writing. You may discover new relationships between ideas, and often some new insights which should be followed up. Open questions emerge and it is easy to see what still needs to be done. Often it is possible to see how the thoughts expressed in the text could be usefully restructured.

Similiar things happen if a memo is reread or analysed. Analysis in research is a kind of rereading of existing data with the intention of reorganising, interpreting and evaluating them with respect to your research interest (see Chapter 6). Although it might be tempting to see this as a reason to write the diary using a word processor, an important part of analysis is seeing the original text with emendations. Therefore, if a word processor is used, revisions are best written on to the printout by hand, so that the process and progress of your learning is recorded. Earlier in this chapter, we recommended rereading your own diary entries from time to time and doing a provisional analysis. We would like to discuss some important features of such an analysis under the following three headings:

- *Theoretical notes* These put forward explanations relevant to the research question or issue being investigated. Relationships between events are identified and noted for further research.
- *Methodological notes* These record your reflections on the research methods used. Ideas for alternative methods and procedures are noted to help develop your own competence as a researcher.
- *Planning notes* When writing or rereading diary entries, new ideas emerge for the improvement of practical action. For example, you

remember things that you wanted to try out some time ago, or flashes of thoughts from the last lesson which have simply been forgotten.

a) Suggestions for *Theoretical Notes* (TNs)

Research is more than collecting data. It is also about making connections between data and understanding them. When you reflect on data, various ideas come to mind. Theoretical notes in a research diary try to capture these ideas and save them from oblivion. Sometimes they are an integral part of memos, as in our example from the English teacher's diary: the researcher marked the theoretical notes with the symbol TN and with a key term or label, which indicates the main theoretical idea for subsequent analysis. Ideas for theoretical notes also emerge while analysing data, while thinking or talking about your research plans, or as sudden flashes of understanding on the way to work, etc.

There are a number of purposes for which writing theoretical notes is useful. These include:

- clarifying a concept or an idea (see 'TN2' in the example from the English teacher's diary on p. 11);
- making connections between various accounts and other bits of information (see 'TN5' in the example);
- identifying surprising or puzzling situations worth following up later (see 'TN5' in the example from the English teacher's diary (p. 18) and 'TN6' in the Cosmopolitan Café example (p. 19));
- connecting your own experience to the concepts of an existing theory (see 'TN1' and 'TN7' in the examples);
- formulating a new hypothesis (see 'TN4' in the example);
- realising hitherto unconscious assumptions and formulating their theoretical implications (see 'TN3' in the example).

For practical purposes in making theoretical notes, we suggest you might:

1 Date each theoretical note and give it a label or key term indicating its content (see the examples in the English teacher's diary extract, p. 16).
2 Clarify the relationship between a theoretical note and the data it relates to. If necessary, the relationship may be qualified (for example, by writing 'uncertain', 'examine'); and cross-references to other theoretical notes and data may be added.
3 Priority should be given to writing theoretical notes over other research activities (such as observation, documentation, formal analysis, etc.). Whenever you have an idea for a theoretical note, other activities should be interrupted to record it in as uncensored a form as possible – even if it sounds rather fantastic or daring. These ideas may turn out to be keys to understanding the issue being researched.

b) Suggestions for *Methodological Notes* (MNs)

Methodological notes record the researcher's self-observation when doing research. As with theoretical notes, sometimes they can be an integral part of the diary entry and sometimes may be added later as part of preliminary analysis. For example, they might address these questions:

- What were the circumstances in which I used particular research methods (see 'MN1' in the example from the English teacher's diary)?
- What role did I play in the situation under investigation?
- What comments arise from my experience of specific research methods and strategies (see MN2 in the example)?
- What decisions did I take about the future course of my research, and why?
- What conflicts and ethical dilemmas did I encounter and how did I deal with them?

Doing research on the research process itself might seem too complicated and self-indulgent – or even a first step to madness (as a result of infinite self-mirroring). In moderation, however, there are good reasons for making methodological notes:

1 *Pragmatic reasons* Even unintentionally, discussions about a research project and written memos cover both research experiences and reflections upon them (see 'MN1' in the example). It would be a pity to lose these ideas instead of using them to improve your research skills.
2 *Reasons derived from the theory of research* Methods of action research do not claim to produce unambiguous results regardless of the context. Therefore, it is important to reflect on research methods while doing research, and to build up a stock of methodological knowledge which action researchers can draw upon in future investigations.
3 *Educational reasons* Documenting and reflecting on methodology while carrying out action research may be of particular importance for people working in both pre-service and in-service teacher education, such as lecturers and tutors, advisory teachers and consultants. Such records provide them with knowledge and practical examples, which are useful when working with other teachers and students who want to reflect on and improve their teaching.

c) Suggestions for writing *planning notes*

When writing memos and reflecting on data, we often 'automatically' generate ideas about, for example:

- alternative courses of practical action;
- how to do it next time;
- what was forgotten this time and must definitely be made up for in the next lesson;

- what has to be thought through more carefully;
- what additional information seems essential and needs to be gathered.

Jotting down planning notes in the research diary makes more systematic use of the stream of ideas which, as we all know, goes as quickly as it comes. The diary, thus, becomes a 'memory bank'. It reminds us of plans that we want to put into practice at some later date. At the same time, it facilitates the shaping of a plan by recording the context of the original aspirations and thus helping us to keep its purposes clear in the course of development.

Some practical suggestions are:

1 As in everyday life, you should not make too many plans. Plans which are not put into practice often induce feelings of frustration and failure. On the other hand, you should not suppress evolving ideas too early just because they seem 'unrealistic' (see also Chapter 7).
2 We mark 'plans' by the symbol □ in the margin. A date may be added to the □ if planned activities have to take place at a specific time. It can be ticked when a plan has been carried out (see the example in the English teacher's diary, p. 18). In this way, the □ provides quick reference to which plans have still to be put into practice, and it makes it easy to check on the ratio of completed to uncompleted plans.

d) *Ethical issues* relating to keeping a diary

Like all data, a diary constitutes a record. Diaries are usually private to the researcher and contain intimate accounts and reflections, akin to private thoughts. Data of this kind cannot be made public (i.e. used in written or spoken accounts of the research) without clearance from the participants.

When diaries contain interview data or observation notes made by someone else (as in the extract from the English teacher's diary), it is usually best to clear the data immediately with the person concerned. This can be done by photocopying the relevant passage, or even by handing over the diary open at the relevant passage (though this has the disadvantage that the person is not able to reflect on it except in your presence – since the diary as a whole is confidential). When diaries are kept in loose-leaf folders, this problem may be more easily overcome.

A helpful ethical rule is never to allow research to become covert. Diary notes of conversations in the staffroom or in casual situations, such as on the way to the swimming pool, are often the most useful of all; providing colleagues and children know that the research is being undertaken, they do not all need to be cleared. To ensure research is not covert, first tell colleagues and children that you are undertaking it and, second, clear any data before you refer to it or quote it publicly. These issues are further dealt with in Chapter 5 on data collection and Chapter 8 on reporting.

In-depth reflections

When you read a diary, you will not only find entries that describe clearly defined situations in great detail, in the way that we have been describing for memos above; you will also come across sections of text which are the result of in-depth reflections, not focusing on a specific situation but drawing on a range of experiences over an extended period of time.

In-depth reflection and other creative-introspective methods may be important for action researchers to gain access to and reach an understanding of our 'tacit knowledge' (which is the result of our experience but, normally, not directly and consciously at our disposal; see further discussion of this in Chapter 9, p. 203ff.). The process of writing often helps to unlock this kind of in-depth reflection. It may be particularly helpful for exploring recurring situations that are problematic in some way, for example:

- situations that occur frequently but which you do not fully understand;
- situations that end up in problems and conflict again and again;
- situations that you repeatedly feel uneasy about although no obvious conflicts surface: for example, dilemmas, ethical uncertainties, difficult decisions, 'vicious circles' in which you feel trapped into behaving in a particular way, etc. (see further discussion of this in Chapter 6, p. 146ff.),
- problems with pupils which do not seem to have any logical reason.

In-depth reflections in diary entries can contain descriptive and interpretative sections, just like memos. Since these reflections usually refer to longer timespans, the descriptive element is sometimes neglected, but you should be aware of the danger of losing touch with reality if you allow your thoughts to range too widely. Therefore, it is important to link passages of in-depth reflection, with their roots in events and actions.

To illustrate in-depth reflection we include here an extract from a particularly ingenious example. A teacher of a special class, for pupils with learning difficulties, used this method to explore her experiences during breaks between lessons (Bergk 1987: 2). We suggest that while reading it, you keep a check on how this example relates to the points we have made above. In addition, at the end of this chapter you will find some further practical suggestions for your own in-depth reflection.

Diary extract illustrating in-depth reflection

. . . in particular, my twelve students' ways of modifying closeness and distance – both among themselves and towards me – during the breaks inspired me with some ideas of how to do them (and myself) more justice in the classroom. Using [one child] as an example to illustrate what I mean, I will describe not persons and situations but what was impressed on me through my observations: perceptions and subjective images influenced as much by my will to see and learn as by what was really taking place.

I have used the following procedures to reproduce these images as authentically as possible:

1 When thinking of one particular child, I display my *associations* in the form of 'clusters'. These serve as a starting point for the next steps (although not every idea is followed up).
2 I sketch some impressions of a *typical situation* during breaks in which this particular child was involved.
3 In doing so, I reconstruct *my part* in these situations as far as I am conscious of it.
4 *Comparisons* with the situation during lessons then indicate starting points for improvement which emerge from the observations during breaks.
5 Finally, I roughly describe the *development* in the course of the school year and, in particular, my reflections on the observations in order to learn from them.

Winfried: a distorted mirror-image of myself

1 Associations

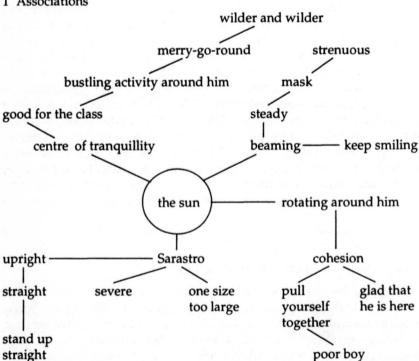

2 Behaviour in breaks

Winfried occupies the centre and smiles, beamingly. Smaller children cling to him, drag him around. He laughs: 'You will tear me to pieces!' Like a mother whose children are tugging at her. His peers struggle for his attention. He distributes it equally in the circle around him, provides judgements and laughs at somebody fooling about in front of him. What he says, counts. He is a source of tranquillity – amid all the to-do around him. Apparently, he has nothing to do with it. And yet, it arises from the competition for his attention.

3 My part

In addition to that, I put him on a throne. It is so comfortable. If I want to re-establish discipline I merely need to express my displeasure standing close to Winfried. He will immediately reprimand his classmates in an appropriate manner. The wrongdoer is embarrassed, the case is settled. 'I'm glad that he is here!' comes to my mind again and again. But it is also a strain on him. He is tugged to and fro, not only physically. Sometimes his smiles go in all directions and seem to be a mask. This is linked with a certain aloofness from the others. He is there for everybody, but would he also be able to cling to anybody who is there for him?

I notice the similarity with my own role. Do the right thing and be available for everybody! That is what I always have to do – and it is a strain.

4 Comparison with the situation during the lesson

Winfried rarely starts any disruption. But many children want to talk to him or show something to him during the lesson. This interferes with my plans when I want to talk or show the class something. It is a repetition of the situation during break – only this time I don't like it. Again, Winfried is under strain as a result. He cannot concentrate on his own writing, picture or maths problem. Therefore he is slow. His neighbours, competing for his favour during the breaks, surpass him during the lessons and even prevent him from catching up when he falls behind. Winfried really grieves about his learning difficulties. On two occasions I found him shedding silent tears.

5 Development in the course of the school year:

Winfried clearly demonstrated a typical teacher's problem to me by adopting parts of my role: being the authority who judges and evaluates is exhausting and produces unrest all around. His peers sucked assurance out of Winfried which – had their self-confidence been greater – they could have gained more efficiently from their own work, self-reflection and self-appraisal. I could support Winfried best by helping all the students to develop more independence in their learning . . . . If I stepped down from my judge's or master's throne and furnished all the children with spacious masters' seats, Winfried could also leave his throne and take a position among the others.

At first it was difficult. The children's minds were set on hierarchical structures and teacher-oriented instruction. Winfried sat in the of the first row, appropriate to his 'task' as 'co-teacher' and 'mother'. At first, my attempts at pair and group work failed because the younger ones, in particular, did not accept each other as 'partners' but sought feedback from Winfried. Only as the groups became more independent and I removed him physically from the centre stage, did Winfried calm down slowly . . . and so did I.

(Bergk 1987:2)

GETTING STARTED

Familiarity with action research can develop in various ways: you can read about practical methods and theories, or you can study what other teachers actually did in order to reflect on and improve their practice. The wealth of examples in this book, as well as collections of action research case studies (for example, Elliott and Ebbutt 1986; PALM 1990/1), may enable you to do this. However, the royal road to action research is to explore it by doing it yourself. Thus, the most meaningful way of reading this book would certainly be to exploit it as a reservoir of tools and ideas, and test its usefulness while reflecting on and developing some issue from your own practice.

Among the descriptions of *Methods and Strategies*, some act as *Starters* (M1, M2, M4, M6 and M9). These are particularly useful as ways of getting started on research. They arose from our experience in in-service courses, university workshop conferences and innovative projects. We realised that teachers, overwhelmed by the complex aim of researching, developing and documenting an aspect of their own classroom, often did not easily find a worthwhile starting point for their work. Often they needed specific suggestions of ways to get started. Because of their preoccupation with their grand aim, they were unable to begin their research and find small-scale progress rewarding. However, our experience also tells us that action research does not lend itself to precise pre-planning. On the contrary, every action researcher must find his or her own path according to the specific research question and the particular working situation. There are specific methods and approaches from which to choose, but these need to be selected and tailored by the individual. Too many tasks, too precisely defined, hamper the development of an individual research path and press action researchers on to a generalised course of research which often does not fit the particularities of the situation. Our suggestions try to balance these extremes.

The Starters are intended as 'suggestions': they attempt to formulate some ideas and recommendations about how to approach the complex task of researching your own practice. You should use these recommendations to get you started. As soon as you have found your own way, which will be bound to deviate from the suggestions, you may confidently abandon those ideas that are no longer helpful. Just as Lawrence Stenhouse (1975) claimed for all curricula, recommendations are, at best, intelligent proposals which have to be tested and developed by reflective practice.

We assume that different and original methodological patterns will develop as your research progresses. Thus, you will find some Starters proposing small research activities at the beginning of the book.

M1: RESEARCH DIARY (1ST STARTER)

Use a research diary during the whole course of your research. We recommend a notebook with large margins, at least 40 pages in length. You can record here all your observations and experiences during your research. Every idea or reflection that comes to your mind in connection with research activities – be it positive, ambivalent, negative or simply yet unclear – could be important for your subsequent work and provide a starting point for development and improvement. Jotting down all experiences, striking events and ideas in your diary means preventing valuable information from being lost in the further course of project work.

A diary develops into a valuable research method only if it is used regularly. If you notice that there has been no single entry in your diary for a full working week check:

- whether you can reserve a period of time during the week which is relatively free of disruption;
- whether diaries really fit your research plans.

However, remember that difficulties are bound to occur with something new (and, according to our experience, they are particularly frequent for novices in diary-writing). Don't be discouraged too quickly. Don't forget to make use of the suggestions for diary entries contained in the whole of this chapter.

Our second Starter results from our experience that it is often frustrating to wait too long to see the first research activitity materialise. We recommend embarking on a small research activity even before you have begun to formulate a starting point for your research, to warm up your research muscles, as it were. This helps you start the diary and gives you the feeling that something has been achieved. You have begun your research even though it is not yet focused on a specific issue for reflection and improvement. As a bonus, such small exercises – even if they seem to be selected at random – sometimes point the way to an issue that becomes the starting point for further research.

M2   EXERCISE TO WARM UP YOUR RESEARCH MUSCLES (2ND STARTER)

1 If you have not yet definitely decided on your research issue ('This is what I am going to study and nothing else!'), we suggest that you carry out one of the following five exercises:

- Select one of next week's lessons. Write a memo about the course of events in your diary. Include all thoughts that come to your mind during reflecting and writing.
- Tape one of next week's lessons. Select 5 minutes of the tape for transcription (see M21 and M22 if you need help for this activity). Leave a margin for comments beside your transcription. Then note in the margin all associations that come to your mind when reading specific sections of the transcript (it is not the 'correct' interpretation of the event which is at stake – allow every association).
- Prepare a 'cluster' of all associations that come to your mind when you think of the phrase 'Being a teacher' (for a description of the 'clustering procedure', see M3 which follows).
- Every day next week cut out from a newspaper some words, phrases or pictures which you intuitively like or which you spontaneously feel concern your profession. At the end of the week prepare a collage from the cuttings. Feel free to complement the collage by handwritten words and your own drawings.
- Imagine an extraterrestrial visitor entering your classroom (or your personal workroom) from the top left corner without being noticed by anybody in the room. Describe in a short piece of writing what he or she would see and think.

2 To close this warm-up exercise, we suggest:

- If you are working on your own: read what you produced again after a few days. Add a sentence that concisely expresses the impression you have when rereading your own writing.

- If you are collaborating in a group, what you produced might be read to the group. However, sharing should always be voluntary. Alternatively, you could report back on the exercise in a few sentences. Other group members might ask questions but should refrain from making comments and putting forward interpretations. (For further ideas on this, see also the analytic discourse method in M7.)

M3 IN-DEPTH REFLECTION

In-depth reflection is an opportunity to think through your own actions and make your 'tacit knowledge' accessible to yourself (see Chapter 9, p. 203). The following procedure, known as 'clustering' (based on the work of Rico 1984), provides one way of starting this process.

1 The procedure of 'clustering' begins with a *core word* (or *phrase*) which is written in the of a blank sheet. For example, a possible core phrase at the beginning of an in-service course might be 'Being a teacher'. Other stimuli may be used in a similar way: a situation which has been of concern to you for some time, a picture, some writing, a dream, a piece of music, etc.

2 Note down all associations to this core word as *word-chains*. These start from the central concept and display your associations in various (linear or branched) graphic arrangements. A core word plus word-chains is called a 'cluster'. The following example, taken from Bergk's example on p. 26, indicates what clusters might look like:

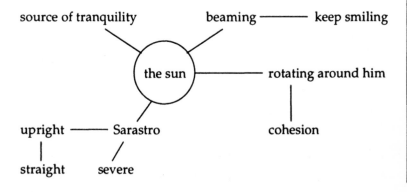

3 When you have noted down the most important associations, the next step is to switch over mentally from the flow of associative images to the recognition and systematisation of patterns. Let the cluster inspire you and use its elements as the basis for some writing. This writing might either be rather prosaic or emphasise creative elements – just as you feel (see points 2–5 in Bergk's example, p. 27).

4 Later on, you might do some editing of the text. You might also read it to others (colleagues, family) and discuss it.

Chapter 3

Finding a starting point for your own research

The first step in a research process is to find and formulate a feasible starting point. What issue in my practical experience is worth studying over a period of time? Does it fit my capabilities and do I have the resources? Is there a fair chance I can get somewhere if I research this issue? These are questions a teacher needs to ask when beginning research. In this chapter we provide some suggestions and ideas to help you to answer them.

WHAT DO WE MEAN BY 'STARTING POINTS FOR RESEARCH'?

What does a feasible starting point for action research look like? How do teachers reach such starting points? Let's have a look at the beginning of a case study written by one of the authors, Bridget Somekh (1983a).

Extract from a teacher's case study

I have chosen to study my teaching of English for the CSE examination because it is the area in which I have least experience. The pupils are assessed 50 per cent on a file of course work undertaken over two years, and 50 per cent on written and oral examinations which they take at the end of the course when they are 16. The group consists of 25 pupils: 11 boys and 14 girls. It is parallel with a second group taught by a colleague, but I am experiencing more problems. Is this due to my inexperience and inappropriate teaching methods? From preliminary enquiries it seems that there may be other reasons. My class includes ten pupils who give trouble frequently with bad behaviour or truancy, three of whom come from families visited by a social worker. The Upper School Tutor could only think of four other pupils in the year group whom she would place in the same category.

When I began teaching the class, I was influenced by my recent experience of teaching for CSE. In particular I felt that I had let some pupils down by failing to ensure that they had sufficient work in their files at the end of the course to achieve a good CSE grade. So, I adopted a definite policy, recorded in my research diary. There would be:

1 Very clear expectations of homework and I would always follow up those who failed to do it by giving them 'extra help' after school.
2 Regular inspection of files at intervals during the course to ensure that they were kept in good order and no work was lost.
3 Emphasis on the 'O' Level English Language examination as a possible extra option for anyone who achieved the necessary standard.

I believed that if I established a good habit of working while everyone was enthusiastic at the beginning of the course, there would be no problems later on. Unfortunately, by the end of the first term it was clear that this habit of working had not been achieved by all members of the group (about eight pupils regularly missed homework) and, by February, I had to admit that many students were not enthusiastic and that a discipline problem existed.

At this point I decided to analyse the evidence I had collected: the entries in my research diary, my lesson plans, and records of pupils' work. From these I developed hypotheses about the problems:

1 By following up every piece of missing homework, I had instituted a system of after-school 'help' which the pupils saw as 'detention' and which provided a clear pattern of negative reinforcement. Much time in lessons was wasted on discussions about missing work and compiling lists for individuals of what they had to do to 'catch up'. The atmosphere in the class was spoilt by each lesson beginning with recriminations about missing work. In addition, written work was often short and of a poor standard, because pupils felt the emphasis was on 'getting it done'.
2 I was probably not employing appropriate teaching methods for a mixed ability group. I might be demanding too much of the less able, both in quantity of work and in setting 'high-risk' learning tasks rather than routine tasks (see Doyle 1979). I might also be failing to stimulate the more able.
3 Those who worked regularly were getting very little of my time since so much was spent on following up the unreliable workers. In practice, I spent part of lesson time teaching the whole class as a group and part talking to individuals while the class continued with work I had set. Of the time spent talking to individuals, little was left for actual teaching or encouragement since it was taken up with 'following up' missing written work.

Starting points for action research have a developmental perspective. In an area that seems important to the researching teacher, she wants to improve a practical situation (for example, the motivation and self-image of pupils in the class) and to develop further her own competences.

Typically, starting points for research begin with experiences of discrepancies. They can be:

- discrepancies between plans and expectations on the one hand and actual practice on the other hand (for example, following up to check they had done their homework was intended to establish good working habits but the written work was often short and of a poor standard);
- discrepancies between the present situation and a general value orientation or an aim (for example, the teacher's aspiration that all the pupils should do well in the examination caused him to set challenging tasks but this led to their falling behind with homework and actually induced a sense of failure for many. This was the reverse of what the teacher intended);
- discrepancies between the way in which different people view one and the same situation (for example, extra 'help' after school was interpreted by pupils as 'detention').

In teachers' experience, such discrepancies give food for thought once they are consciously recognised. Action research begins with reflection upon such discrepancies and tries to save them from being forgotten in the maze of everyday work. They become the focus for further development of the teaching process and for the generation of knowledge about that process. Such discrepancies need not always be negative and problematic for the teacher. Action research can also focus on trying out good ideas for improvements or on the further development of one's own strengths. Marion Dadds (1985), for example, mentions three types of starting points for research without prioritising any one of them:

1 an *interest* – for example, trying out a promising idea, developing a strength, or coping with a routine obligation in a more considerate and economic way;
2 a *difficulty* – for example, wanting to improve a difficult situation, solve a problem, or compensate for a deficiency (in, say, the quality of teaching materials);
3 an *'unclear' situation* – teachers often begin their research with bigger or smaller 'puzzles': situations which are neither clearly positive nor negative, neither enjoyable nor burdensome, but which raise an issue they want to understand more fully. Often their work begins with unexpected experiences in the classroom which they are unable to interpret, but believe might serve as a useful starting point for further developing their teaching.

It is very likely that every starting point contains characteristics of all three types in various combinations. In our example, the teacher wants to improve the opportunities for all the pupils in the class to achieve a good qualification (point 1 above); but faces the problems caused by the poor motivation of a sizable minority (point 2); and is unclear about the appropriateness of the learning tasks she is setting (point 3).

What kind of issue is an appropriate focus for action research? Broadly, any professional situation about which teachers or others want to gain a deeper understanding, and which they want to change, is a potential starting point. Here are some examples:

- A teacher investigated parents' perceptions of the innovatory relationship she had established with them – seemingly successfully – over several years.
- A lecturer at the university researched her own teaching of a new course and developed modifications of teaching and learning strategies.
- A modern languages teacher researched the differing levels of participation of her pupils in classroom work with the aim of improving their ability to communicate in a foreign language. To her surprise and dismay, she found that self-initiated contributions from girls were much rarer than those from boys.
- A teacher who had taken over a difficult class in a vocational school studied relationships between pupil behaviour and his teaching style.
- A teacher experimented with a new form of assessment of her pupils' work and carried out action research to improve and refine it.

These examples are drawn from a wide range of different levels of the educational system. They also demonstrate that case studies can focus on curriculum or social issues, or even on issues beyond the confines of the school, such as the establishment of productive relationships with parents and the community.

All of the examples of research and development above have one characteristic in common: they refer to the scope of action of a single teacher. However, action research can also tackle issues of institutional development:

- In Chapter 1 we referred to a school which developed as a result of collaboration between a number of teachers each focusing upon their own classroom, co-ordinated by a deputy head (Wakeman 1986).
- A secondary teacher researched the processes of decision-making and the operation of power in the school where she worked, drawing colleagues into collaboration in the process, first by eliciting their views in interviews and later by inviting them to contribute to redrafting the written report (Somekh 1987).

- In a primary school, the team of teachers responsible for teaching the youngest children focused on the use of computers to support language development in their pupils, for the majority of whom English was a second language (Ourtilbour 1991). Their collaborative research resulted in changes in the schools policies and practice.
- A secondary teacher, responsible for co-ordinating colleagues' professional development in the use of computers as educational tools, carried out action research upon her own role in bringing about institutional development (Griffin 1990).

In general, institutional issues are more difficult to tackle than classroom issues. The practical, theoretical and political problems of action research tend to increase greatly when the focus moves beyond the classroom to institutional development. These can really only be tackled if the teacher-researcher is already experienced, or if the research is undertaken in the context of a project involving a number of teachers from the same school.

FINDING STARTING POINTS

Those who decide to engage in action research fall into one of the following three categories:

1 They have one very specific question in mind, often needing urgent attention.
2 They have many different questions in mind, none of which constitutes an obvious starting point.
3 They have no concrete ideas from which to begin an investigation.

The suggestions and ideas below are especially intended for categories 2 and 3. However, they can also be useful for category 1, especially if someone is beginning this kind of research for the first time and wants to check the feasibility of tackling a question by comparing it with alternative possibilities. We have suggested the following approaches to teachers we have worked with:

- formulate more than one possible starting point;
- consider all the potential starting points in relation to everyday practice, over a period of time;
- invest sufficient time to make the exploration of possible starting points as wide-ranging as possible.

The ease and speed with which a meaningful question is likely to be found is frequently miscalculated. Some time may be necessary before any single issue relating to an individual's professional practice emerges as the one of greatest importance and can be clearly formulated (see Hull et al. 1985: 88). The amount of time needed will differ from person to person and from context to context. On research-based courses at the University of Klagenfurt, which last for four months, the first two weeks are reserved for finding starting points. Teachers in the PALM project in East Anglia, which lasted for two years, in some cases took over a term to select their focus. Even within tightly scheduled projects (as is often the case in courses or INSET activities), there should be opportunities for individual variations in the amount of time spent on this important stage.

Your personal search for a starting point could be facilitated by the following exercises:

M4   INDIVIDUAL BRAINSTORMING: FINDING STARTING POINTS (3RD STARTER)

One step towards finding a starting point for your own research could be individual brainstorming:

1 Think of your own practical experience as a teacher:

- Is there any question which you have been wanting to investigate for a long time already?
- Which of your strengths would you like to develop?
- Are there any aspects of your work which you find puzzling and which have already been a focus for your reflection?
- Are there any situations which cause difficulties and which you would like to cope with more effectively?

Let your thoughts flow freely and write down your first spontaneous associations in the form of catchwords. You might like to use your diary to record these. Don't spend more than 6–8 minutes!

2 Once you have recorded your initial ideas, you may be able to stimulate further ideas for starting points by using these incomplete sentences (Kemmis and McTaggart 1982: 18):

- I would like to improve the . . .
- Some people (pupils/parents/colleagues) are unhappy about. . . . What can I do to change the situation?
- I am perplexed by . . .
- . . . is a source of irritation. What can I do about it?
- If I . . . I am completely worn out afterwards.
- Again and again I get angry about . . .
- I have an idea I would like to try out in my class.
- How can the experience of . . . (recounted by a colleague, or found in my reading etc.) be applied to . . . ?

---

3 If you have already started to keep a research diary, read through what you have written and see whether it generates additional ideas for starting points for research.

4 You can enrich the formulation of your potential starting points – and at the same time carry out a first provisional analysis of each situation – if you use these questions to identify the most important characteristics:

- What happens in this situation?
- Who does what?
- Which contextual factors are especially important in understanding this situation?

5 Try to condense the results of this brainstorming exercise by formulating a question for each possible starting point as precisely as possible.

M5 GIVING CONSIDERATION TO SEVERAL STARTING POINTS
(modified from *Developing Teaching* 1984: 12)

We recommend that you don't make an immediate decision on a starting point, but instead keep several starting points in mind to test their feasibility in the light of everyday experience. You can do this in the following way: take the list of possible starting points which you generated from the brainstorming exercise and select 3–5 situations which seem the most interesting to you. Write down on a card the specific issue that interests you in each of these situations. For example:

Card A I am interested in the amount of time which I devote to different pupils in my class, and whether these differences are justified or should be changed.

Card B I am interested in whether boys get more time to talk in my class than girls. If that is so, I would like to find out why and how I can change it.

At the end of each day over the next week, take your cards and shuffle them. Then take the first card and for about 3 minutes reflect on the day and think about any events which seem relevant to the issue recorded on it. Write down your ideas in key words, either on the cards or in your research diary. Afterwards spend a minute on each of the remaining cards to think briefly about the other issues, possibly making brief notes.

APPROACHES TO CHOOSING A STARTING POINT

How can I choose a starting point from the many interests and questions that come to mind in relation to my own practical experience? Are some starting points more or less suitable than others? How can I identify the more suitable ones?

M6   CHOOSING A STARTING POINT (4TH STARTER)

You can examine the available starting points in the following way.

1   Remember that action research has a developmental perspective. Check your starting point against these questions

- What is your focus for possible development?
- What might you want to try out?
- What might you want to change?

Doing action research does not mean that you have to change everything. But, nevertheless, it is important that when you embark on action research you have a genuine interest in development. Sometimes the main change is in your perception rather than in adopting specific new strategies.

2   Look at the starting points that you have formulated so far in the light of the following criteria, and write brief notes to record for each the pluses and minuses of adopting it as your main research focus.

(a) *Scope for action*   Does the situation come from my own field of experience? Can I really do something about this? Do I have any possibility of influencing this situation and/or taking action? Or am I too dependent on other people and institutional structures? Would an improvement in this situation depend primarily on changing the behaviour of other people?

(b) *Relevance*   How important is this situation to me and to my professional concerns? Is this issue worth the effort in an educational sense – is it concerned with important educational values? Is it likely that this situation will still interest me in a few weeks' time? Am I willing to invest a certain amount of energy in dealing with this situation? Am I interested in this situation in order to change and improve something?

(c) *Manageability*   Do I have the time to cope with this? Are there too many preparatory or related tasks to be coped with before I can start this project? Will it make too many demands of me? When you begin research, don't choose a question which is 'too big'. When in doubt, opt for the smaller or more limited project.

In general, it is better to build on successes, even if they are small, rather than having to reduce one's aims because they prove impossible to fulfil. There may be time later to extend your work.

(d) *Compatibility* How compatible would this question be with the rest of my activities if I select it as my research focus? Would it involve things that I have to do anyway? How well does this intended research fit in with my forward planning? Would it be possible to build some research activities directly into my teaching (for example, students interviewing each other, group discussions, etc.)? If you are in doubt, decide on a starting point that fits thematically with those things that you do anyway in your teaching.

3 Now select the starting point that comes closest to these criteria. The result will not always be clear-cut, but sometimes may involve weighing up the advantages and disadvantages of two or three options. However, we believe that this process in itself can be important in helping to identify the question that best fits your personal situation.

4 Next, try to document your starting point as vividly as possibly in your research diary. Formulating your starting point for research generally has two elements (see Kintner 1986: 8ff.):

- *A short description of the situation*: What happens in this situation? Who does what? Which contextual factors are especially important in understanding this situation?
- *Questions which indicate the developmental perspective*: What would I like to try out? What would I like to change/improve?

Although this may all sound rather complicated, it is in reality relatively simple. Here are some examples of starting points (adapted from Kemmis and McTaggart 1982):

- When they are doing group work, the students seem to waste a lot of time. How can I increase the amount of task-oriented time for pupils engaging in group work?
- My pupils are not satisfied with the methods I use to assess their work. How can I improve assessment methods with their help?
- Most parents want to help their children and the school by supervising homework. What can we do to make their help more productive?

The following example illustrates some of the difficulties which can occur if you choose a starting point without being clear about your reasons:

Case study – Astrid

Astrid is a participant on a course entitled 'Teachers Investigate their Teaching'. Halfway through the term she wants to give up her research because she doesn't see any meaningful possibilities for action and she is 'getting sick of' the situation. By looking at the formulation of her starting point, we can examine the practicability of her choice (see M6).

Astrid teaches a second form in an elementary school. She wants to focus on a girl who is already a cause of concern in only her second year at school. She formulates the question: How can I work with this girl in a way which is productive for us both? This statement seems to provide a promising starting point for action research:

- The situation comes from her field of experience as a teacher; the scope for action initially seems considerable because her interaction with the girl happens for the most part within the classroom (criterion a).
- An interest in change is expressed, specifically in looking for a more productive way of dealing with the situation; the problem seems to be important, because Astrid talks about the situation with a lot of emotional involvement (criterion b).
- The focus seems manageable because within the complexity of class-room events there is a concentration on the relationship with one student only (criterion c).
- In addition, the questions should be easily compatible with Astrid's normal work because the problem recurs daily anyway (criterion d).

In group sessions during the course, Astrid reports on her research, primarily drawing on memos about her interactions with this girl. Little by little it becomes clear that she was already strongly involved with her in the first form, but at that time had come to the conclusion that she was 'underdeveloped, physically and intellectually'. This educational diagnosis, which would usually have led to a transfer of the child to a special school, had been rejected by all those concerned – from the father of the girl, to the school's medical officer, to the principal of the school. Only the school psychologist shared the teacher's opinion. Astrid writes: 'I turned to some people from whom I expected help, unfortunately I was mistaken because nobody wanted to admit the problem.' She had given up hope of improving her relationship with the child a long time ago; the question which obviously worried her, her 'real issue', seemed to have been a different one: 'How can I persuade others in this school that my edu-cational diagnosis was the right one?' Her interest in change obviously had nothing to do with the internal situation in the class, but was concerned instead with her relationships with colleagues in the school.

Although her problem appeared at first to be very important (criterion b), she was unable to identify any real scope for action and, what was worse, the whole situation was interwoven with an unpleasant prior professional experience: this is a situation in which in reality she sees herself not as an actor in the field but as one who is acted upon (criterion a). The study Astrid presented at the end of the term fits this retrospective analysis: in a vivid, moving narrative it documents a journey of personal and professional suffering, but it contains almost no new understandings reached by Astrid through the process of her research. She formulates no new strategies to cope with the problematic situation, but instead says that she would 'do the same again in a similar situation', trying only to be more 'persistent' in pursuing her aims and pushing them through. She concludes her study with the words: 'All in all I believe that this case is unique and will not recur in the same way.'

This example illustrates two further important characteristics of action research:

1 Whatever is formulated as the starting point can only be a first view of a situation which is very likely to change in the course of the research process (see Brown *et al.* 1982: 3). Action research tries to avoid the dogma of fixed hypotheses which, in more traditional research approaches, cannot be modified once the research has begun (see Cronbach 1975). Instead, the researcher remains open to new ideas which may influence the course of the research while it is taking place. In this way, any development of the initial starting point becomes an important indicator of the learning of the teacher carrying out the research.
2 Whatever is formulated as a starting point often touches only the surface of a problem. A more detailed clarification of the problem situation and a further development of this 'first impression' develops a deeper understanding of all the related factors and opens up new possibilities for action.

Chapter 4

Clarifying the starting point of research

A starting point for action research is best thought of as the *first impression*. In this chapter we give some suggestions for going beyond this first impression to a deeper understanding of the practical theories which govern our actions.

FROM THE 'FIRST IMPRESSION'

A story from the experience of one of the authors serves as an introduction to our theme. The Nuffield Physics course for GCE 'A' Level (Nuffield 1971) set out to stimulate pupils aged 16 to 18 to learn through exploration, reflection and discussion. The main teaching strategies recommended for the course consisted of two central ideas:

- Pupils should observe demonstrations given by the teacher and engage in a series of exploratory experiments in which they themselves should solve problems.
- experimental work should be followed up by pupils engaging in discussion with the teacher and other pupils, presenting short talks and demonstrations to the group, and reading a range of books.

Bridget Somekh was commissioned to undertake action research by the head of Physics in a large comprehensive school (see Somekh 1983b). He said he was having problems in teaching the course because he was unable to get his pupils to engage in discussions about Physics. Teaching by the Nuffield methods was also proving time-consuming and he was worried that pupils were not gaining a clear understanding of the concepts. Bridget observed two teaching sessions and afterwards interviewed three pupils. From the observations a key teaching pattern appeared to be:

- to ask a question and repeat it several times in slightly different forms until a pupil answered;

- to ask further questions on the same theme in response to any answers received;
- to reteach the points in a short didactic session after the 'discussion' before going on.

From this it appeared that the teacher was acting upon interpretations of classroom events based upon certain assumptions:

- that he could initiate discussions and encourage open debate by asking questions;
- that supplementary questions would move the discussion forward;
- that the pupils' failure to answer questions indicated that they did not understand the concepts.

However, when Bridget interviewed the pupils, these assumptions were challenged by the reasons they gave for not answering the teacher's questions:

- Fear that in giving wrong answers they would expose their own ignorance to their peers and the teacher: they saw the teacher's questions as a test of their knowledge rather than as an invitation to express tentative views, and felt inhibited: they did not want 'to appear ignorant' because of 'the fear element of everybody else if you get the answer wrong' and because they felt that the teacher would be irritated by a wrong answer.
- Fear that if they answered a question, the teacher would 'pounce' on them. Often they knew the answer to the question but chose not to answer it because they felt punished for right answers as much as for wrong ones. 'If you say a wrong thing he tends to "pounce" on you. If you say a right thing he'll say, "Why?" . . . and then you try and think "why?".' The tape-recording of one of the observed sessions clearly showed an example of this 'pouncing' effect in an instance when a pupil gave the right answer but was immediately challenged to justify it.

At least three points in this story are of special interest. The first one is so obvious that it is easily overlooked: what a teacher thinks about an issue and what he or she says and does may not be wholly consistent. In putting changes into practice, teachers may be unaware of the implications of some of their established practices. For instance, in the example, the teacher is unaware that his practice of asking questions to test pupils' knowledge is incompatible with getting them to express their opinions openly in a discussion.

The second point is closely related to the first: what a teacher intends by what he or she says and does can be interpreted quite differently by the pupils. The fact that the teacher's intentions and actions affect pupils only via their perceptions and interpretations can lead to problems when a teacher introduces something new, as happened in this example. Pupils interpret the events in class on the basis of their previous experience of schools and teachers. If new teaching strategies involving changes in the roles and behaviour of teacher and pupils are sprung upon pupils without explanation, there will be a fair chance that they will fail. The introduction of new teaching strategies presupposes a change in the routine perceptions and actions of teachers and pupils. This is often a long-term process in which all the participants have to become conscious of the new roles, explore them, and test their reliability.

We want to look a little more closely at the third point arising from this story. The first interpretation of a situation does not always get to the heart of the matter, even if it sounds plausible and even if new strategies for action can be derived from it, as illustrated in the example above. Our first impression often relies on familiar assumptions and long-standing prejudices. If we want to bring about improvements in school or classroom situations, it is important to test the quality of the first impression in order to establish a sound basis for development. Answering the following questions can serve this purpose:

1 *Does the first impression neglect any existing information?*
   The first impression often gives a plausible picture because we use data selectively and ignore information that contradicts or deviates from our view of the situation. Perhaps – elaborating on our original story – the teacher has picked up indications that the pupils are nervous of one another and of him. He may have considered them unimportant because they didn't fit into his view of the situation which is already dominated by his perception that young people aged 16–19 are confident and self-possessed.

2 *Does the 'first impression' contain any vague, ambiguous concepts?*
   Often the initial interpretation uses everyday concepts whose ambiguity may have been a contributory factor to the problem. In the story above, it seems clear that there would have been no progress in coping with the problem had the teacher continued to believe that discussion consists of question-and-answer sessions in which the teacher asks the first question and responds to every answer with a further question. Discussion is an ambiguous term in this context. The teacher interprets it, in the classroom, in terms of question-and-answer sessions, whereas the students do not recognise this as discussion, since they retain the everyday meaning of open-ended, wide-ranging debate.

3 *Does the 'first impression' deal only with the surface symptoms of the situation?*
   The first interpretation of a situation sometimes consists of a detailed description of diverse events and actions without uncovering or explaining their underlying implications. One could say that such a

representation sets out the surface symptoms but does not progress to an in-depth interpretation. Surface symptoms comprise all observations and empirical generalisations that refer directly to the problem, for example: 'the pupils don't engage in discussion'. An in-depth interpretation puts forward a broad pattern of interpretation that appears to explain different phenomena and relate them to one another. For example, the teacher assumes that discussions about Physics consist in testing every statement against evidence. 'Physics is about asking "why?".' But the pupils assume that the teacher is asking questions to test their knowledge and that when he asks a supplementary question, he is trying to 'catch them out'. Both levels are connected with each other: in order to grasp a problem fully, an in-depth interpretation is essential because it reveals the interconnections between different factors in a situation. Often it is not the event itself that creates a problem but the interpretations and tacit assumptions that individuals bring to the event. On the other hand, the reliability of interpretations can be tested only by means of surface symptoms (see M12).

4 *Has the 'first impression' been accepted without testing it against other competing interpretations?*
The story from the Nuffield 'A' Level Physics classroom illustrates this question quite clearly. The first impression, fed by tacit assumptions and previous experiences, provides a seemingly plausible interpretation – that the pupils' failure to participate in discussions is due to their inability to understand the Physics concepts they have been taught. This interpretation is neither doubted nor questioned in the light of possible alternatives – such as the pupils' nervousness of exposing their ignorance in response to questions which they assume are asked to test their knowledge rather than to encourage them to explore ideas. This results in time being wasted on repeating questions and reteaching points the pupils already understand.

Facing problems and dealing with discrepancies between plans and their implementation in practice is not pleasant. We tend to try to forget about them as soon as possible. By confronting first impressions with alternative interpretations, action research slows down the process of problem resolution. This, in turn, increases the chances of more reliable interpretations which can be used as a basis for improving practice.

ACTIVATING ADDITIONAL KNOWLEDGE EN ROUTE

It is easy to draw false conclusions from a first impression. To help you avoid this, we suggest you spend some time on clarifying the starting point. What happens when we clarify the starting point for research? Two processes generally characterise this phase:

- on the one hand, the researcher tries to get access to additional knowledge and to use it for reflection;
- linked to this, and often at the same time, the first impression or initial formulation of the starting point is questioned by this additional knowledge and refined, extended or changed.

In the case study at the beginning of this chapter, the teacher of Nuffield 'A' Level Physics gained access to additional information on the starting point through Bridget's interview with pupils. The information from these interviews served to question his interpretation of the situation and suggested an alternative meaning. Besides interviews, there are a number of other ways of tapping additional knowledge.

Activating tacit knowledge

Whenever you take action in a situation, you gain experience. From this experience, routines of action and assumptions develop which are not always conscious and accessible to reflection (this will be dealt with more fully in Chapter 9, p. 203). There are a number of methods available that help to make this knowledge accessible to self-reflection:

- *Activating tacit knowledge by introspection* Memos or diary entries can help you to formulate new interpretations and cross-links which were missed in the first impression of the situation.
- *Activation of tacit knowledge by conversations and by being interviewed* Story-telling facilitates introspection because we have to order our experiences before we can tell someone about them. It helps to clarify the situation further if the listeners can contribute actively to generating the story, for example, by posing questions, asking for additional information, and reflecting back to the narrator their provisional understanding of the situation. Analytic discourse (M7) tries to create such a conversational situation by means of a few simple rules. A conversation with a critical friend (M8) is useful in a similar way for teachers who do not have access to a support group of colleagues.
- *Activating tacit knowledge by ordering conscious knowledge* A procedure for finding patterns in knowledge and establishing categories to locate and formulate new information is described in M10. In addition, by generating graphic representations of our knowledge, we can often formulate existing experience more completely and identify blank spots in our awareness (M9).
- *Activating tacit knowledge by reading one's own actions* An example should illustrate what we mean by this mysterious phrase.

Pavani often organises group work on a division of labour basis and is generally satisfied with the results. However, she is not satisfied with the sharing of information between groups: at the end of the day, either there is not enough time for groups to report back to each other, or the pupils are too tired to do it well. A colleague's proposal that reporting back on group work should be done the following morning, and her intuitive opposition to this proposal, provide her with a new perspective. The teaching strategy which she has been putting into practice seems to say: 'The reporting back from groups is a tail end, a kind of time-buffer which can be dispensed with in case of time pressure.' She found that it would be difficult to change this practice, despite the contradiction with her conscious aims.

Reading an action implies that there is a kind of knowledge embedded in action which has been previously ignored because it does not conform with familiar meanings and stated aims. We can gain access to this knowledge through a naïve reading of our actions:

+ rejecting the familiar meanings and stated aims which we normally associate with an action;
+ revisiting an action as if it were something strange and exotic, pretending to know nothing in order to know better.

Sometimes teachers formulate starting points and state aims that are contrary to their deeply rooted practices. This contradiction remains undiscovered if the knowledge hidden in action does not become conscious. In such cases, new action strategies to improve a situation (for example, a new plan for storing resources, or a new strategy for improving the way groups report back to each other) cannot easily be put into practice because of their tacit contradiction with established routines of action.

Collecting additional information which is available in the situation

One possible way of testing our knowledge of a situation we want to improve and develop is to obtain additional information – perhaps by carrying out an observation or by interviewing other people involved. The whole inventory of data collection methods can be used for this purpose (see Chapter 5).

Collecting views on similar situations from non-participants

To discover alternative interpretations of a research situation we suggest you:

• ask colleagues about similar situations;
• read relevant books and articles in magazines and journals.

As we have seen, other people's views can provide starting points for our own reflection, helping to actuate our tacit knowledge or to stimulate us to collect additional information. It is important to remain clear that such explanations are hypothetical, providing stimuli for research and development rather than replacing them.

Experimenting by introducing changes in existing situations

'One of the best ways to understand the world is to try to change it' said Kurt Lewin (quoted in Argyris *et al.* 1985: xii). By introducing changes, trying out new actions, and observing their results, our view of the situation in which we find ourselves is often deepened. Chapter 7 provides information and suggestions for trying out this strategy.

TOWARDS ELABORATING PRACTICAL THEORIES

Clarification of the starting point for research provides a practical theory (see Chapter 9, p. 207) of the situation to be studied. The next section deals with some characteristics of such practical theories, while the section after that provides strategies for developing them further.

Individual elements of practical theory and their inter-relationships

Which questions are usually asked when 'clarifying the starting point for research'? Normally the clarification is attempted in two areas:

1 Formulating individual elements of the practical theory

We need to find a pattern in the complexities of the situation identified as the starting point for research. First, we try to identify the most important individual elements of the situation, to distinguish them from less important elements, and describe them as vividly as possible. We ask:

- What is happening in this situation?
- Which events, actions and features of the situation are important?
- Which people are involved, and in what kind of activities?

Let's try to illustrate the process of clarifying a situation by an example. A possible starting point for the research could be the statement:

> Pupils seem to be very noisy during discussions in class. How can I organise the discussion so that it is less noisy?

The starting point begins with a statement that describes the situation (M6). We can now investigate this more carefully:

- Which pupils are noisy?

- What are they doing when they are noisy?
- Does their noisiness result from taking part in the discussion or from something else?
- Why does it matter if they are noisy?
- How can I define exactly what I mean by 'noisy'?
- Is there a particular time of day, or a particular environment when discussion is noisier?
- How do I respond when they are noisy in discussions? Do different responses from me have different effects on them?

When we formulate important individual elements of the practical theory, we should not restrict ourselves to what happened, but also take account of the context. Action research doesn't take place in a laboratory in which the researcher controls most of the context. Teachers do research in the real world of schools. Their own actions are embedded in a framework of other people's interests and actions. Their research and development activities in turn have consequences for others. Guiding questions for clarifying the context could be:

- Which other people are affected by my research and development activities?
- Who do I need to consult to ensure that I have freedom to act with the greatest possibility of success?
- Which features of the institution in which I work are likely to have an influence on the question I want to investigate?
- What are the broad social and political determinants that I need to take into account in relation to my question?

2 Formulating the connections between elements of the practical theory

Such questions lead step by step to the second area that needs to be addressed in clarifying the situation: we are interested not only in single features of the situation but also in the connections between them. We need to engage in analysis (identifying the constituent parts), and also in synthesis (drawing threads together). The point is that we need to become aware of our tacit theories which make connections between individual elements, and of how they influence our interpretation of the situation:

- How does this situation come about?
- What important connections are there, in my opinion, between events, contextual factors, the actions of individuals and other elements of this situation?
- What is my instinctive personal interpretation of this situation?

On the basis of these questions it is possible to formulate statements of this kind:

- The greater the expectation in a school that well-disciplined class-rooms should be quiet places, the more difficult it will be to conduct classroom discussions without giving rise to discipline problems.
- If a teacher always follows up the answer to a question with a supple-mentary question, pupils can be prevented from answering questions even if they are sure of the answer.

Sentences like these establish connections between individual elements of a situation (for example, between the teacher's comments and the level of the pupils' participation in a discussion); and they put forward a possible explanation for these connections.

In scientific literature, such statements are usually called hypotheses, and this term is useful in action research as well. Hypotheses can be used to express aspects of someone's practical knowledge (see Chapter 9, p. 207). It is important to be clear about their nature:

- A hypothesis does not have to be correct. The term itself implies that the explanation needs to be tested against experience.
- A hypothesis throws light on only one aspect of a complex situation, rather than the whole situation. As hypotheses are derived from a specific situation, even when they have been verified, they will still need to be re-examined in new situations (see Cronbach 1975: 125).
- A hypothesis tells us about the relationship between specific features of the situation and actions or events which result from them. Therefore, they can be used as a basis for planning future action (see Chapter 7).

Commonly held views which influence our practical theories

In our experience, there are some commonly held views which influence practical theories about what happens in schools. These views are like glasses that we look through without being aware of them. Of course, it is not possible for any human being to do without these glasses: for example, we are all influenced by theories and explanations prevalent in our time. However, it is a good idea to try to identify some of these 'glasses' and the unconscious influence they exert on the way we interpret situations. When clarifying the starting point, it is important to try to become more conscious of these hidden attitudes and preconceptions. Useful questions to ask yourself include:

- Could things have been different?
- Can I interpret this situation in another way?

We want to go on now to describe some of these commonly held views in order to illustrate our point.

Positive and negative influences

Most of us think of negative factors first when we try to explain educational situations. Every analysis tends to focus on negative experiences, often because the starting point has been chosen in response to a painful experience. But this is not enough to solve the problem.

First, it is important to take into account the positive aspects of the experience because they offer possibilities for positive action and improvement. One way of getting a better overview is to make a table that places these positive and negative influences side by side for comparison. Second, the distinction between positive and negative influences is useful for another reason: often, on closer inspection, it turns out that something which on the surface seems to cause problems is a hidden opportunity. Here is an example from a teacher's research:

> After a serious conflict with his class in which the teacher became verbally aggressive, he asked his pupils to write about their perceptions of the event. Their writing gave a very negative view of what had happened and of the teacher's use of 'insulting' words.

When you read this, your attention may be drawn to the negative points of the situation. However, on closer inspection, you may find some positive points: only in a relationship in which there is a lot of trust would the pupils dare to express such open and emotional criticism.

The teacher as originator or pawn

Richard DeCharms (1973) distinguishes between two opposing self-images that people can hold: the originators who see themselves as responsible for their own actions, and the pawns who see themselves moved by powerful hands. Action research encourages the researching teacher to develop strategies for action to improve the situation, so – sometimes unnoticed – it encourages a self-image of the teacher as originator. This needs to be balanced by an understanding that situations cannot be fully controlled by teachers but are conditioned by multiple forces. To achieve this balance, it is useful to pose some critical questions:

- What possibilities for action are there in different situations?
- In what situations do I feel confident to effect change?
- In which situations am I mainly dependent in my actions on other people?

On the other hand, many people, including teachers, see themselves as dependent on external forces and underestimate the contribution they can make to the situation. For these people, action research tends to challenge their self-concept, inviting them to explore possibilities for action and encouraging them to show greater autonomy.

A causal or a systemic view

Another approach which elaborates on these ideas is helpful in determining the starting point more precisely. Positive and negative influences are not seen as separate, but stand in either a causal or a systemic relationship to each other.

The *causal* relationship needs little explanation. A is the cause of B. Pupil X disrupts the lesson because she knows that this gives her status with her classmates. Pupils are not willing to take initiatives because my authoritarian predecessor conditioned them to react only to pressure. The advantage of causal interpretations is that they suggest definite reasons and apparently simplify the complexity of a situation. They also help us to place a moral interpretation on events by assigning guilt (to the pupil, a colleague, the parents, or ourselves). However, causal interpretations have their problems. One is that situations are usually caused by a number of contributing factors: for example, a pupil's bad behaviour might be traced back to preceding events involving other pupils, parents and two or three teachers. Her behaviour can therefore be regarded partly as a reaction to other, preceding events. This is not an argument against causal interpretations, but it does mean that we must be careful not to settle quickly for one which is too simple, because each cause may itself have layers of further causes.

Let's take the case of a young teacher taking a new class for the first time. She will be a bit nervous and, either instinctively or consciously, want to win them over and gain control. This purpose will be expressed in her behaviour. Let's look at the pupils: they sit tensely, perhaps rather sceptical, keyed up and interested in holding their own against the teacher, individually and as a group. This purpose will be expressed in their behaviour. At the same time, they will watch every action of the teacher closely and their interpretations of her behaviour will influence their own behaviour.

The noisiness of some pupils is interpreted by the teacher as a threat to her control of the class. The pupils notice the irresolute appearance of the teacher and it makes them feel insecure. Is the pupils' noisiness caused by the wavering appearance of the teacher or vice versa? This question cannot be answered as there is some evidence for both possibilities. Looked at from the pupils' point of view, the first answer will be more plausible; from the teacher's, the more plausible is the second. As it is impossible to know whether the noisiness or the wavering came first, we cannot tell which should be regarded as the cause of the other. If we identify a cause, it will be arbitrary.

What happens if we decide that there is no point in searching for causes and the people responsible? An alternative is the *systemic* view (see Selvini-Palazzoli *et al.* 1978: 48). According to this view, a class is regarded as a system in which each member of the class (the pupils and the teacher) have a relationship to one another. Each person influences the other members and is influenced by them. A change in the behaviour of one member leads to a change in the whole system. Every kind of behaviour can be regarded as both the result of feedback from the behaviour of others and as an influence on their further behaviour. Even 'non-behaviour' (for example, the silence of classmates when one pupil disturbs the lesson) can in this sense be seen as information for the 'troublemaker', the teacher and the pupils.

A system is a network of mutual relationships (expectations, kinds of behaviour, perceptions) in which the teacher is caught up. It is easier to understand if we imagine the network consisting of threads which are alive. A particular action of a pupil, or of the teacher, is affected by all the threads of the network as well as influencing them. But there is limited room for each thread to move if the network is not to be destroyed. There are longer and shorter threads, and there are knots in the network. These are the points at which threads intersect. Therefore, an occurrence in the classroom originates from the whole network, even if some parts of the network play a more important role than others. An extreme example of this is what happens when you introduce a computer into a classroom. Teachers usually find computers difficult to use at first, not only because they need to master some technical skills and decide which software to use, but because the computer disturbs many different aspects of class-room life, all at the same time. For example, there is a shift in the pupils' attention away from the teacher towards the computer; whole-class teaching is likely to have to be replaced to a large extent by group work; the nature of classroom work may need to change (pupils' energies can be devoted to interpreting graphs instead of drawing them – a more challenging task which does not have the same potential to keep them usefully occupied for a fair period of time); the teacher may no longer appear to know more than the pupils in everything and may become more of a partner in their learning (see Somekh 1992). Of course, teachers do not necessarily make all these changes, but the computer has some-times been seen as a 'Trojan horse' because it pulls on many threads of the web: it has the power to challenge us to make a number of changes, which together add up to a substantial shift in our teaching approach.

What can we learn from the systemic view? It enables us to ask new questions; not questions which search for causes of events, and attribute blame, but questions like: Which threads (for example, other pupils' and the teacher's expectations) contribute to the event (for example, a pupil's disruptive action)? What is the function of a pupil's disruptive behaviour for other pupils (and for the teacher)? Which are the sensitive spots (knots where many threads meet) in the event?

The systemic view also has another advantage: it can help us to arrive at a less emotional, more detached and, therefore, probably also fairer approach to situations in class, because it broadens our view beyond the concrete cause of trouble to its environment (of which the teacher is part). The interdependence of the elements in a system leads to a kind of balance (the tension of the net) to which the quiet pupils as well as the troublemakers contribute. The actions of a troublemaker can cause the 'normality' of the 'good' pupils and vice versa (thus many teachers have noticed that when a disruptive pupil leaves the class, another will often emerge to take his or her place.)

If we pursue this perspective, it can also offer suggestions for action. In any situation, the system is kept in balance by feedback from its interacting elements (pupils and teachers). However, this feedback can also change the system. That means, for example, that it is important to know what feedback (from other pupils, or the teacher) reinforces a 'troublemaker' and what does not (it may be that any form of attention acts to reinforce the bad behaviour). We can start to solve the problem by influencing the nature of the feedback (for example, by giving other pupils a chance to express their opinions, or by the teacher voicing his or her own perceptions of a situation).

A focus for analysis is to find the knots where the threads interact and particularly influence events. For example, there may be pupils whose reactions are very important for the pupil who disturbs the lesson, or there may be occasions which bring about the kind of interaction that causes a difficult situation (such as, an occasion when the teacher – from the pupil's point of view – has upset or humiliated a pupil).

Holistic and analytic perspectives

In this chapter we have given a number of hints for clarifying the starting point of research. This process of clarification is not value-free. By clarifying or analysing situations and problems, we are necessarily rather selective and reductionist (see also Chapter 6, p. 120). We reduce the complexity we face at school to a few central features whose relationships are then interpreted oversimply. Often this results in a rather mechanistic view of reality. This tendency has to be counteracted from time to time during the research process. We must not equate the reductionist and mechanistic model with the reality in which we live and act, which is much more complex than our model. The following suggestions may help to prevent this:

- Once you have developed hypotheses, don't view them in isolation from one another, but always look for possible links between them.
- Try to keep in mind the specific situation from which the hypothesis was derived initially, by asking from time to time: Under what

conditions would the prediction of my hypothesis be likely to be valid? Under what conditions would it be likely to stop being valid?

SUGGESTED METHODS FOR CLARIFYING THE STARTING POINT OF RESEARCH

Before introducing methods and exercises for clarifying the starting point, we want to present some of our own experiences of this phase of research:

1 It is important to engage consciously in clarifying the starting point but at the same time its importance should not be exaggerated. After all, clarifying the situation is the task of the whole research process: if we aimed for absolute clarity about all aspects of a situation before beginning, we would never start at all. 'The process of analysis is an endless one, but in action research it must be interrupted for the sake of action. And the point of interruption should be when one has sufficient confidence in the hypotheses to allow them to guide action' (Elliott 1991: 74).
2 The time needed for clarifying the situation can vary considerably. It will depend on the complexity of the problem to be investigated, the researcher's prior experience and depth of reflection, the accessibility of crucial information, the relative ease with which explanatory patterns and theories emerge, etc. There is a comforting rule of thumb. The total time needed in research for clarifying the situation will always be nearly the same: if you take less time in the earlier stages, you will have to invest more time later on, and vice versa.
3 Even if a lot of effort is invested in clarifying the situation in considerable depth in the early phases of research, understanding will change during the process of further research – not because the initial understanding was 'wrong', but because this is an outcome of the research. The researching teacher is interested not merely in confirming insights once they are gained, but in further development in depth and analysis of understanding. All actions – those that are primarily to do with teaching and those that relate to the research itself – can open new insights, no matter whether they happen at the beginning or at the end of the process. To neglect and discount these insights – as sometimes happens in academic research aimed at confirming or refuting initial hypotheses – is not sensible for the practitioner. Repressed problems will come back sooner or later and waste the time and energy of teacher and pupils.
4 Sometimes clarifying the situation is the single most important result of the research. For example, for one teacher, a taped interview with an apparently difficult pupil led to clearing up a misunderstanding and seeing the pupil in quite a new light. Because of seeing her in a new

light, the relationship between the teacher and the pupil became more relaxed, which in turn changed the way the teacher treated the pupil. In this case, the situation changed at the time of clarifying the situation, because interview data enabled the teacher to see the pupil differently. There was no need for a systematic testing of new strategies of action.

In the following section we suggest some concrete methods for clarifying the starting point of research.

CONVERSATIONS

M7   ANALYTIC DISCOURSE IN A GROUP

This procedure allows us to increase our awareness of the important characteristics of any situation and to enhance our understanding of their interdependencies. However, it presupposes that the analysis is carried out in a group rather than individually. In analytic discourse, a problem or issue is analysed in the following way:

1 It is the task of the teacher who wants to analyse a problem to provide the group with basic information on the issue to be discussed (in about 5 minutes); and subsequently to answer questions put forward by the group as comprehensively as (s)he deems possible or feasible.
2 It is the task of the remaining participants to gain a comprehensive and consistent impression of the situation by means of asking questions. The following rules have proved to be important in carrying out analytic discourse:

   • There should be questions only: statements concerning similar experiences should be avoided. This rule aims at focusing attention on the situation of the reporting teacher.
   • Critical comments (including those in the form of questions) should not be permitted. This rule, of special importance at the beginning of a discourse, aims at preventing the reporting teacher from becoming defensive rather than reflective.
   • Suggestions for solutions should not be permitted. This rule is to ensure that the search for an increasingly profound understanding of the problem is not cut short by a compilation of recipes.

3 Adherence to these rules, discussed beforehand with all participants, should be monitored by a moderator (usually one of the participants, who is prepared to assume that role). He or she

is allowed to ask questions and may use this as a means of opening up new perspectives.

4 For the analysis of a situation, three types of questions are predominantly suitable:

- questions concerning the concretisation of remarks (for example, the request to give an example or provide more details);
- questions concerning the underlying theories (for example, a request to give reasons for any action described, or any interpretations of events put forward);
- questions concerning an expansion of the system (for example, the request to give more information about people or events who may be related to the problem but have not so far been mentioned).

An *analytic discourse* has proved to be an effective method of gaining in-depth understanding of a problem. Through it, the interrelationships of the elements of the problem, including the 'headache areas', become apparent. This can provide a basis for solutions or for a new line of enquiry. An analytic discourse can lead to a deeper understanding of the problem – particularly for the person reporting but also for the whole group.

It usually takes some time for an analytic discourse to open up a problem in depth and become an intellectually worthwhile and personally enriching experience. The personal enrichment has to do with the seriousness, the sympathy and the personal concern that may develop in the group. The intellectual value derives from a growing understanding of the intricate relationship between observations, tacit assumptions and evaluations which are specific to one person's situation, but which have many implications for the other participants' self-understanding.

Usually the greatest benefit from an analytic discourse is gained by the teacher for whom it is organised. Apart from the deepening relationship with colleagues that results, the reporting teacher develops a clearer and more analytical view of the problem or issue. Sometimes this can be experienced quite dramatically, if the teacher's perception of the problem changes fundamentally, or if approaches to its solution emerge. At the same time, a more analytical view of a problem is usually accompanied by an emotional relief.

The role of the moderator is not always simple, because it involves seeing that rules are observed which are against the practice of everyday conversation and which therefore are 'forgotten' easily. The moderator must see the rules are kept or run the risk of the discourse remaining at a superficial level.

It may sometimes be necessary to refuse to accept questions that go too deep and that invite a level of personal and emotional commitment unwarranted by the mutual trust in the group. Too much emotional involvement can also interfere with analysis, because it draws attention away from a systemic view of a situation to a one-sided, causal interpretation (possibly too personally focused).

In the course of an analytic discourse, progress should be made in three areas:

- The situation in which the research problem occurs should be clarified (knowledge of surface symptoms).
- An understanding should develop of 'positive' and 'negative' factors and influences related to the problem (in-depth interpretation).
- An understanding should develop of the potential for change (in thinking and action). To this end coherence and holistic plausibility of analysis is often more important for a researching teacher than the 'objective' quality of individual arguments.

It has proved to be helpful, if there is still some time left at the end of an analytic discourse for discussion without the rules. Often there is strong interest by the group in talking about the experience. If this opportunity is announced at the beginning of the discourse, when the moderator explains and negotiates the rules, it takes pressure off the process because participants who urgently want to 'tell their own story' know they will get their chance later.

M8 CONVERSATION WITH A CRITICAL FRIEND

If you have no group of fellow teachers willing to take part in an analytic discourse, you can do something similar with a single person whom you trust and feel you can confide in. Of course, one-to-one conversations will not follow the rules as strictly as we have suggested for an analytic discourse. None the less, it can still be very useful to adopt a similar discipline:

If I want to assist a colleague in clarifying a situation, it is useful to devote a period of time to gaining an understanding of the situation and:

- ask only questions that deepen this understanding;
- refrain from any anecdotes, adverse criticisms or suggested solutions that might distract or deflect the train of my colleague's reflective thinking.

Conversations with colleagues play an important part in action research. This holds not only for the stage of 'clarifying the starting point' (discussed in this chapter) but also for the whole research process. The partners in this conversation should be *critical friends*: they should have empathy for the teacher's research situation and relate closely to his or her concerns, but at the same time be able to provide rich and honest feedback.

A small team of teacher-researchers will probably create better conditions for action research than a teacher working alone. Another good way of working is to form research tandems. The partners in each tandem have their own starting points for research but assist each other as critical friends, sharing experiences and helping with data collection (doing observations, interviews, etc.).

USING DIAGRAMS

Normally, theories start with a verbal description (written or spoken) of a situation. After a period of reflection and discussion/writing, the salient points are drawn out and expressed in succinct verbal statements (i.e. the hypotheses). Of necessity, these statements are reductionist, losing much of the complexity and detail of the situation they attempt to explain.

Miles and Huberman (1984: 21) have suggested that narrative texts (and other ways of presenting theories linguistically) overstretch the human capability to digest information and therefore lead to over-simplified interpretations. They make a plea for more frequent use of diagrams and other graphical means of representing theories. Narrative texts organise information according to the sequential structure of language and pose a problem for the representation of non-sequential events. Diagrams, on the other hand, allow us to represent information and its interrelationships in a structured, rapidly accessible and compact form.

Miles and Huberman (ibid.: 33) give some suggestions for constructing diagrams:

- Limit the diagram or chart, whenever possible, to an A4 page.
- Try out several alternative ways of representing the situation. Many changes and modifications may be necessary before you are satisfied. The graphical representation should not be thought of as a straitjacket to limit future work but more like a map of the area which has just been researched. A main purpose of research is to contribute to the development of maps.
- Avoid the 'no-risk framework'. If the elements of the situation are defined only in very general terms, and two-way arrows connect everything to everything else, it will be easy to confirm the theory but

it is unlikely to have any explanatory value. It is better to express your ideas as concretely and definitely as possible. The more exactly a practical theory is formulated, the more helpful it will be for your further work (although it is likely to need considerable modification).

- Use the graphical representation for your own development. Outcomes of practical experience, existing theories, and the results of important research studies can be 'mapped on to' it at a later stage. This will help to identify parallels, overlaps, contradictions and gaps, and in this way refine and deepen your understanding of the field of study.

In the following section, we suggest a practical method for creating a diagram.

M9 GRAPHICAL RECONSTRUCTIONS (5TH STARTER)

Graphical reconstructions help in clarifying the situation but also with data analysis in general (see Chapter 6).

Procedure

1 Read all the data (for example, your short description of the situation and questions that indicate the developmental perspective – see M6).
2 Write the most important features, events and actions which you identify in your data separately on small index cards. Then write on further cards the *most important* contextual conditions of the situation. Try not to have too many cards (particularly at first), or it may be too difficult to keep them all in view: 8–16 cards are ideal as a rule. If you find there is a need to include further items as the activity progresses, new cards can easily be added.
3 Now try to express the kind of relationship between the cards. For that purpose, you can use further cards with symbols for relationships. Probably you will need the following ones most frequently. Other symbols can be written on blank cards as needed.

(A) ⟶ (B)	B follows A chronologically
(A) ⟶⟩ (B)	A causes B
(A) ⟨⟨⟶⟩⟩ (B)	A and B interact
(A) ──[Ind.]── (B)	B indicates A

The point of *graphical reconstructions* is that in presenting the essential elements graphically (and not in a linguistic flow of ideas), you have to restrict yourself to essentials and be clear and concise. This helps to identify the most important features of a situation. Working with movable cards makes it easy to try out different configurations until you find one that satisfactorily reconstructs the situation you are considering. As you move the cards, you go through a process of clarifying the relationships between all the elements of the situation.

4 When you have found a representation of the starting point which really satisfies you, copy the graphic diagram on to a single sheet of paper. Preserve this diagram. In the course of your research you will be able to see how your ideas change. You can also use the diagram to check how plans for actions fit your personal theory as represented in the diagram: From which elements of my theory do my plans for innovative actions originate? Why exactly do I think they originate there and not from other points on the diagram?

An example

This is taken from research on a university statistics course. The lecturer described the starting point she wanted to clarify as follows:

> The students do not ask any questions. My last year's students did ask questions and everything went well. Now, because they are not asking any questions, I do not know whether they have understood or not. If they articulated their problems, I could explain points again more clearly.

In a later discussion with one of the authors, the lecturer elaborated her view of the situation. We quote from notes of this discussion made from memory:

> The teaching process is divided into two phases. The lecturer thinks that her explanations during the first phase are not usually very well understood. But even if the students do not understand her explanations (and as a result cannot solve the problems correctly), they provide the material from which questions can arise to create starting points for the second phase of the teaching process. In this phase the lecturer's explanations are much clearer as she can concentrate on specific aspects of the subject matter. If, however, the students do not ask any questions, she doubts whether they have understood everything and, in addition, she has no way of starting the second phase with her clearer explanations. In this case she

believes it is unlikely that the pupils will understand the subject matter and she finds this frustrating and worrying.

On the basis of this description of the situation, a *graphical reconstruction* exercise led to the production of the *graphic diagram* presented in Figure 3.

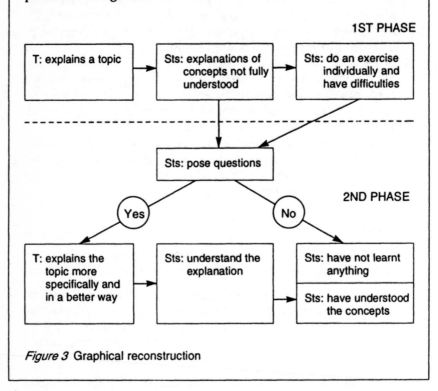

Figure 3 Graphical reconstruction

FINDING PATTERNS IN EXPERIENCE

Diagrams are a means of exploring experiences that relate to the starting point of research, of becoming aware of existing preconceptions and theories, and discovering areas in which information is lacking. The same result can also be achieved with the help of other methods.

M10   A STORY FROM CARDS

Try to observe practical situations that are important in relation to your starting point of research over a defined period of time (for example, between one and three weeks depending on the research question).

1 After each observation, describe the situation as precisely as possible on a large index card.
2 At the end of the time, take all the cards and read through them.
3 Try to write a general explanatory statement which relates to all the situations you have observed.
4 Check this explanatory statement by answering the following questions for each card in turn:

- Is it possible to present the situation described on this card using the concepts in my general explanatory statement?
- How?
- If the situation I observed is distorted or fragmented by this attempt, what changes or additions do I need to make to the explanatory statement?

M11 FROM CATEGORIES TO HYPOTHESES

Hypotheses are formulated in order to make the researcher aware of his or her own tacit assumptions and to provide an orderly framework for the research. The starting point is usually a loosely structured information base (experiences, knowledge taken from books, or data). Working on this information, the researcher tries to impose a pattern by identifying important characteristics or categories, as distinct from unimportant ones, and by making connections between these categories explicit. Unlike in graphical reconstruction (M9), the results of the analysis are not expressed diagrammatically, but linguistically. In what follows, the procedure of formulating hypotheses is split up into steps, each illustrated by an example (see also the practical hints for coding data in M26).

1 First try to identify your assumptions about the situation in question (for example, as they are documented in your research diary, in other data you have already collected, or in your memories from reading or experience). A teacher made the following notes from memory after seeing a video-recording of one of his lessons (for reasons of space only brief sections are quoted).

> The recorded lesson once again shows the problem I have identified: in this class there is no discussion which is kept alive by the pupils themselves for any length of time. Even if I ask questions or express provocative opinions there is normally little response and the topic is closed . . . . Watching the video I became aware of a pattern that occurred

four times (the first time stimulated by a work-sheet which all the pupils had to read, the other times by a question from me). First a genuinely controversial topic is introduced for discussion. Then three or four pupils say something which is relevant to it. Then I put forward my opinion. Then only one or two more pupils say anything further (in one case nobody said anything further). Does the discussion die as a result of my statement?

2   Write down all the *categories* that emerge. To do this we need to know exactly what a category is. Unfortunately, it is difficult to give one overall definition, but here is an attempt:

- A category is a concept, usually represented by a noun (with some additional phrase). It can be used as a key to a text: it helps us to order the ideas in the text.
- The order is created by using the category to stand for several phenomena, which in the text are likely to be expressed in quite different forms.
- By putting them in a category, phenomena which are regarded as important are differentiated from unimportant phenomena (i.e. those that are not put in a category) within the framework of the research question.

It is easier to understand the concept of a category with the help of examples. As an exercise, we suggest that you reread the teacher's notes in point 1 above and make a list of categories contained in the text which you think could be important in clarifying the situation (i.e. no in-depth interpretation of the text is necessary for this exercise).

My list of categories: ....
....
....
....

We have also done this exercise ourselves and made the following list of categories:

- *class discussion* (developed from 'In this class there is no discussion ... ');
- *teacher's questions* (developed from 'Even if I ask questions or express provocative opinions ... ');
- *topic introduction* (developed from 'a genuinely controversial topic is introduced for discussion');
- *pupils' responses* (developed from 'there is normally little re-

sponse', 'then three or four pupils say something,' and 'only one or two more pupils say anything further');

- discussion dying (developed from 'Does the discussion die');
- teacher stating views on controversial topics (developed from 'Then I put forward my opinion').

We see some value in keeping categories close to the wording of the original text, initially; as the analysis progresses, some of these can be regrouped into more general categories. If your list is worded differently or contains different categories, it need not be 'wrong'. Maybe you see a pattern different from ours in this situation. In the end, the 'rightness' of a category is determined by its usefulness (i.e. its analytic power) for further research and action. In any case, comparing different lists of categories drawn up by different people (for example, yours and ours) helps us to understand the alternative perspectives expressed through the selection of categories. If you have the opportunity, discuss these differences with a research partner.

3 When you have made your list of categories, check this interim result:

- Are there categories that actually describe the same phenomenon and that can be summarised in one category?
- Are there any categories that represent different aspects of a more general concept (which is either already included in your list or should be added)? In our example, 'discussion dying' is closely related to 'pupils' responses'. We keep the more general category 'pupils' responses' and cross out 'discussion dying' on our list.

4 When reading the data and making the first list of categories, some connecting patterns between the categories usually emerge which need to be written down. Make a list of hypotheses that express presumed relationships between these categories. Usually hypotheses are formulated in an 'if . . . then' form.

Try this out by taking two categories from your list and writing down a possible connection in the form of a hypothesis:

My hypothesis: ....
....
....
....

For example, from our list of categories we set up this hypothesis:

If there is more 'teacher stating views on controversial topics', then there will be less 'pupils' responses'.

Or in a stylistically more elegant form:

If the teacher expresses opinions on controversial topics more frequently, then the frequency of pupils' responses (to the controversial topic) will be reduced.

5 Examine the list of hypotheses which you have drawn up, using the following criteria:

- Which categories do not appear at all in the hypotheses or only figure marginally? Why not? (Is it because you don't have a theoretical concept of these categories – in other words, that you don't really know what they mean? Is it only possible to identify trivial connections between them and other categories? Is it only possible to identify connections that cannot really be investigated?)
- To which hypotheses can you already bring a lot of experience (examples?) and which ones are very speculative?
- In order to test these hypotheses, what action could you take in your teaching and what data would you need to collect?

Chapter 5

Data collection

How do teacher-researchers get the material for their reflections, their *data*? The chapters on the research diary and on finding a starting point have already presented some methods of data collection. This chapter deals with it more systematically. We begin by discussing what data are and the relationship between data and the situations we want to research. Next we discuss four criteria for judging the quality of action research. The main body of the chapter is taken up with presenting various data collection methods.

GAINING EXPERIENCE AND COLLECTING DATA

We are able to take skilful action in daily routines as a result of our experiences. Experiences are events, and our interpretations of them, that have taken place in the environment in which we are participants. We use them to plan, carry out and evaluate later actions. Some of them we soon forget, others are stored in our mind as knowledge (*practical theories* about specific situations) and can be retrieved to inform later actions. We can draw in this way not only on our own experiences, but also on other people's, to which we have access through listening to or reading their accounts.

All the different kinds of empirical research, including action research, are based on experiences. Traditionally, great importance is attached to profound reflection and verification. However, experiences can only be verified if they are not unique, but accessible to the researcher and others again and again. Experiences can be verified in different ways:

1 if the event the experiences refer to can be repeated;
2 if the event has left some traces, independent of the researcher, which can be investigated by the researcher and others;
3 if the researcher has used some means to represent the experiences (for example, a diary or audio or video tape-recording) and these representations are available to the researcher and others independent of the original context of time and place.

In most cases, it is complicated or impossible to repeat events (point 1), and in any case reflection takes more time than is generally available during an event, so research depends heavily on *data* which give *indirect* access to events (points 2 and 3). Data have two important features:

- They are material traces or representations of events and therefore are givens in a physical sense (from the Latin 'datum'), which can be passed on, stored, and made accessible to many people.
- They are regarded as relevant by a researcher, providing evidence with respect to the issue investigated.

What are or are not data depends on the research question. If the research concerns pupils' use of language, then their written work or a tape-recording of their verbal utterances will be important data. If the research is into group work and its consequences, then observation notes, tape-recordings of discussions with pupils about their work, and the group's products (written or otherwise) will be important data.

Three characteristics of data are important:

1 Data can only represent events selectively: the tape-recording pre-serves verbal utterances from the area within range of the microphone for the period of time during which it is in operation; the questionnaire gets the opinions that people give in answer to the questions asked. During the process of becoming data, either by being produced (for example, photos, transcriptions of interviews, memos) or by being selected (for example, pupils' writing, worksheets, school rules), some aspects of reality are stressed as important while others are neglected. To some extent this happens on purpose, as part of interpreting the research question or choosing a particular methodology; to some extent it happens accidentally, as a result of the researcher's uncon-scious prejudices, or some known or unknown bias of the methods chosen, or some restriction in the research situation (for example, the timetable making it impossible to interview a particular pupil).

2 Whatever is produced or selected as data depends on interpretative processes by the researcher. The extent to which the researcher's inter-pretation contributes to the production of data can vary considerably. It is very slight if the researcher selects existing material as data because they seem important to the research question (for example, a letter to parents from the head selected as data for research into home–school links). But when the researcher transforms personal experiences into data, the degree of interpretation is much larger. For example, in order to produce a memo, an event is observed, interpreted (that is conceptualised) and finally recorded in written form. Data coming into being like this are events that have been interpreted by the researcher; that means the events are reconstructed, even if only by being

described in terms of concepts (= meanings) already familiar to the researcher. In that respect, experiences which have been recorded by the researcher are theory-laden.

3 Finally, data are static because of their material character. Events lose their dynamic quality and cannot develop any more (for example, the photo taken in assembly).

The following example will illustrate these three features. Let's assume we decide to audio-record a lesson. By choosing this method of data collection, we already express a certain view of the situation investigated: it is seen as a linguistic interaction, with less importance placed on non-verbal communication or on the thoughts of the people involved in the situation. By placing the tape-recorder, a certain section of reality is chosen and marked as meaningful in understanding the situation: the tape-recorder's position may pick up more of the teacher's talk, or the talk of a particular group of pupils nearby. The recorder itself embodies a specific observation theory in that, depending on the type of microphone, sound is picked up within a nearer or farther radius, with the consequence that the observed reality is selected differently. What has been recorded can be listened to again and again, but the relationship between teacher and pupils which has been made storable by the tape may have developed in the meantime: the results of our analysis based on this material may still be historically interesting, but may have become unimportant in understanding the current situation.

We can summarise: data typically provide us, as researchers, with access to a reality to be investigated. We take them as representing reality, but must bear in mind that they are not reality itself, but only its traces. They are always chosen or constructed from a certain perspective, and are therefore – to varying extents – theory-laden. This would not matter if we could make ourselves aware of all the theories (prejudices) involved in collecting and selecting data. However, we can be aware of only some of the theoretical perspectives contributing to the research process, while others remain unnoticed or tacit, although they still shape our research activities.

The practical consequences of these considerations are small but at the same time wide-ranging. As our insights are built on data containing theoretical assumptions which, to some extent, are tacit:

- we must be modest in our claims and make clear the preliminary and hypothetical nature of our insights:
- we must re-examine and further develop the situational understanding we have gained (see the following section on criteria for judging quality in action research).

M12 THE LADDER OF INFERENCE

An aid to understanding the degree of reliability of data is the 'ladder of inference' (Argyris *et al.* 1985: 56). This ladder consists of three rungs or steps to be climbed one after another – like a normal ladder. Each step of the ladder symbolises data of a certain quality. Each step differs in the extent to which data are accessible to examination by people other than the researcher.

The first step of the ladder symbolises data that can be regarded as relatively unambiguous representations of events, as they are accessible to observation. For example, with the help of a tape-recording, we can check if the teacher has uttered the words quoted on the first step in Figure 4. The second step gives an interpretation of the teacher's words which is shared by everyone in a defined cultural domain. We assume that the teacher's utterance 'John, your work is poor' would be interpreted as criticism by everyone in our cultural context. The third step contains individual interpretations, which are probably not shared by everyone because they contain a number of additional assumptions.

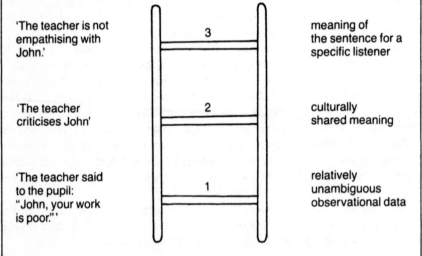

Figure 4 The ladder of inference

From step to step, the likelihood increases that different observers will interpret the same event differently. In order to avoid differences in the interpretation of events, we recommend the following:

- Start by examining the reliability of data on the lowest step of the ladder: identifying which data are factual observations, accessible to cross-checking by others.
- Move on to examining the reliability of interpretations on the second step, asking yourself if you are sure that they will bear scrutiny by others.
- The first two steps have provided relatively 'hard data'. Only now are you ready to proceed to the third step for further, more individual interpretations and conclusions.

You can approach it the other way around if you want to judge the reliability of an interpretation on step 3 ('the teacher is undermining John's confidence'):

- try to get information about the first step (what was said or done?);
- find out if the interpretation of the data on step two will bear scrutiny by others;
- then it is useful to continue the analysis, possibly identifying more than one alternative interpretation at the third step.

The ladder of inference serves three functions (Argyris et al. 1985: 247):

- It enables a careful scrutiny of interpretations based upon data drawn from a particular event.
- It clarifies the relationship between interpretations and more factual data.
- It facilitates reflection on action, by allowing us to trace interpretations of actions to the events to which they refer.

Can we say that the typical means of generating knowledge in research is through the collection of data, and that this distinguishes research from other activities? Unfortunately, we cannot draw such a clear line between research and everyday life, for the following reasons:

1 Data (as material traces and representations of events) do have a central position in the research process, but research results are not only and perhaps not even primarily dependent on the data. They spring also:

- from the researcher's consciously formulated theories;
- from the researcher's tacit theories based upon personal experiences (for which there may be no evidence in the data);
- from the collective tacit theories of the researcher's professional culture (for which there may also be no evidence in the data).

In a similar way, all daily routines (for example, a teacher's work in a classroom) are governed by a mixture of conscious and currently unconscious knowledge.

2 Data also have a central place in our daily routines. For example, tests are set and pupils' answers are collected and analysed (becoming accessible to other persons). By this means pupils' knowledge is assessed, and the results recorded in written records.

We want to emphasise that data collection does not (and cannot) replace what we learn from everyday experience, but is based on it and should support it where this is useful. For example, data collection is particularly useful when we want to understand and cope with difficult situations in which we are not satisfied with our routine actions, or when we want to re-examine our practical knowledge, develop it, and make it accessible to our fellow teachers (see also Chapter 9, p. 207).

CRITERIA FOR JUDGING THE QUALITY OF ACTION RESEARCH

What are the criteria by which research decisions should be made and data collection methods chosen? What counts as quality clearly depends on the aims of the research. In action research there are four important objectives:

- to develop and improve practice through research in the interests of all those concerned;
- to develop the knowledge and practical understanding of those involved in the research process;
- to develop the professional knowledge of teachers as a whole;
- to develop and improve education as a discipline (see Chapter 9, p. 207).

We want to put forward four wide-ranging quality criteria. They are in the form of questions to inform the research process. They cannot be fulfilled in terms of an initial research design, but should be used to shape and challenge the conduct of the research as a whole.

1 Considering alternative perspectives

Have the understandings gained from research been cross-checked against the perspectives of all those concerned and/or other researchers?

Why do we believe considering alternative perspectives is an important criterion in judging the quality of action research? In traditional empirical research, objectivity, reliability and validity are usually regarded as central criteria for judging quality. (Altrichter 1986a presents a detailed comparison between the methods of empirical science and other forms of research.)

These three quality criteria in empirical research are derived from the basic idea of making close comparisons. By 'repeating the research' (e.g. having different people looking at the same event, using different research methods – interviews, classroom observations, etc.) it is possible to make a detailed comparison at each stage. Discrepancies can be identified as they would be if a second photograph were to be superimposed on the original one. Any such discrepancies in the research process are interpreted as indicating quality deficits; and conformity as indicating quality.

These quality criteria are also important for action research, although some of the procedures for testing them, developed for research in experimental settings, can hardly be applied to action research in naturalistic settings:

- *For practical reasons* (see also the section on practical compatibility): complex procedures for testing validity require time, effort and resources that are not available to a teacher-researcher. Even considering alternative perspectives by drawing on a second observer may give rise to insurmountable difficulties in some cases.
- *For theoretical reasons*: in action research, reliability is only possible in a very restricted sense. Naturally occurring situations are usually changeable: it is seldom possible to observe comparable situations at different times because the situation will have developed in the meantime. In addition, the action researcher sets out to destabilise a situation by developing and putting into practice action strategies to change and improve it (see Chapter 7).

However, the quality criterion 'consulting alternative perspectives' is in the spirit of the central idea of the traditional quality criteria of empirical research: namely that the quality of research can be raised by 'repeating the research' in order to discover discrepancies. Teacher-researchers can discover weak points in their research and raise its quality, if they confront their findings with alternative perspectives of the situation. If discrepancies arise, these can be used as starting points for further reflection and development.

In practical terms there are several sources of alternative perspectives available:

- *Other people's perspectives* Our own understanding of a research situation (as it emerges, for example, after clarifying the starting point of research, or after the first activities of data collection and analysis) can be confronted with other people's views. These can be people who are directly or indirectly involved in the situation (e.g. pupils, headmasters, parents), or people who are relatively uninvolved (e.g. external observers).
- *Perspectives drawn from other research methods* Another research

method can be used in relation to the same situation: for example, a classroom observation can be complemented by interviewing pupils.

- *Perspectives developed in other comparable situations* These can lead to the discovery of flaws in our own research process. Other teachers' accounts, research papers and books, and the teacher-researcher's own experiences are all sources of alternative understandings of the situation being investigated.

Discrepancies between different perspectives can have two main causes:

1 They can result from poor methodology and misinterpretations. For example, our own observations of a pupil's behaviour can be different from an external observer's observations. This calls for two possible courses of action. First, we can identify and correct mistakes in our own observations or, if there is no way of knowing which data are more reliable, we can provide alternative interpretations which express the ambiguity. Second, we can learn from this experience and adapt, or add to, our 'rules of thumb' for carrying out research.

2 If discrepancies cannot be explained by re-examining the research process, they are probably caused by different perspectives inherent in the situation being researched (see Chapter 3, p. 35). In this case, the practical theory emerging from the research will need to be extended to explain why the situation is seen differently from different perspectives. This is illustrated by the following example.

   A teacher begins a lesson by asking questions. In an interview, he explains his intention: the questions are meant to stimulate the pupils to think about the subject matter and discover links between different ideas. But he is not satisfied with the results. To him the pupils' answers show very little 'thinking' and no 'links between ideas'. During a group interview with the pupils, it emerges that they interpret the teacher's questioning as a test. In this situation, they want to give an answer that is 'correct ', and which 'reflects the views they believe the teacher holds'. They do not want to take any risks. In this case the reason for the discrepancy between the teacher's and the pupils' views cannot be explained in terms of the research methodology. The discrepancy 'is inherent in the situation'. It will be important to explain the existence of the divergent explanations in the practical theory of the situation, for example, by saying:

- The teacher interprets the situation in terms of his immediate motives for action.
- The pupils do not perceive the teacher's motives in this situation, but interpret his action in terms of their own experiences of similar situations in the past (their socialisation as pupils).
- The result is the observed 'misunderstanding'.

- This finding does not suggest any different interpretation of the teacher's motives. However, if he takes seriously the pupils' understanding of the situation from their socialisation in the classroom, he will have to take into account ways in which, over time, he can improve the effectiveness of his questioning.

2 Testing through practical action

Have the understandings gained from research been tested through practical action?

There are two ways of scrutinising theories: *critical analysis* (reflection, dealt with in the previous section) and *investigation through action*. The quality of theoretical insights can be judged by their contribution to the improvement of practical action. Developing action strategies and testing them by putting them into practice is an integral part of action research and is dealt with in Chapter 7.

3 Ethical justification

Are the research methods compatible with both educational aims and democratic human values?

In action research, the end does not justify the means. Research interferes in a social situation: many research methods are 'reactive' (i.e. they make people do things they would not otherwise have done); and people involved in the situation learn things as a result of the research process. Thus, when we carry out action research, it is very important that our activities abide by ethical quality criteria.

1 The research should be compatible with the educational aims of the situation being researched, rather than working against them. For example, data collection based on competitive tests would be incompatible with the educational aim of fostering co-operation between pupils. Similarly, covert observation would be incompatible with supporting openness and trust between teachers and pupils.
2 Action research is based on the belief that effective change in practice is only possible in co-operation with all the participants in the situation – it cannot be achieved against their will. Therefore, research methods should help to develop democratic and co-operative relationships. Chris Argyris (1972) shows convincingly that many research designs do not contribute to democratic and co-operative responsibility. Action research tries to overcome this problem:

   (a) The research methods are governed by *ethical principles*, in particular:

- *Negotiation* Research techniques may be used only with the consent of all those concerned. What does this mean in practice? In classroom research, the pupils are told the aims of the investigation and are asked for their co-operation. If the effects are likely to go beyond the classroom, fellow teachers and the head are similarly approached. This process of informing and asking for co-operation is repeated at every stage. If the methods of data collection are not acceptable, alternative procedures have to be negotiated. Before an interview, the pupils (or other interviewees) are told what use will be made of the data, and afterwards they are given the opportunity to think over what they have said and asked if the data can be used in the research. If they refuse permission, this has to be accepted (e.g. by handing over the tape to the pupil). In our experience, it is very rare for pupils to refuse to co-operate if they believe a project is important for them and their teacher and if they are asked for their co-operation explicitly. They usually want their views to be considered. It is worth noting that the rather vague category of 'all those concerned' is likely to include both those immediately involved and others whose significance may emerge only after the research begins (for example, a fellow teacher who taught the class in a previous year – see Posch 1985: 55).
- *Confidentiality* The data are the property of those from whom they originate. Data have to be treated confidentially and may not be passed on to others without permission. Research reports and case studies must not be published without giving participants the opportunity to comment: this may lead to changes being made or to the comments being incorporated in the writing. If individuals can be identified, they must be asked for permission before the report is passed on to others. Making data anonymous by leaving out or changing the names is often not good enough. Walker (1985: 24) has shown that while this practice protects the researcher, the participants can often be easily identified.
- *Participants' control* Those who participate in the situation keep control of the research. This ethical principle is of great importance in building trust between a teacher-researcher and external facilitator, or between teacher and pupils. Lawrence Stenhouse (1975) has argued convincingly that control over research and any changes resulting from it should be in the hands of those who have to live with its consequences. This principle requires facilitators to support but not dominate the teacher-researcher.

(b) The ethical principles are set out in an *ethical code*.

When teacher-researchers collaborate with external facilitators, it is important to draw up an ethical code defining the rights and duties of all parties. This should be discussed with participants beforehand and revised if necessary. Some external facilitators sign a contract with the teacher-researchers setting out their aims and principles for democratic collaboration. For example, in the PALM Project (Pupil Autonomy in Learning with Microcomputers) the following Code of Confidentiality was drawn up to safeguard the interests of all those involved (teachers, their schools, three Local Education Authorities (LEAs), the four-person central support team and the project's sponsors, the National Council for Educational Technology).

PALM Project: Code of Confidentiality

1 It is understood that the use of any evidence or data collected by teachers will be fully negotiated with the individuals concerned.

2 It is also understood that the discussions of formal or informal meetings remain confidential to participants in the meeting until they have given permission for more general release (but see 3 below).

3 It is understood that children will have the same rights as teachers to refuse access to data that they have provided (e.g. notes taken of interviews with them).

4 Pupils' anonymity will normally be safeguarded at all stages of the research. Individuals will be mentioned by name only with their prior agreement or, where appropriate, with that of their parents.

5 Information relating to a school will only go on public record with the agreement of the head teacher.

6 To facilitate cross-LEA research, it is understood that release of evidence (data), and/or discussions at meetings, to one member of the central team constitutes release to the whole team, unless a further limit is placed by those concerned.

7 The central team will be reporting both formally and informally to the sponsors. However, these reports will not infringe the ground rules outlined above.

8 The PALM schools and the central team will work within the framework of LEA policy. Teachers, schools and the central team (within the limits outlined above) will release the outcomes of PALM research to the LEA advisory teams at the earliest opportunity.

9 Wherever possible (within the limits outlined above), PALM teachers will share the outcomes of their investigations, first with their school and with the central team, then across the participating LEAs, and finally more widely where appropriate.

10 All reports produced by teachers will be published under their names

in order to give full credit to them for their work. All such reports will be subject to negotiation with the sponsors. The central team will assist teachers with this work as and when required.

(PALM 1990)

An ethical code of this kind will always need to be negotiated between all those concerned, so that it is tailored to the particular context. The PALM Code of Confidentiality was drawn up to fit a funded project within the British educational system in 1988–90; a similar ethical code in the United States during that period would probably have had to include a clause specifying the rights of parents more clearly. You may like to adapt some of the items from the PALM Code for your own use, but don't forget that PALM was a large project involving many people and you may not need as many clauses if you are working with just one partner or a small group.

(c) The conduct of the research remains open to negotiation.

Even if those concerned have been fully informed from the start, and principles for collaboration have been written down, misunderstandings and conflicts can emerge in the course of the research. Therefore 'negotiation' continues to be important *throughout the entire research process* and, in the event of conflict, existing agreements must be open to further negotiation (see Johnson 1984: 10).

4 Practicality

Are the research design and data collection methods compatible with the demands of teaching?

To ensure that the action research is of high quality, the research design and individual research methods should be:

- compatible with the economies of time imposed by the teacher's main responsibility for teaching;
- compatible with the professional culture of teachers; building upon the experienced professional's ability to make numerous, finely tuned decisions in a process of 'practical reflection'.

It is often possible to use research methods that are integral to the teaching and learning situation. For example, an interview with a student can be both a learning experience for the student and a means of collecting data on a research question. Working in pairs on a mathe-matical problem can improve pupils' mathematical competence and at the same time provide the teacher with data on their specific learning problems. Asking pupils to keep a diary (for example, as part of a project) can be a good way of improving their language competence while, at the same time, providing the teacher with rich data relevant to a research issue.

COLLECTING EXISTING DATA

Teachers have access to a variety of existing material which can be used as data. This material can provide evidence of past events relevant to a research question. *Written documents* are the most obvious, for example:

- pupils' written work: homework and school work (essays, exercises, tests, etc.) and a variety of less formal writing (such as class magazines, graffiti on the walls or desks, etc.);
- teachers' writing: worksheets, lesson plans, corrections and comments on pupils' writing, mark books, desk diaries, notes of pupils' progress (for example, assessments of oral work, etc.);
- other documents: the class register, letters from parents, absence notes, school rules, circular letters, newsletters, notices, textbooks, etc.

There is also *unwritten evidence*: for example, the appearance of a classroom after the pupils have left, the cover designs and binding of books as well as their state of repair, signs of wear on the furniture and so on. Here are two suggestions of ways to collect and use these existing data:

M13 MAKING A DOSSIER

A dossier is a set of materials collected according to certain criteria, for example:

- A teacher can collect the work of a particular pupil in order to study his/her development (all the work, or a selection of the best, or an arbitrary selection).
- Each pupil can be asked to make a representative selection of his/her school work.
- A whole class could put together a dossier of its work: first collecting all of the work and then selecting what is relevant for the dossier.
- A teacher can collect an agreed number of papers over a certain period of time (for example, one per week) selecting them because of their interest (topic, quality, the way in which they illustrate a specific problem, etc.).

(After Brennan 1982)

Here is an example of one way of using a dossier for research. A French teacher wanted to study the mistakes most commonly made by low-achieving pupils in order to identify possible causes and develop teaching strategies to help overcome them. She collected the exercise books of a selected group of pupils and listed the mistakes they had made over the past three weeks. She then analysed the kinds of mistakes, their context and frequency. The list provided clues to possible causes. She then handed out the list to the pupils and discussed it with them in order to get a more complete picture of specific causes and possible teaching strategies.

Dossiers are useful in many ways:

- as reference material to be used in discussions with pupils, parents, or fellow teachers;
- as a database for a class conference on ways of improving work patterns (both in terms of the teacher's organisation and the pupils' activities);
- as a stimulus for pupils' reflecting on their work and becoming more aware of educational aims and criteria for success in learning. This often has the effect of involving pupils in the research process, by raising their awareness of their own learning and increasing the care with which they carry out their work;
- parents who have access to this kind of dossier of their children's work are better able to judge their achievements, progress and difficulties.

M14   RECORDING AND MAKING USE OF CLUES

It is often easy to neglect available data because they are embedded in everyday routines. They are so 'normal' that it is difficult to notice them and they seem too banal to be taken seriously. We can learn from Sherlock Holmes. The secret of his method lay in his ability to detect clues in the most inconspicuous things. Dr Watson had just bought a new surgery, choosing from two located in adjoining houses. Without even entering the building, Sherlock Holmes congratulated him on his choice. He had discovered that the steps leading up to Watson's surgery were much more worn than those of the surgery next door.

Here is an example of how clues can be recorded and used in action research. A teacher who was annoyed by pupils' careless treatment of the school furniture decided to carry out an investigation. He began by asking how the problem manifested itself. Where did it happen? How did it show itself? He began in 'his' class and inspected the desks, the floor, the 'designs' on the walls; then he inspected the halls, looking for signs of wear on the window sills, graffiti, etc. He took photos of what he saw, and he also took photos of places where similar furniture, etc. was in good condition.

He used this data to start a discussion with the pupils in his class, not in order to 'preach' but to find out their point of view and get more information about the situations in which damage occurred. This led to further speculation about contributory factors, such as how careless behaviour was sanctioned: for example, many offences of this kind went unnoticed when older pupils were responsible but were punished when younger pupils were involved. He followed up with interviews to try to find out more about the reasons for the pupils' behaviour.

Using existing data has some advantages over data collected through a contrived process. In most cases it has higher credibility because it is independent of the teacher's research activites. A further advantage is that it can often be collected relatively quickly. Finally, it provides evidence of events which may not be accessible by other methods (for example, pupils' ways of doing homework).

On the other hand, using existing data has some disadvantages. Often it contains much more information than necessary, making its analysis very time-consuming. Furthermore, even if the data have not been influenced by the research process, there will have been other influences which often can no longer be reconstructed in sufficient detail (e.g. the person who lived in Dr Watson's surgery before his predecessor). This makes interpretation difficult. Documents also contain mistakes, omissions and prejudices, and can even be deliberately misleading. It is difficult to discover these flaws and to take them into account if the circumstances in which they came into being are no longer known. For these reasons it is important to combine this method with other methods of data collection.

OBSERVING AND DOCUMENTING SITUATIONS

Observation is a normal process. Teaching entails continuously looking for answers to practical questions: What is happening here? What does this situation 'demand' from me? What happens if I act in a certain way? Will the situation develop in the way I expect? These observations are normally intuitive and unfocused. Professional action requires an 'eye for the whole situation' (a kind of intuitive 'seeing' that is different from a carefully aimed 'looking'). However, this kind of 'seeing' has some draw-backs as a basis for developing professional competence. For example,

- it is diffuse – the focus is wide-ranging, details get lost;
- it is biased – observations are acted upon with a minimum of reflection. There is a danger of seeing 'what one wants to see';
- it is ephemeral – observations are held in memory for only a very short period of time so that it is difficult to subject them to detailed ex-amination.

These weaknesses can be overcome by using systematic observation procedures. Diffuseness can be countered by observing something specific for a particular purpose. Bias can be controlled if observation is used to test assumptions against the 'reality'. Finally, the ephemeral nature of 'seeing' can be overcome by using techniques that 'capture' events. There is a price to be paid in a reduction in the integrity of vision of the situation as a whole, so it is important that systematic observation procedures should not replace intuitive 'seeing', but rather complement and correct it.

Here are suggestions for trying out four ways of observing and docu-menting a situation: direct observation, audio-recording, photography and video-recording.

Direct observation

Direct observation of a situation does not require any technical tools except perhaps pencil and paper. It can be thought of as a form of *participant observation*, a well-known method used by anthropologists and ethnographers. Normally, participant observers are professional researchers who become part of social situations in order to investigate them. However, for teacher-researchers, the prime task is not observation but teaching. When teachers observe lessons systematically, they are taking on a second task which sometimes fits in with their teaching but may sometimes conflict with it.

When teaching requires the teacher's full attention or emotional in-volvement, it is difficult to achieve the 'distance' necessary for systematic observation. There is strong pressure either to abandon the attempt or to introduce technical aids (e.g. tape-recordings). On the other hand, there are times in many lessons when some form of systematic observation is possible: for example, during group work, or when pupils are 'reporting back' to the class.

The most important skill in observing is sensitivity to what is observed. Observers have to cope with a dilemma that is normally insoluble. On the one hand, reality is what is reconstructed from the observer's current under-standings; on the other hand, reality has its own 'stubborn' character which resists interpretation and reconstruction. This dilemma is only 'solvable' by 'double vision' – by being aware of one's assumptions and expectations and at the same time approaching each situation as if it were a totally new one (see Chapter 9, p. 204). The temptation to make quick and simplistic assumptions about a situation based on one's own prejudices is very strong, particularly for a teacher who is under pressure to take action.

In spite of these difficulties, we believe that there are particular advantages in teachers' using direct observation as a method of data collection, in particular because it relates well to the complex processes of teaching and learning. Here are some ideas to help you get started:

1 Preparing to observe

Observation always involves selecting from a stream of events. So that this does not become a matter of chance, consider in advance:

- *What* are you going to observe? Is it the sequence of events, a pupil's behaviour, or one specific aspect of your own behaviour? The more limited the focus of observation, the more precisely it can be observed. However, the more limited the focus of observation, the more likely it is that the outcomes will shed light on only a small, possibly even minor, aspect of the original research question.
- *Why* are you carrying out the observation? What are the assumptions and expectations on which it is based? Observing is not a mere registering, but also a theoretical reconstruction of a situation. The observer's assumptions and expectations are theoretical tools for this reconstruction. They are her or his 'pre-judices' (pre-judgements), but striving for objectivity in observing does not mean that prejudices can be completely avoided; rather they should be clarified as far as possible, so that the part they play in producing an understanding can be taken into account at the stage of interpretation.
- *When* will the observaton be carried out, and how long will it take? It is particularly important for a teacher-researcher to decide beforehand at which times in the lesson it is likely to be possible to devote attention to observation.

The simple method suggested below is a useful way of preparing to observe, both to increase sensitivity and to focus the observation on a chosen research question.

M15 GETTING TUNED INTO DOING OBSERVATIONS

1 First of all write down the focus for your observation (e.g. 'the level of pupils' oral participation').

2 Write down what you would like to see in relation to this focus (what kinds of evidence do you hope to get?).

3 Write down what you suspect you will probably observe (e.g. 'Only A – if anybody at all – will ask a question without being asked'). In doing this, try to be as precise as possible (e.g. 'B is going to call out an answer without putting up her hand' instead of 'B is going to behave badly').

4 Choose one of the expectations listed above which relates closely to your research question and which you expect to be able to observe during the lesson you have chosen.

5 Decide what is the best way of writing notes of some or all of your observations (during the lesson or afterwards).

2 Recording observations

The main problem in direct observation is keeping a record for later use. The record can be made either during or after the observation.

Keeping a record *during* the observation

Time is a rare commodity for teachers during lessons. It may save time to use an observation schedule with predefined categories. In the lesson each relevant event is then assigned to a category and thereby recorded.

Let us take an example. A teacher thought that she might be paying more attention to pupils in certain sections of the classroom than to pupils in other sections. She decided to keep a record of the pupils she called on and to note in each case whether or not they had given any signal that they wanted to be called upon. She made a plan of the seating arrangement in the class and marked a sign against the name each time a pupil was called on (e.g. a '+' for 'called after having given a sign' and '-' for 'called without having given a sign'). After a while, a pattern began to emerge on the plan. During the observation she was already becoming aware that she called on some pupils more often than others. She responded by distributing her attention more evenly. Although this 'distorted' the result, it served the purpose of her investigation.

This example illustrates the essential elements in using an observation scheme of this kind:

- Categories must exclude each other: e.g. calling a pupil with/without a signal.
- There needs to be a schedule or pro-forma of some kind on which observations are recorded.

- There have to be rules for recording observations. In the example given above, the rule was: whenever the teacher called a pupil, she marked a sign against the name on the class seating plan.

The categories in the example can be related to the observed situation quickly and with a minimum of interpretation. This is very important if observations are to be recorded reliably without unduly disturbing the progress of a lesson.

Pupils can be asked to help with simple observation tasks. For example, an English teacher asked one of his pupils to mark each pupil's utterances on a class list during ten lessons. Afterwards the teacher compiled the results and found that the number of utterances during these ten lessons varied from pupil to pupil between 12 and 107. He was then able to talk to the three pupils with the lowest number of utterances and try to identify possible reasons and develop ways of increasing their participation.

There are a large number of schedules for direct observation (see Hook 1981). However, we believe that it usually works better for teacher-researchers to design their own schedules, matching them closely to the purpose and subject of their observation. The existing schedules are generally designed for use by observers who are not teachers and who do not have to cope with any other demands in the situation. Consequently, the schedules are often extensive and may require observers to be trained in how to distinguish categories correctly. By designing their own schedules, teachers can avoid these disadvantages. However, as the examples show, schedules provide only relatively thin information. A schedule is most useful for an initial survey, which is then followed up by other methods (e.g. memos of the observed lesson, see Chapter 2, p. 19).

Making a record *after* the observation

It is usually much easier for teacher-researchers to make a record of the observation *after* the event, even though this may mean that some details will be lost. In most cases, the teacher will not be able to write a full record immediately after the observation. However, the most important observations should be recorded as soon as possible, at least in the form of brief notes (perhaps in the form of a résumé of data, as described in M25) to make it possible to produce a fuller reconstruction at a later time.

One of the most important methods for recording observations is the 'memo' (see Chapter 2). If the observations recorded after a lesson do not relate to single events but follow a research question over a longer period of time, they will develop a diary-like character (see also Chapter 2). Other methods are suggested later in this chapter.

M16 ANECDOTES

An anecdote is a story about an event which is striking or surprising. Here is an example told by a secondary teacher:

> I decided to investigate the quantity and level of difficulty of homework given to members of my class (11 year olds) and began talking to Benjamin in 'tutorial time' one day. He was considered one of the less able children, but he became very animated telling me about making 'sugar volcanoes' in Science: 'We got a . . . some baco foil and we made a column cone-shaped with a pencil . . . put it like a hole inside, the shape of a volcano, and poured some sugar into it and put them under the bunsen burners – and like lava come out! It was all different colours.' But he was worried about Science homework: 'I don't know if it's effort . . . it's hard to finish all my homework and that'. I asked if he could turn to anyone for help and he said he sometimes asked his Dad, but really his Dad expected him to get his homework done himself. When he came in from playing at about 9 pm he tried to do it in the bedroom he shared with his elder brother who always had the TV on. It seemed that although he enjoyed Science, the work was too difficult for him, especially as his home background was not supportive. But then he said something else: 'If I get homework before break, I do it at break, or I do it at dinner time. So I don't have to do so much homework at home. I get confused and that if I get a lot of homework. Like the last two lessons at the end of the day, I can't do that at school, so I take that home and do it . . . I get confused . . . I remember quite a lot of it then, at school. See it's not so long away from that lesson. See when you've been out at play and that you forget some.' Suddenly I realised that I had completely misunderstood the nature of his problem. It wasn't so much that he couldn't *understand* the work as that he couldn't *remember* what he was supposed to do. What I needed to do was to help him write down his homework and get him to practise reading it aloud before he went home.

Anecdotes usually arise from surprising experiences rather than from planned observations. Because things have not happened as expected, the experience stands out from the stream of familiar events. There is a discrepancy between expectation and reality which can help us to develop a new practical theory as the basis for changes in our practice. (See the discussion of discrepancies in Chapter 3, p. 35.) Recording a surprising event as an anecdote saves it from oblivion and makes it available for further analysis and discussion (perhaps with pupils or fellow teachers). Writing anecdotes is not difficult and is a good way of recording first-hand experiences by describing situations and kinds of behaviour.

An anecdote should contain the following:

- a description of where and when it occurred and the people concerned;
- enough background information to give the context of the event;
- an account of the event (it should be written in a narrative form; important utterances (statements, answers, questions) made by the main participants should be quoted exactly in order to retain the authenticity and immediacy of the situation. The sequence of actions should be clear so that they can be easily imagined in their context);
- some commentary giving the observer's spontaneous under-standing of the situation. (It is important that this is clearly distinguished from the account of the event.)

M17 SELECTIVE OBSERVATION USING TOPIC CARDS

This method of recording observations is directed by carefully chosen questions:

1 Write down on about ten separate cards some issues about which you want to collect data (for example, pupils' attention span, pupil A's behaviour).
2 At the end of the school day, shuffle the pack and deal two or three cards. Reflect on what has happened during the day in relation to these issues and write observation notes for each in your research diary. This should take no more than 10 to 15 minutes.
3 On each subsequent day, deal a further two or three cards until you have written observation notes about each issue. Then start again from the beginning, possibly reshuffling the pack so that you take the issues in a different order.

What is special about this method is the combination of systematic and random elements of observation. During the day the teacher knows all the issues that may become the subject for observation notes, but does not know which ones will be chosen when the cards are dealt at the end of the day. This serves to raise the level of readiness and sensitivity in observing. As time goes on, connections emerge between observations. Some issues can be dropped if they prove unproductive and new ones can be included, for example, by splitting some of the existing issues into two (see Hook 1981: 132).

M18 OBSERVATION PROFILES

In an observation profile, notes are recorded on a two-dimensional chart using criteria that closely refer to the research question(s).

The example in Figure 5 was drawn up by a teacher who was researching how to organise role play. The profile has a horizontal axis, dividing the lesson into phases chronologically (before, start, rehearsal, etc.). The vertical axis sets out the things you are interested in looking at (children's activity, concentration level).

Profiles like these help with recording observations after the lesson, as the blanks on the profile stimulate the memory. Observation profiles can also be useful if another person takes the role of observer. By giving a profile to the observer, a teacher can indicate what he or she considers to be important. Profiles can also be used when analysing transcripts of lessons and interviews (see M26).

TEACHER'S PROFILE (Miriam)

TABLE 1 – teacher's profile (Miriam)

	Before	Start	Rehearsal	Performance	Discussion	Clearing up
My activity	Informal chat. Some direction of activity re collection of equipment.	Semi-didactic discussion/ lecture to ascertain the comprehension of particular part.	Helping with ideas and problems with equipment. Conveying information. Encouraging activity among those reluctant.	Watching. Helping with odd equipment and queries. Altering what happened by passing written messages to particular people.	Adding to ideas already brought up by Ros. Encouraging new ideas from kids. Helping to take vote on idea for next week.	Seeing that equipment put back, that room left tidy. Listening with half an ear to other ideas
Children's activity	Seating themselves. Talking. Making enquiries as to the nature of the afternoon's activity. Moving about. Slow flow of children into classroom.	Some listening. Some restlessly whispering. Some quietly carrying on with written work.	Heavily involved in preparing their ideas physically and mentally.	Watching with a high degree of intensity. Acting out their ideas. Janice and Susan acting as a link. Using me and Ros to confirm ideas. Acting on messages.	Quiet, controlled but very lively interest and contribution.	Some taking equipment back some helping to clear up. A milling around and breakdown of activity.
Noise level	Fairly high	Low but mumbly	Very high	Extremely quiet except for actors. Quiet talk at breaks.	Moderate	Fairly hign
No. of children	–	20 really involved. 6–7 uninvolved	All except 3–4 opters-out	All – either as audience or actors	All	

Figure 5 Observation profile
Source: adapted from Walker and Adelman (1975: 22–3)

3 Using other people as observers

As paradoxical as it may sound, most teachers know too much to make good observers in their own classrooms. Observation requires a certain 'naïvety', a 'stranger's view' (Rumpf 1986), an ability to see the un- expected and uncommon in daily routines and in what is considered 'normal'. As a teacher-researcher, you need to distance yourself from the situation.

Every situation in the classroom can be seen from different perspectives:

- *The teacher's perspective* The teacher is responsible for organising what goes on in the classroom and will tend to want to judge the lesson (and him/herself) as more or less successful, according to particular aims.
- *The pupils' perspectives* They may see themselves in a number of roles, for example, as partners (or opponents) of the teacher in organising and enacting what goes on.
- *Another person's pespective* An outsider will want to experience the situation and understand it.

Knowing the perspectives of the pupils or of another person helps teachers to distance themselves from the situation. By acting as an observer, a fellow teacher or an external critical friend can provide a new perspective on the classroom, if only by having 'blind spots' different from those of the teacher.

In addition, someone who is not teaching is able to observe more precisely, having time to do it without any responsibilities for the lesson. Such an observer has access to information that is not easily accessible to the teacher-researcher and which may, on occasions, be hard to handle. For that reason you need to choose an observer whom you can trust. Once trust is established, you should not be content with trivial comments, but ask the observer to describe in detail what she or he has seen. If you ask specific questions and/or define your expectations before the observation (e.g. What does A do in the course of the lesson? Or: I expect A will only write down calculations copied from the blackboard) it is easier for the observer to focus attention on the events that are important to you and write observation notes that will be genuinely useful.

Ask the observer to give you written notes as soon as possible, and take time to look at these and consider what additional information you need. Writing notes requires the observer to impose an order on impressions and some things may have got lost in the process. If you talk to the observer about particular points, keep a certain distance and don't apologise for things which were 'bad' in your opinion, or try to justify yourself. If your perception deviates from the observer's, don't engage in any arguments (except perhaps to provide counter-examples without any comment) because the purpose is not to win an argument but to understand and learn as much as possible about another person's observations and interpretations. You may find it useful to look at the rules for analytic discourse (M7).

M19   NOTES ON LESSON OBSERVATIONS

What is important in writing good lesson notes? Here are some suggestions, modified after Grell and Grell 1979: 297.

1   Describe what happens as precisely as possible:
   • what teacher and pupils say – use quotations;
   • what teacher and pupils do – be as precise as possible ('pupil A is in tears' instead of 'pupil A is sad'); What exactly is the task set? What page of the book the pupils are working on, etc.

2   Use abbreviations for words that occur frequently (e.g. we use T = teacher, P = pupil not identified by name, PP = several pupils, initials for identified pupils, B = blackboard, HW = homework). Draw a seating scheme with the pupils' abbreviated names on it, or a number for each pupil so that you can easily identify him or her.

3   Check your notes after the observation in order to correct mistakes, make things clearer, and add additional remarks. Possible additions are:
   • your feelings about specific events (friendly/unfriendly, encouraging/discouraging);
   • ideas which came into your mind, e.g. things which might have been done differently.

4   Intensive observation throughout a whole lesson is very exhausting, so it's a good idea to alternate intensive phases with phases that demand less attention (e.g. 5 minutes trying to note as much as possible followed by 5 minutes taking brief, summarising notes). One way of changing the demands on your concentration is to change the focus (e.g. observing one group in depth and the rest of the class more cursorily).

5   There is a need to distinguish between descriptive and interpretative reporting. Descriptive reporting describes the behaviour 'as it is' (what has been said and done) with as little explanation, judgement and evaluation as possible. This kind of reporting refers to the lowest step of the 'ladder of inference' (see M12). Interpretative reporting clarifies the effect of an event or a piece of behaviour on the observer (the feelings which were evoked, how she or he understood it, etc.).

6 A helpful way of ensuring that you record both descriptions and interpretations is to fold your paper down the middle and use the left-hand side for descriptions and the right-hand side for inter- pretations and personal responses.

M20 SHADOW STUDY

When an observer works alongside a teacher, there is the opportunity of carrying out a more precise investigation by using some additional methods of data collection, for example *shadow study*. In a shadow study, the observation is concentrated on one individual or a small group and carried out over a longer period of time. The observer shadows a pupil, a group of pupils, or the teacher-researcher, for perhaps a day or more.

For example, Robinson (1984) observed a child during her first three days at school from 20 minutes before school started until 20 minutes after the end of the last session, and made detailed notes. His study showed that at first the child was keen to start 'working' from the first minute of the day, but because she was made to do 'admin' and boring repetitive tasks, her enthusiasm quickly cooled. According to Robinson's interpretation: 'Alienation begins as soon as pupils arrive at school'. The study resulted in the headmaster and teachers restructuring the beginning of the school year.

While carrying out a shadow study, the observer should be as close as possible to those being observed (e.g. a group of pupils) without being seen as a part of the group and without being involved in the pupils' work.

Using a tape-recorder to observe

Tape-recordings capture the sounds of a situation. Compared with direct observation, some information is lost in a tape-recording: in particular, the surroundings and and all non-verbal communication (movements, facial expressions, gestures, etc.). However, a more complete record is made of the sounds than is possible in direct observation. There are two ways of using tape-recordings:

- recording complete teaching sessions, to give an overview or to help in identifying possible research questions;
- Recording interactions which are narrowly limited in time, and care- fully selected to throw light on a chosen research question (e.g. a

teacher explaining a concept to one child, a session with the whole class revising a concept taught in a previous lesson, or a small group carrying out an investigation).

An example: teacher–pupil interaction on tape

This is taken from an English teacher's study of methods of teaching poetry to 15 to 16 year olds preparing for public examinations (see Somekh 1986b). Instead of reading and discussing poems with the class as a whole group, she experimented with giving each pupil a choice of poetry books and a choice of ways of responding, including: drawing or collage work; writing their own poems; and writing critical interpretations. The last of these was essential preparation for the examination, so pupils were told that they must choose to respond to some of the poems in this way. Although the rubrics of the examination (which was innovative at the time) instructed pupils to 'write in any way you like about this poem', the teacher knew, from her experience as an examiner, that marks were allocated for a particular kind of response which needed to be taught. The extract from the transcript below gives the interaction between the teacher and a British-Chinese boy who is preparing to write in this way about a poem he has chosen.

My Old Cat

My old cat is dead
Who would butt me with his head.
He had the sleekest fur,
He had the blackest purr.
Always gentle with us
Was this black puss,
But when I found him today
Stiff and cold where he lay,
His look was a lion's
Full of rage, defiance:
O! he would not pretend
That what came was a friend
But met it in pure hate.
Well died, my old cat.

Hal Summers

Lup:	I don't understand the last four or five lines.	1
T:	My Old Cat. Can I read the whole thing a minute . . . (quite a long pause followed by a laugh). Oh . . . well, down to 'full of rage, defiance' it's all right, isn't it?	
Lup:	Yeah.	5
T:	That's just a description of his cat.	

Lup:	He's saying that the bloke coming in to inspect it, he hated him. The old cat hated the person that's coming in, you know, to look at him. But how can he see that if he's snuffed it . . . all dead? 10
T:	Well, if anybody dies you tend to think back about them and what they mean to you and their good points and their bad points, don't you?
Lup:	Yeah, that he never liked him.
T:	What? 15
Lup:	I think that the cat never liked the human – well, you know, these last lines, saying that he didn't pretend that he hated humans but actually showed it.
T:	But . . .
Lup:	Then he goes, 'Well died my old cat', so I think the old 20 bloke here wants the cat to die.
T:	Oh look, I've just got an idea, Lup. I don't think I've seen enough in this. Do you see what the cat looked like when he was dead?
Lup:	Yes. 25
T:	'Stiff and . . . His look was a lion's full of rage and defiance'.
Lup:	The person who's come to – 'I', whoever 'I' is.
T:	Yes – or death, maybe.
Lup:	Oh yeah (tone of suddenly seeing), I see.
T:	I suddenly saw that. It's good, isn't it? 30
Lup:	Yeah, when you put death into it, it really fits in well.
T:	And that makes sense of 'Well died my old cat'. In other words, none of this nonsense about, you know, he went gently and it was all for the best.

Although this extract from the transcript is short, it contains a lot of information and we recommend that you read it two or three times to begin to uncover what it shows about Lup's learning and the teacher's method of teaching poetry. Then read on to see how your interpretation compares with that of the teacher concerned. In some respects, your view as an outsider is likely to be different from hers as a partner in the interaction. (Further information on the analysis of such texts can be found in Chapter 6.):

At first Lup is puzzled because the cat who is dead appears to be having feelings, 'but how can he see that if he's snuffed it?' At this point his reading of the poem is very literal.

Next, once again searching for a literal explanation, he presumes that the cat's hatred and anger, at the time of his death, must be directed against the author, the 'I' of the poem, who is the only other 'person' in the poem. In turn this leads Lup to think that the man disliked the cat

and wanted him to die. He presumably reasons that it was likely that
the feeling of hatred would be reciprocal. This is, of course, a serious
misreading of the poem.

Up to this point in the conversation, I myself had assumed that the cat's
anger was directed against dying in the abstract and the world in general,
but Lup's literal approach here gave me a new insight – perhaps it is the
approaching figure of death who the cat hates. After I suggest this, Lup
says 'Oh yeah' with a tone of voice expressing sudden understanding. He
goes on, 'Yeah, when you put death into it, it really fits in well'.

During the conversation Lup had understood the poem and I, too,
had come to a new understanding of it.

(Somekh 1986: 30)

This analysis shows that tape-recordings can be valuable in giving
insights into pupils' thinking. Tape-recordings also provide a way to
begin helping pupils with problems: for example, they can be given a
transcript like this and asked to read it carefully and make a list of what
they do to solve a problem. If this is followed up by discussion with the
teacher, pupils can have a closer look at their problem-solving strategies
and try to improve them themselves, as well as trying out new strategies
suggested by their teacher. When Lup read the transcript quoted above,
he told the teacher that he had learnt an approach to reading other poems.

I just learnt how to understand. I don't know how to put it in words
. . . . What I'm trying to say . . . is that . . . you give us an idea . . . you
know, try all the different things, and see if the poem actually, you
know . . . see if it fits in with the poem – and if they do then it's
probably the right answer.'

(ibid: 31)

He then went on to read Dylan Thomas' powerful, but difficult, poem
about the death of his father, *Do not go gentle into that good night* and was
able to write about it without any further help from the teacher.

Usually, pupils only remain conscious for a short time that their work
is being taped, especially if it happens frequently. However, they are
likely to be a bit less communicative than usual at first. The extent to
which a situation is changed by a tape-recording also depends on how
pupils have been prepared in advance, how important they believe the
recording to be, and whether or not they think the purpose is worthwhile.
This is especially true for older pupils.

Technical suggestions

We recommend the use of small tape-recorders with batteries and normal
size cassettes (the size of a Walkman). They take up very little room and

the cassettes are easily available. The quality of the recording is important and we recommend an external lapel microphone which will not pick up the sound of the recorder's own motor. The recorder can be slipped into a pocket (of pupil or teacher). The microphone can be clipped to a lapel or on to a shirt front (at the height best suited to picking up the pupils' voices – teachers always talk louder than pupils!). For 'whole class' recordings, we recommend you use a tape-recorder with a high quality microphone, perhaps suspended from the ceiling by attaching it to a light fitting.

Before using the tape-recorder, check it is working (batteries charged and microphone switched on) – we have all had bad experiences. Afterwards, label the tape immediately (place, date, class, topic). You may find it useful to write a brief note to yourself highlighting the main points of interest so that you can locate this tape quickly when you need it (see data summaries, M25).

Suggestions for transcribing tapes

It is easy to make a tape-recording and it actually takes very little extra time. The problems only start afterwards, when you try to make use of the information. If you decide simply to listen to the tape, you will need to play it to yourself two or three times (preferably making brief notes) before you will be able to make any sensible use of the data.

For detailed study, it is worth transcribing parts of the tape, although this is very time-consuming. Good quality recorders with headphones and foot-operated switches for playing the tape help to save time. Because it takes so long, only relatively short extracts should be transcribed unless you are lucky enough to have some secretarial support.

M21 PARTIAL TRANSCRIPTION OF RECORDINGS

An economical way of making good use of tape-recordings is to transcribe selected passages. We recommend the following steps:

1 Listen to the whole recording to get an overview.
2 Listen a second time and make brief notes of the structure: give each individual scene or phase of the lesson a catchword and note the corresponding numbers on the tape counter so that you can quickly relocate the passages.
3 On the basis of these notes, select the sections that are important and relevant to the research question and transcribe these fully.

There is the tendency for people to leave out the first and sometimes the second of these three steps under time pressure. However, this 'saving' can cost a lot of time afterwards, and can reduce the quality of the research. The first two steps are an important part of the process of constructing theory from the data. They also structure the work and enable sensible choices to be made about how best to reduce the effort expended on transcribing.

M22　USING ABBREVIATIONS AND ANNOTATIONS WHEN TRANSCRIBING

Here is a list of examples of abbreviations and annotations we use to save time and space when transcribing. You could adapt these as convenient. What is important is to have a system which is quick to use and consistent, so you know exactly what abbreviations mean when you come to read the transcript.

T	teacher
Ca	Caroline (named pupil)
P	unidentified pupil
PP	several pupils
(inaud.)	inaudible
(Let's add the 3?)	words guessed because difficult to hear
(surprised)	transcriber's note of non-verbal data (e.g. tone, laughter) or summary of an untranscribed passage
(. . .)	words or phrases omitted
. . .	short pause
(pause, 6 secs)	long pause (in this case 6 seconds)
this point	emphasised by stressing the word
as – a – result	spoken slowly

Photography

'An image tells more than a thousand words.' This is an exaggeration, at least in relation to classroom research, but none the less photographs capture aspects of situations which – although they *can* be observed – are more fleeting and more easily missed than verbal utterances.

What is the value of photographs for teacher-researchers?

Photos can be useful for teacher-researchers in a number of ways:

- to supplement observation notes or tape-recordings of a situation: photographs bring back a holistic impression of what took place and where;
- as an aid to studying non-verbal aspects of situations and events;
- as a means of raising questions and stimulating ideas to find a starting point for research.

Photos are most valuable when used in conjunction with other sources of data (especially interviews and tape-recordings). They can also provide access to other data – for instance, photographs make good starting points for interviews – younger pupils especially may be stimulated to talk by the concrete character of pictures. 'Tell me about what you were doing when this photograph was taken' has the advantage of being a fairly specific question while not being a leading question.

Taking photographs in a classroom can be disruptive, but this can be minimised. It may help if the teacher – or one of the pupils – takes the photographs (rather than a visitor) and if the pupils know why the photographs are being taken and come to see being photographed as routine. Any nervousness can be further reduced by making the photographs available afterwards and discussing them with the pupils. If the photographer is one of the pupils, it is very important for the teacher to explain the purpose of the photographs carefully beforehand.

Technical suggestions

The quality of photographs mainly depends on the quality of the camera. It is important to be able to take photographs unobtrusively and without any delay. An automatic focus and lightmeter are therefore important. It is useful to have a zoom-lens (if it is not noisy) to take photographs at different distances without having to move. Flash can be very disturbing, so it is best to use a highly sensitive film (e.g. 400 ASA) which does not need flash. For some purposes it is essential to use a polaroid camera so that the photographs are available immediately, but in general the disadvantages of polaroid cameras (the flash, the noise, the rather low quality of the pictures and the relatively high cost of films) outweigh the advantages.

As soon as possible after taking the photograph, a data summary should be made (see M25), including a brief description and comments on the situation in which the photograph was taken. This contextual information is essential, because the 'frozen frame' nature of a photograph provides no information on what came before and after. After the film is developed, the photographs should be labelled immediately (place, date, class, topic) and any necessary additions or changes made to the data summary.

Making video recordings

At first sight, video-recordings (made with a camcorder) combine the advantages of tape-recording and direct observation as well as providing a record of movement. However, they also combine the disadvantages of both. The main advantage is that a relatively holistic record is made of the situation – seen from the perspective of the camera. By representing the sequence of events in time, video-recordings can make the context and causal relationships more accessible than other methods of data collection. Behaviour patterns become visible, including the relationship between verbal and non-verbal behaviour (audio-tapes are actually better for analysis of verbal patterns alone). Video-tapes are also an excellent way of presenting a situation to others (for example, to pupils) to open up discussion.

These advantages must, however, be weighed against several disadvantages. Video-recordings involve the use of a lot of equipment which can be very distracting in a classroom (this can be minimised by using the camera in a static position and using it sufficiently frequently for it to become routine). More seriously, video-recordings can be misleading because they give the appearance of being a complete record of events when, in fact, they are highly selective (the camera has been pointed in one direction and there is no indication of periods of time when it has *not* been recording).

Making good use of video-recordings takes a lot of time. A careful analysis concentrating on events that appear to be essential in terms of the research question requires repeated playings of the tape. Transcribing extracts (see M21 and M22) is more time-consuming and technically ponderous than transcribing audio-tapes: first, because foot-operated switches for playing the tapes are not available; and second, because pictures and sound together contain a lot of information and this makes it necessary to spend time sifting useful data from much that is irrelevant.

If someone is operating the camera, it is possible to use a range of shots, including close-ups and panning. However, it is usually counter-productive if an attempt is made to imitate the conventions of television. For the teacher-researcher, a broader view of the situation can be much more informative than a face that fills the screen 'as on TV'. Sometimes a fixed camera is sufficient, positioned on a tripod at the (window) side of the classroom and allowed to run for the whole session without pause. It can be focused on a whole area of the room, on a group of pupils, or on one pupil. Recordings of this kind make rather boring viewing for people not involved, but they provide a more complete record of the session for purposes of analysis or discussion.

Sound is also a problem with video-recordings. The radius of the camera microphones is usually too small to record a lesson involving a whole class, so an additional high quality microphone is necessary. The positioning of the camera will depend on what is being researched: e.g. focused on a group of pupils if group-work is the subject of investigation. Afterwards the tape should be labelled immediately (location, time, subject, topic of investigation) and a data summary made, as with audio-recordings.

The ethical considerations discussed earlier in this chapter, which are always important in collecting data, are more sharply focused when using video, because the apparently more holistic and authentic record of events increases the chances of invading the privacy of individuals and representing them in a way that goes against their interests.

INTERVIEWING

Interviews have developed from everyday conversation. They give access to other people's perceptions, including crucially the thoughts, attitudes and opinions that lie behind their behaviour. Behaviour and its manifestations are ambiguous. Behaviour which the teacher regards as disruptive in a pupil may mean something quite different to the pupil herself. Questioning, orally or in writing, offers more direct access to the meaning it has for the pupil than do other methods.

However, even this access is limited. The interview, at its best, only brings to light what the interviewee *thinks* – his or her interpretations at the time and under the circumstances of an interview. Even interviewees who wish to tell the 'truth' will, in some sense, misinform the interviewer by 'withholding' information: they cannot be conscious of all the motives for their behaviour and are engaged in their own process of reconstruction in answering the questions.

Interviews as a relationship between people

Interviews are communications that aim at getting to know points of view, interpretations and meanings in order to gain greater understanding of a situation. The key precondition for the success of an interview is to make it clear to the interviewee that what he or she has to say will be important in at least one of two respects:

- important for the interviewer: the interviewee should feel that his or her views will 'count' for the interviewer.
- important for the interviewee: the interviewee should believe that the outcomes of the interview may be useful for him or her.

How can we set up the right preconditions for an interview? Watzlawick *et al.* (1980) distinguish between two levels of communication: the level of content and the level of relationship. These levels influence each other:

the relationship between two persons (e.g. mutual trust) influences their understanding of what is said (the content). Vice versa, the interpretation of what is said influences the relationship. The interviewer can exert influence on both levels, but only to a limited extent. If a teacher interviews a pupil, the interdependence of the two levels can cause problems: teacher and pupils do not just build up a relationship during the interview, but have already developed various attitudes towards each other (on a continuum of trust and mistrust, affection and animosity). This framework of relationships provides the context in which the interview starts. It influences the way in which the pupil understands what the teacher says. If the pupil sees the teacher as someone who is interested in answers to questions only in so far as they demonstrate what has been learnt (repeating what the teacher already knows), the interview questions will be viewed in that light: i.e. the pupil will not assume that the teacher really wants to know something she does not yet know, for example, the pupil's own personal perceptions. This problem can be partly overcome by asking a third person to do the interviews (for example, a fellow teacher) – someone the pupil does not know, or know well, and who will therefore have a better chance of building a new relationship during the interview.

If relationships between the teacher and pupils are strained or difficult, a third person acting as interviewer can be indispensable in getting access to the perceptions and views of pupils. But, ultimately, the teacher-researcher should interview the pupils him- or herself. Although action research usually starts from the teacher's research interest, in the course of time it should become a common concern of the teacher and pupils. We suggest this not only for ethical reasons, but also because it is our experience that the quality of understanding and potential for development are greatly enhanced if teachers and pupils become research partners. An important side-effect of establishing the kind of relationship needed to interview pupils is almost always a permanent change in the relationship between teacher and pupils which is likely to be supportive of teaching and learning.

Preparing for an interview

The aim of an interview is to learn from one or more people what you do not yet know, but consider to be important. So you need to reflect carefully on what you want to know and why. The aim is to decide upon the issues that will be the focus of the interview. We recommend that you formulate questions either that are central to the research question, or that will enable you to reflect more deeply on sensitive issues. However, this does not mean that you should ask the questions in this form in the interview, because preformulated questions tend to take your attention away from the interviewee and the dynamics of communication.

In this chapter we will only discuss *unstructured interviews*. Unlike structured interviews, they give interviewees room to develop their own concerns in answering the questions. Hron (1982: 119) distinguishes two kinds of open interviews: focused and narrative. For the teacher-researcher, the focused interview is probably more useful. These interviews ask for perceptions and interpretations of specific events (e.g. things which occur during a lesson = the focus). However, they allow fluent transitions to the even more open narrative interview. The latter generally has very little structure. Often it simply puts forward a broad topic (e.g. 'learning') which is then developed by the interviewee.

The choice of the interviewee depends on the research question. For some questions, it is important to interview several pupils who somehow differ from one another (for example, some who are achieving well and others who are underachieving or working erratically, etc.). For some questions, individual interviews are more appropriate; for others, group interviews. The group interview is a more normal situation for students: the social pressure to talk is lower for the individual because of the presence of others, and if one student talks, this can stimulate comments from the others. However, if there is a danger of pupils being ridiculed by others during the interview (for example, because they express themselves awkwardly), it is better to interview them individually.

The choice of place and time for the interview also depends on the research question as well as on opportunity. Secondary teachers may be able to interview pupils during a free period if a colleague is prepared to release them from class for a short period. Primary teachers may be able to carry out interviews with the support of a colleague in a team-teaching situation. Sometimes interviews can take place during teaching sessions by setting tasks which require students to work independently of the teacher, either alone or in groups.

Carrying out an interview

Starting the interview

It is important to explain the purpose of the interview at the start and to enlist the interviewee's help. This does not take long and is recommended for several reasons:

- *ethical reasons*: it is not ethical to use the information from the interview for any purpose without the knowledge of the interviewee;
- *reasons relating to quality of the information*: an interviewee who knows what it is all about is more likely (in most cases) to be able to give the information the interviewer needs;
- *motivational reasons*: an interviewee who is treated as an equal and fully

informed (becoming a kind of partner) is more likely to confide in the interviewer.

It is essential for pupils to be clear that the interview situation is different from other question-and-answer sessions with the teacher. If pupils perceive the interview as a kind of exam, they will probably say only what they believe the teacher wants to hear. We recommend tape-recording interviews for two reasons:

- the record of what was said will be more authentic;
- you will be able to concentrate fully on the interview and not be distracted by having to take notes.

It may not be possible to tape-record: interviewees' permission should be asked and may be refused; on some occasions the tape-recorder may make interviewees so nervous that continuing will adversely affect the quality of the interview. In this case, the best strategy is to take brief notes during the interview and use these to write more detailed notes later. It may help during the interview to use one half of a folded sheet for catchwords and the other half for quotations, as this makes the subsequent reconstruction easier.

Listening

It takes two people to generate the information: one who tells and one who understands what is said. Communicating honestly about complex matters requires particular qualities of the listener: empathy, disciplined imagination, sympathy, attention, patience, distance, a feeling for truth, and a willingness to understand (see Bedford in MacDonald and Sanger 1982).

During an interview, listening is as important as asking questions. Non-verbal messages communicated by the interviewer's manner of listening are as important as the questions in indicating to the interviewee whether he or she is being taken seriously as a partner in the interview. These are some of the ways of showing seriousness and respect:

- by not interrupting trains of thought;
- by accepting pauses as a natural part of reflection (this can be difficult for a teacher-researcher as pauses are often interpreted quite differently in the classroom);
- by accepting whatever is said, however unexpected and regardless of the interviewer's own views. This kind of neutral attentiveness can be difficult for teachers: they may not be used to accepting statements with which they do not agree nor, on the other hand, to withholding approval when the interviewee meets their expectations. Both approval and disapproval of utterances can show the interviewee that

the interviewer does not want to know what they really think but wants only confirmation of previously held views. This can lead to interviewees trying to gain the approval of the interviewer, perhaps by guessing what he or she want to hear. Approval and appreciation should refer not to what is said, but to the interviewee's willingness to communicate.

Asking questions

The questions should make clear what the interviewer wants to know, while at the same time helping the interviewee to explore his or her mental space. The beginning of an interview is particularly important because it establishes a relationship between the interviewee and the interviewer. It indicates to the interviewee what the 'real' intentions of the interviewer are. A good beginning may be to recount an event (for example, something that happened in the classroom) and ask: 'Why do you think that happened? What do you think lay behind it?' A personal approach of this kind shows that the researcher is interested in the interviewee's opinion.

It is important to ask open questions, especially at the beginning of an interview. They allow the interviewee to shape the answer and take responsibility for structuring the information. By telling the interviewee the issue and asking for comment, he or she is free to decide on the best linguistic form for presenting the ideas. This is another way of showing that it is what the interviewee thinks that counts.

Closed questions (where the format and structure of the answer is already predefined) could tell the interviewee (irrespective of what has been said beforehand) that the prime purpose of the interview is to confirm or disconfirm the interviewer's expectations, or that the interviewer is not interested in any details. Closed questions are useful only if the interviewer knows exactly which answers are possible for a question and wants to cross-check possible interpretations. But if such questions (for example, expecting yes/no answers) open the interview, the whole discourse can become a '(short) question and (short) answer' game.

However, openness can also go too far, for example, if a bundle of issues is packed into one question. This may seem very open to the interviewer, but the interviewee will more likely regard it as a request to be superficial and get the impression that the interviewer wants to know a little about a lot, but nothing in depth. It is better to focus on one issue at a time.

Answers to questions can be either more descriptive or more interpretative. The balance is partly determined by the way the interviewer asks the questions. It may be best to shift the direction as time goes on. At the start of an interview, it is often better to ask for matter-of-fact and descriptive information, leaving room for more personal and interpretative comments when the necessary confidence has been built up. Questions should not be suggestive, and interviewers should not prompt to elicit particular opinions. Leading questions have negative consequences for the interview, as they undermine the credibility of the interviewer. The younger the pupils, the more sensitive and receptive they are to suggestions (e.g. 'Don't you think . . . ?'). Transmitting the interviewer's expectations to the interviewee (sometimes without either of them being aware of it) is one of the most common pitfalls in carrying out an interview.

Expansion and clarification

The process of expansion and clarification is one way of showing the interviewer's interest in what the interviewee is saying. It demonstrates a desire to learn about details, to clarify apparent contradictions, and so on. There are many ways of doing it:

- Repeat what the interviewee said in your own words to find out whether your understanding is in line with what he or she wanted to communicate ('What I'm hearing you say is . . .'). This is especially important if the interviewee has difficulties with self-expression.
- Ask the interviewee to give an example as illustration.
- Ask for interpretations of causes, reasons or aims.
- Ask for clarification of contradictions.
- Have a pen and paper to hand and ask for diagrammatic representations of some ideas.

There are some pitfalls. Attempts to expand and clarify can give contradictory messages: a request for more details can be interpreted either as a strong acknowledgement of the importance of what has been said, or as an indication that you are questioning its truth. When expanding and clarifying, it is important to make clear that you are interested neither in finding fault nor in confirming your own prejudices, but only in understanding.

After the interview

The most important task after the interview is preparing the data for further analysis. If the interview has not been recorded on tape, the interviewee's statements should be reconstructed as literally as possible with the help of the notes taken during the interview (the sooner this is done the better, as it is remarkable what you can remember within 24 hours). If the interview has been recorded on tape, you should label it (interviewee, place, date, topic) and write a data summary (see M25). Sometimes it is useful to transcribe some sections of the interview (see M21 and M22).

Some suggestions for learning how to interview

Interviewing is not very easy to learn as it depends more on developing an approach than on learning a set of techniques. One good idea is to study interview transcripts and analyse how the interviewer and interviewee influence each other. Video-recording and analysing interviews on television or radio can also help. The most important way of learning, however, is through preparing, carrying out and analysing your own interviews. M23 contains some suggestions.

M23   FIRST ATTEMPTS AT INTERVIEWING

1   Write notes on issues or questions that spring to mind from your own teaching: pleasant or less pleasant experiences, hopes and fears, wishes and plans.

2   Ask a pupil with whom you have a good relationship, and whose work is of a good standard, to let you interview her (him). Enlist support from colleagues to enable this to happen during school hours with as little disruption as possible. (Choose an older rather than a younger pupil if you have the choice.)

3   Explain to the pupil that you want to research and develop your teaching, and for that purpose you need to see things from a pupil's point of view. Tell her that you want to record the conversation on tape because otherwise you would have to take written notes, but that the tape will not be heard by anybody else except your colleague, X, with whom you are engaging in joint research.

4   Give your pupil interviewee your own impressions of lessons with this class (very briefly – don't pre-empt 7 below). Then remind her of one or two events that took place in a recent lesson containing pleasant and/or unpleasant features.

5   Ask the pupil to tell you her impressions of the lessons.

6   Be careful not to interrupt the pupil while she is talking and to give her time for pauses. If she stops talking, repeat her last statement and ask for more details (or for an example).

7   If you have time for more questions, you might ask her what she thinks your aims are in teaching the class, and how she views them or what kind of difficulties she (or others) experience in your lessons.

8   Thank the pupil at the end and ask her for suggestions regarding whom you might interview next.

9   Write brief notes of your experience in this interview and what was striking about what you found out.

10   Listen to the tape several times when you have time to relax. Try to get a feel for your own contributions, for their influence on the pupil, and for how her statements influenced your questions. Make notes on what you have noticed (rather than on all the good intentions which come to mind!). Compare these notes with the ones you wrote immediately after the interview (has anything changed?).

11   Now have a critical look at the suggestions for interviewing earlier in this chapter and compare them with your experience.

12   It can also be helpful to play the interview to a colleague and ask for comments. Probably by now you will notice much more than your colleague, but in spite of that, someone not directly concerned may be able to see things you have failed to notice.

13   Invite another pupil to an interview and reread your notes on the first interview again before you begin.

M24 'STANDARD QUESTIONS' FOR THE ANALYSIS OF CLASSROOMS

These questions can be used for interviews with teachers and pupils, or for lesson observations, as follows:

• to start a discussion on teaching without pre-empting the outcomes in any way;

• to explore ideas about teaching before deciding on a clearly defined research question or starting point ;

• when trying out interviewing for the first time.

If you are interviewing a teacher, these are 'standard questions' you might ask before a lesson:

1 What are your aims in this lesson?

2 What do you expect to be problematic in this lesson?

You can also ask the teacher these questions after the lesson (What were the aims . . . the difficulties?). Or you can adapt them for pupil interviews:

1 What were your teacher's aims today, do you think? What was your teacher wanting to get out of this lesson?

2 Were there any parts of the lesson when you got lost? Or bored? Were there any parts of the lesson which you particularly enjoyed?

These apparently simple questions often lead to profound discussions of teaching because they are quite open and allow the interviewee plenty of opportunity to explore ideas. They can, of course, be easily adapted for other situations.

Sources of misinformation in interviews

A basic criticism of interviewing as a technique is that what people say they do is not always the same as what they do, or what they intend to do (either consciously or subconsciously). If intentional misrepresentation is excluded, there are many other reasons for misinformation, for example: selective memory, rationalisation, difficulty of the topic, personality and status of the interviewer, the presence of a tape-recorder, and the social and environmental framework in which the interview takes place (often very different from normal conversation). .

Some of these problems can be addressed as follows:

- When people contradict themselves, it often indicates a tension in their thinking. Talking about the contradictions can sometimes resolve them.
- Pauses indicate that the speaker is thinking or that something is being left out. Careful questioning, without interrupting the train of thought, can help to stimulate the interviewee's memory.
- An important method for avoiding distortions is to ask for details (What did you do? What did you say?). Because of their background knowledge, teachers can easily jump to the wrong conclusion and fail to ask any further questions, believing that they already know the answer.
- Misinformation can be reduced by confronting interview data with other data (e.g. observation notes), or by comparing accounts given by different people (see 'Triangulation' at the end of this chapter).

There is also a deeper reason for distortions in interview accounts: interviewees are not always sure how to interpret situations, or why they have done certain things. The interview can be an opportunity for them to understand the situation better. This illustrates a more general point: interviews are not only about collecting data, they constitute a more or less meaningful, more or less conscious learning process for interviewees. The interview creates a framework within which the interviewee is made to think about a situation or issue and interrelate experiences, thereby potentially gaining a deeper understanding. Collecting data in this way can contribute to a change of attitude and, indirectly, to a change in the situation itself.

THE WRITTEN SURVEY

The written survey is a kind of formalised interview. The most important difference is that in a survey the interviewer cannot respond immediately to the answer or specify new questions.

Sample questionnaires

Roger Pols (n.d.: 16–18) used a simply structured questionnaire to investigate how his pupils (10 year olds) were coping with group work.

Questionnaire on group work

Please underline the answer you want to give. If you are not sure, underline the answer which comes closest.

1 How much of the lesson did you enjoy? All of it /Some of it /None
2 How much do you think you learnt? Nothing /Something / A lot
3 How much did you understand? Most of it /Some of it /Nothing
4 Could you find the books, information, equipment your needed? None/Some of it /Most of it
5 Did other people help you? A lot / A little /Not at all
6 Did other people stop you working? A lot /Sometimes /Not at all
7 Did the teacher help you? Enough /Not enough
8 How long did the lesson last? Long enough /Too long /Not long enough
9 Was the lesson boring /interesting?
10 Did you need anything you could not find? Yes /No
11 Where did you get help from? Teacher /Group /Someone else
12 How did you find this work? Easy /Hard /Just about right
13 Write down anything which made it hard for you to learn.
14 Write down anything you particularly enjoyed about this lesson.

The teacher's aim was to learn how the pupils assessed (1) the task, (2) their success with it, and (3) the conditions (material, time, help from the teacher and classmates, distractions). His immediate purpose was to improve the planning of the next lesson. In the long term, he wanted to find out which changes, if any, take place when group work is done more frequently. He asked the pupils to fill in the questionnaire (in about 5 minutes) after each group work session. The quantitative analysis took him half an hour. One of the findings was:

At first 63% said they were only hindered a little compared with 48% at the end, while none said at first they were hindered a lot, but by the end this had risen to 16%.

The teacher commented on this result:

Left to their own ideas, some children are not capable of working without direction and become a distractive influence. They therefore need direction – but in a large class inevitably some children must wait.

One of his long-term conclusions was:

There is also a need for a careful plan and structure (again only if required) for the less-able children to fall back on if their own ideas are frustrated. Again these must be well backed up with resource material.

Suggestions for the design and use of questionnaires

Compared to interviews – which are often seen as difficult, hard to organise, and time-consuming – questionnaires seem to be a quick method for data collection, easy to develop and administer without any problems. This widespread impression is not quite correct. The usefulness of a questionnaire depends principally on the quality of the questions, as follow-up questions are possible only in a limited way, if at all. Even if the questions have been well formulated, so that they are understood as intended, the insight gained with the help of the questionnaire is often much smaller than expected. In general, the more structured a method of data collection is, the more formal and meagre in content are the answers. In spite of this basic problem, questionnaires can be useful to teacher researchers. The following suggestions should be helpful. (For further information, see Hook 1981: 159ff.)

Before starting work

Effort spent on thinking through the problem you want to investigate before developing the questionnaire saves a lot of time and effort in subsequent analysis of the data. Consider in detail why you are asking these questions, what answers you expect, and what you are going to use them for. The more precisely you know your intentions in advance, the better structured the questionnaire can be. Vice versa: the less you reflect beforehand, the more open the questions will be and the more difficult and time-consuming the analysis will be.

Formulating the questions

A questionnaire can consist of open or closed questions. If closed questions are used, the informant chooses the answers that apply to him/her; with open questions, the informant must formulate answers. In both cases a number of decisions have to be made when constructing the questionnaire.

Decisions on content

- Is the question really necessary? How useful are the expected answers likely to be in solving the problem?
- Does the question cover the topic? Will you need further information (more questions) to be able to interpret the answer? Be careful not to ask 'two questions in one' as this makes the answers difficult or impossible to interpret.
- Do the respondents have the information they need to answer the questions? If you have doubts, no useful answer can be expected.
- If you ask for subjective information (opinions, attitudes) have you followed this up with a supplementary question asking for factual information? For example, the question, 'How satisfying was the group work for you?' can be followed by a question asking exactly what the group did.
- Questions concerning very personal, intimate or taboo topics, or topics where personal interests or social pressures are dominant, tempt respondents to give an expected answer or one that will show them in a good light (if the question is answered at all). If you need to ask questions on these topics, it is useful to begin with a more general question (e.g. 'What, in your opinion, do most pupils think about the new dress code?') before asking a direct one ('What do you think?').
- Does the way you have constructed the questions restrict the range of possible answers? For example, check you have asked for both negative and positive experiences.

Decisions on the wording of questions

- Could the wording be misunderstood? Are the concepts easy to understand for pupils in this age group?
- Does the wording suggest a particular answer?
- Are there any emotionally loaded words? These might have negative consequences for the validity of the answers.
- Does the question ask for a factual account or subjective opinions? Either is quite valid, but it's important to know precisely what you are asking for in each question.
- Which is more suitable – a direct or an indirect question? Direct questions ask about a person's opinion on an event or situation, for example: 'Did you enjoy the lesson?' Indirect questions ask for reactions to other

people's opinions, for example: 'When he was talking to Sanje about group work, Peter said: "I don't bother to do much in group work because the others do the work anyway." What do you think of Peter's statement?'

Decisions on the form of answers

- Should the questions ask for 'multiple-choice' answers, short responses (closed questions), or freely worded answers (open questions)? Combinations of open and closed questions are often possible, e.g. 'Do you prefer working on your own – with a classmate – or in a group (please underline your choice)? Why do you prefer to work in the way you chose?'
- In multiple-choice answers, are all the alternatives useful in relation to your research question?
- In multiple-choice answers, are all the choices clear and distinct from one another, and are all the important options covered? Notions like 'generally' and 'well' are ambiguous and difficult to interpret.
- Is it clear what kind of response is expected? For example, in multiple-choice answers, is it clear whether only one or more than one alternative should be chosen?

Decisions on the sequence of questions

- Will the answer to the question be influenced by the content of the preceding questions?
- Does the sequence of questions allow the respondent to move gradually into the topic of the questionnaire? Factual questions should come at the beginning and questions asking for attitudes, feelings, etc. should follow later when the respondent has had a chance to focus as fully as possible on the situation.

Advantages and disadvantages of closed questions

The questionnaire can be a useful method of data collection for teacher-researchers. Its most important advantages are:

- It's easy to distribute to pupils, parents, fellow teachers.
- It need not take much time to fill in.
- A large number of individuals can answer the questions simultaneously.
- The impersonal nature of the questionnaire and the possibility of answering anonymously make it easier to be completely honest.
- The social pressure on the respondents is not as strong as it is in an interview, which makes it easier for respondents to reflect on the questions before answering.

However, there are also disadvantages:

- There is no way of ensuring that questions are understood as intended. This problem can be reduced by testing the questionnaire in an interview situation before it is handed out, or by including more than one question on the same topic (to enable answers to be cross-checked).
- Questionnaires are not always taken seriously by everyone, particularly if the topic is not important to the respondent. This can also show up in the formal answers, for example:
  - in that yes/no or true/false question are more frequently answered 'yes' or 'true';
  - in the selection of 'middle of the road' answers rather than those that express clear views.
- Answers may be distorted by factors of which the respondent is not at all or only partially aware. Attitudes and emotions are closely linked to self-image and self-esteem. This can lead to a subconscious tendency to paint a positive picture of oneself, or at least to avoid giving a negative impression.
- When questionnaires are not returned anonymously, there may be a tendency for the respondents to confirm the researcher's expectations (for example, in questions asking for information about a teacher-researcher's own teaching).

These problems are equally true of the interview but are more easily recognisable through the personal contact between the interviewer and the interviewee. One important way to reduce these disadvantages is to win over the respondents to the aims of the research. For example, if the pupils understand the reason for the research and are interested in its outcomes, a questionnaire can produce very reliable data and, at the same time, make a contribution to improving the situation. A questionnaire can also raise pupils' awareness of issues for further research.

COLLECTING DATA AS PART OF CLASSROOM WORK

Using open questions, it is easy to collect pupils' perceptions in the course of classroom work. Pupils' essays, for example, can perform the function of a questionnaire with one open question. After an unpleasant argument with pupils as a result of disappointing work on a project, one teacher asked his pupils to write their reactions to the lesson for homework. The resulting writing was the most important source of data on this lesson, as these three examples indicate:

'He [the teacher] practically roared. He asked every single pupil what she had done for the project. I said: "Questions" and he wanted to know "Which ones exactly?" Of course I couldn't remember exactly and didn't say anything. He said (loudly): "Well, this is great – saying nothing and then moping." I was very angry because I wasn't moping. But I hid my anger and didn't say anything, and I was sulking on purpose. I wanted to tell him what I thought to his face' (Alexandra).

'First I was very angry. How could he talk to us like that? He shouted at us and called us "schemers" and other names. I'll show him! But after a while I realised that the conflict was our fault too, not only his' (Kerstin).

'I got angry when we were called "idiots of this day and age" – lacking in character, lazy, scheming, deceitful, mean, and whatever. That we would never find a job because we lacked character. Of course we realised that we had not done everything we should, but was it necessary to threaten to keep us back a year?' (Sabine).

(Schindler 1990)

Commenting on his pupils' essays the teacher wrote, among other things: 'I was surprised at the words I had used according to my pupils. I was not aware of having used some of these words. I was also surprised that they had evoked such strong emotions. It was my intention to make them think about it and maybe even to hurt them. After all I felt hurt by their lack of work. But in fact I had only caused helpless anger and put many pupils into a situation where they had to reject me, because some of my expressions had damaged their self-respect.' (Schindler 1990)

One way of collecting data regularly on pupils' perceptions is the pupil's diary. Entries in a diary can be answers to open questions, for example, 'What happened at school today that made you think?' One primary teacher used diaries both as regular homework for her 6 year old pupils and a source of data for research on her teaching. She also started a dialogue with some pupils by writing short comments after their entries.

A COMBINED METHOD: TRIANGULATION

We have already said that for many research questions it is useful to combine different methods of data collection. A typical combination of methods is the so-called 'triangulation' (see Elliott and Adelman, n.d.; Somekh 1983b). In most cases, triangulation consists of a combination of observation and interview, whereby data on a particular situation are collected from three perspectives ('corners'):

- the teacher's perspective (by an interview);
- the perspective of individual pupils (by interviews);
- the perspective of a neutral third party (by observation).

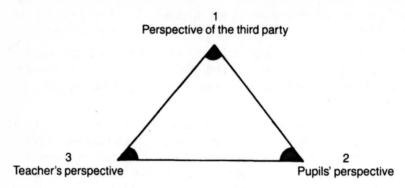

Figure 6 The three corners of triangulation

An example of triangulation

As teacher in charge of Information Technology in his school, Vince Moon (see Moon 1990) wanted to try out and evaluate the use of computers and a video-camera in a 'Newsdesk' project with his class of 10 year olds. 'News' from a simulated press agency was printed out by the computer at random intervals (using the *Newsdesk* program). The children had to work in groups to handle the writing (on other computers), presenting and video-recording of a television news broadcast. The project was set up as a special activity and took a whole day. An outside facilitator or *critical friend*, Jon Pratt, was available to help with data collection. A triangulation exercise was carried out.

1 The teacher and the critical friend planned the day together, deciding on the aims of the activity and drawing up a list of concrete issues and questions as the focus for data collection. (They started from the 'standard questions', see M24.)
2 On the day, the critical friend observed the activities, spending part of the time taking notes and part taking photgraphs (1st corner of the triangle).
3 A short time later, the critical friend interviewed three pairs of pupils chosen by the teacher, using the photographs as a way of starting the discussion, as well as the original issues and questions (2nd corner of the triangle).
4 After the lesson, the teacher used the issues and questions as a framework for writing detailed notes of his perceptions of the day (3rd corner of the triangle).
5 In this way they arrived at three sets of data: the views of the six pupils

(as a partially transcribed interview), the teacher's perception (in writing), and the observer's notes. The data were then juxtaposed, enabling a comparison of the three different points of view to be the focus of the analysis.

6 The results were fed directly into plans for a second Newsdesk Day with a parallel class. The value of having three points of view became clear in analysing the extent to which the teacher should structure the day: initially it was the teacher's view that more structure had been needed to enable the groups of pupils to work more effectively, but the pupils felt it had been important that they had been allowed to organise themselves. The critical friend was able to contribute his view that at one point an intervention from the teacher had come too soon and may have impeded the group's decision-making.

Advantages and disadvantages of triangulation

Triangulation is an important method for contrasting and comparing different accounts of the same situation. Through identifying differences in perspective, contradictions and discrepancies can emerge which help in the interpretation of a situation and the development of practical theory (see chapter 3). In addition, where the different perspectives agree with one another, the interpretation is considered more credible (see earlier in this chapter, p. 91).

Triangulation has the following advantages:

- It gives a more detailed and balanced picture of the situation.
- The contradictions which are often hidden in situations become visible, enabling a more profound interpretation.
- It breaks the 'hierarchy of credibility', which limits our understanding, by giving equal status to people from different ranks. 'Hierarchy of credibility' means that individuals of a higher social rank are more credible (reliable) than individuals of a lower social rank: the teacher is more reliable than the pupil, the headmaster is more reliable than the teacher, and so on. Triangulation regularly shows that pupils are able to help explain a situation by providing relevant information hitherto unknown to the teacher (however good his or her relationship with pupils may be).

But triangulation also has its disadvantages:

- Many teachers see it as threatening. It obviously demands a high degree of self-confidence to confront your own perceptions of a situation for which you feel responsible (and which you feel is a 'part of yourself') with other people's perceptions, and in doing so to question them. It seems that a neutral observer's perception is seen as less threatening than the pupils'. John Elliott (1978) recommends teachers new to research not to begin with triangulation, but to start with less threatening methods of data collection, such as free observations recorded in a research diary, or tape-recordings of lessons.

- A further disadvantage of this method is the amount of effort required to set it up: a neutral observer has to be invited into the classroom and data on the same situation collected from three different sources. However, it can be helpful to focus data collection within a relatively short period of time – particularly as triangulation provides very rich data which are likely to take some time to analyse and interpret.

Chapter 6

Data analysis

How can we make the best use of data? How can data be processed so that our understanding of a situation becomes clearer, more analytical and more reliable as the basis for planning future action? This chapter – like the one on data collection – is a kind of tool kit. It contains a variety of methods of analysis to make the best use of data.

MAKING SENSE OF DATA

Human beings look for meaning. We are often quick to ascribe meaning to chaotic events: this is one of our most important abilities. It helps us to see the world as a network of interrelationships, coherent and predictable. The more we refine this ability, the more we feel at home in our environment. A very old example of the human need for meaning is mythology. Here is an Australian aboriginal myth:

> Walu, the sun goes down into the sea every evening and becomes Warrukay, the great fish, so that she can swim under Munatha, the earth, and come back to the right place for morning.
>
> (Isaacs 1980: 144)

For the inhabitants of the coastal region, the sun sinks daily into the sea and emerges again on the other side of the world. It must have come to the other side somehow. What is more plausible in magical thinking than supposing that the sun could only do this in the shape of a big fish? This myth resulted from an *analytic process* in which observations were selected, put into relation with each other, and interpreted. The explanation seemed plausible to the people: it corresponded with their understanding of the world, confirmed and expanded it. It was emotionally balanced and made them feel secure.

In another example, meaning is also ascribed to events:

> While a teacher is explaining a point he is observing the classroom. He watches the behaviour of some of the under-achieving pupils, among

others Susie, who from previous experience he does not expect to pay much attention. He notices that Susie is listening. Then she asks a sensible question. The initial impression is intensified and is accompanied by interpretations and feelings: e.g. 'Susie is participating'; 'perhaps she is having a good day'; 'maybe I've been underestimating Susie'. But the teacher is still unsure. 'Is she really on task? Or is she only pretending? After all she isn't taking notes.' He wants to be sure and asks Susie a question which she should be able to answer if she has really been listening. Susie is able to answer the question and the teacher gives her an approving smile.

One of the purposes of analysis is to find explanations which 'fit' our understanding and therefore seem emotionally plausible. The teacher searches for an interpretation of the situation which seems right to him and serves as a secure basis for action. However, plausible explanations cannot necessarily be trusted. Sometimes they are the product of prejudices and wishful thinking and fail to stand up to examination. Another of the purposes of analysis is to check on explanations and test them. As a result, what seems to be plausible at the end of an analytic process often differs from the assumptions that seemed to be valid at the beginning of the process.

The example above illustrates the most important analytic procedures:

- Events are observed.
- The focus of observation is selective. The teacher pays more attention to the low-achieving pupils.
- Events are organised to present a coherent mental picture, that is, a theory of the situation. The teacher relates different observations to each other (e.g. Susie listening, Susie asking a sensible question).
- The situation as perceived is interpreted: the teacher draws conclusions: 'Susie is participating', 'she is having a good day', 'maybe I have underestimated her'.
- The teacher's understanding of the situation is examined critically. Not only is a theory constructed, based on the perceived events, but it is subjected to critical questioning. The critical part of the analysis goes hand in hand with the constructive one. In the example, this takes place through internal questions ('is she only pretending?'), through observations that at first seem to contradict the interpretation ('she isn't taking notes'), and through definite actions (asking a question).

Rather than being clearly separated from each other, all these procedures are interconnected and enable the teacher to cope emotionally, intellectually and practically with daily routines. This kind of analysis of daily routines allows us to react quickly to an initial understanding and use it as the basis for action (e.g. praising Susie). Its disadavantage is that it all happens very quickly so that we can process only a very limited amount of information and carry out a small number of testing procedures. It is therefore insufficient for understanding any major discrepancies between the teacher's expectations and his perceptions of the situation. This requires greater distance from the events and a certain amount of time to concentrate on the analysis.

If you want to withdraw from the stream of events and give yourself time for careful analysis, data are important as a prop for memory: with the help of data, memories can be reconstructed more vividly (e.g. by listening to the tape-recording of a lesson), and be more available to critical questioning, making it possible to correct false interpretations.

The analysis of both data and direct experiences should result in a deeper understanding of the situation, and a 'new' practical theory that can extend existing understanding. Through analysis, data and experiences are restructured and practical theories elaborated. In this sense analysis, theorising, and restructuring are the same. But can this be called research? Is the teacher who is doing the analysis a *researcher*? A sharp line cannot cannot be drawn between analysis in research and everyday analysis. The more systematically an analysis is carried out (based on theoretical and methodological knowledge), the more critical the process (tested against conflicting data and interpretations); while the more communicative it is (the process and the results made public), the more it deserves to be called research. The results of the process of analysis are preliminary and hypothetical, and require further testing through reflection and examination in practice.

The essential elements of the analytic process are summarised in Fig. 7.

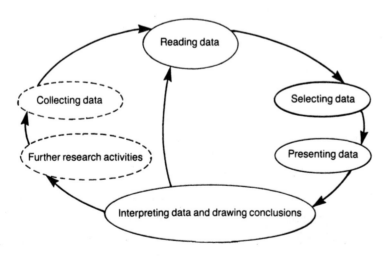

Figure 7 The analytic process
Source: Miles and Huberman 1984: 23

The constructive stage of analysis:

- *'Reading' data*   Data are 'read' (closely scrutinised) in order to recall the events and experiences that they represent: What was done? What was said? What really happened?
- *Selecting data*   Important factors are separated from unimportant ones; similar factors are grouped; complex details are sorted and (where possible) simplified.
- *Presenting data*   The selected data are presented in a form that is easy to take in at a glance. This can be in the form of a written outline or a diagram (see Chapter 4, p. 61).
- *Interpreting data and drawing conclusions*   Relationships are explained and a practical theory (or model) constructed to fit the situation which has been researched. This theory or model should relate to the research focus.

These activities take place not only during a separate stage of analysis, but during the entire research process, with the result that decisions made in each phase have consequences for what follows. This is especially clear with respect to data collection: decisions have to be made about which aspects of events are observed (selection), in what form the data is stored (presentation), and so on.

The critical stage of analysis

Analysis tries to make sense of data. This construction of meaning is accompanied by a critical examination of the analytic process. Each stage of the analysis is tested. Do the data bring the event to mind? Has the data selection focused on the central issues? Does the data presentation clarify the relationships between events and stimulate further analysis? Does the interpretation explain the data satisfactorily? Critical examination often occurs at the same time as the constructive activities. But sometimes it is useful to create a separate stage in the research process specially for testing. The quality criteria for research discussed in Chapter 5, p. 74 provide suggestions for critique at this stage of analysis. We want now to present practical methods which a teacher-researcher can use in trying to make sense of data. We will begin with elementary methods for the constructive and critical stages of data analysis – a kind of basic tool kit for the teacher-researcher (avoiding repetition of the methods of analysis described in Chapters 2, 3 and 4). We will then go on to present two complex methods combining elements of these basic methods: pattern analysis and dilemma analysis.

CONSTRUCTIVE METHODS OF DATA ANALYSIS

M25 MAKING DATA SUMMARIES

It is helpful to review data immediately after they have been collected (tape-recordings, observations notes, documents) and write a
summary, both to provide easy access to the data later and to get an
overview of what they offer concerning the research question
(compare Miles and Huberman 1984: 50). The data summary might
contain answers to the following questions:

1 What is the context in which the data were collected? Why were
   they collected? Why in this particular situation? Why using this
   method of collection?
2 What are the most important facts in the data? Is anything
   surprising?
3 About which research issue are the data most informative?
4 Do the data give rise to any new questions, points of view, suggestions, ideas?
5 Do the data suggest what should be done next, in terms of further
   data collection, analysis, or action?

It is a good idea to cross-reference each answer to relevant passages
in the data (use the number counter for tape-recordings or number
the lines for transcriptions). Summaries of existing data (pupils'
books, newspaper articles) are also useful. A data summary should
take no more than two pages or it begins to lose its value as a quick
point of reference.

M26 DEVELOPING CATEGORIES AND CODING DATA

One important method of getting 'conceptual leverage' on data (see
Schatzman and Strauss 1973: 117) is organising them into categories
(coding them). Imagine a room in which a large number of toys have
been left lying around and it is your job to create order. You will
probably begin by walking round and having a look at things.
According to your interests and the characteristics of the toys, features
will come to mind which help you to order them: for example, colour,
size, shape, state of repair, the age group for which they are suitable,
and so on. Then you will choose two or more features by which to
begin to sort them. Something similar happens when a researcher

wants to create order from a quantity of data. Categories (features) need to be chosen which are relevant to the research question and at the same time partially express the contents of the data. Using these categories, the data are sorted: for example, by ascribing a suitable category to each passage of a text. This process is called coding.

There are two well recognised methods of coding data. According to the *deductive* method, categories are chosen from the researcher's theoretical knowledge and the data is then searched for relevant passages: in this case the development of categories is independent of the data. According to the *inductive* method, categories are chosen during and after scrutinising the data: in this case the categories are 'derived' from the data (see M11).

In action research, it is probably most useful to use a mixture of both methods, capitalising on what you already know but remaining open to the surprises the data can contain. As the inductive method is less common, we will describe one possible approach to carrying it out, split up into six steps:

1 Read through the text you want to code (e.g. the transcript of an interview). Underline or highlight each passage that seems important (interesting, surprising, unexpected) in relation to your research question. This will give you a broad overview of the contents of the data through the marked passages.
2 Go through the text a second time looking only at the marked passages, and decide upon a category (one word or a short phrase) for each passage that expresses its contents.
3 List the categories on a sheet of paper – the category sheet.
4 For each category, write down the passage(s) it refers to, giving the following information:
    • the name of the text you are coding;
    • the page number of the text;
    • the margin number of the marked passage (each marked passage is given a serial number in the margin, starting with 1 on each new page). For example, 'ON1/2/1' in Figure 8 means that a passage in the Observation Notes, no. 1, on page 2, with margin number 1 has been ascribed to this category. A coding system of this kind is important as it enables much more information to be written on the 'category sheet' which ensures that you can retain an overview.
5 Also write the name of each category in the margin beside the passage it refers to. For example, the short form 'WS' in Figure 8 stands for the category, 'working strategy'.

Figure 8 shows a section from page 2 of Observation Notes, no. 1 (ON1) on a group of pupils working together to solve mathematical problems. In the observation notes, interesting passages have been marked by underlining, and given a margin number at the right-hand side of the page. The coding of the passage is noted both on the category sheet and in the right-hand margin of the Observation Notes (in an abbreviated form).

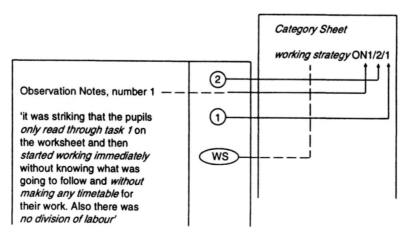

Figure 8 Example of inductive coding

In the process of coding, you begin to hold a reflective conversation with the text. You check whether the categories correspond with what is in the text and relate to your research question, and change them if necessary. Because a number of changes are likely, it is better to do the coding with a pencil. When you have gone through the text a second time, you will have a category sheet containing all the categories you have ascribed to the marked passages on the text, with one or more number codings written beside each category, making it easy to find the relevant passage quickly. The text will also list the categories in the margin, beside the marked passages.

6 Order the categories by grouping concepts which belong together. This gives some structure to the whole by suggesting connections between individual categories (see 'From categories to hypotheses' in M11).

A further step is to write definitions of the categories. A definition expresses your theoretical understanding of the category and gives it a meaning independent of the data. Definitions are useful, particularly if you continue to elaborate and refine them in the course of your work, in relation to both new data and your own developing understandings.

A few practical tips for coding

- Data should be coded as soon as possible, while your direct experience of the event is still fresh. Coding can also be helpful in suggesting ideas of what to do next in your research.
- Categories are key concepts which form the nuclei of ideas. Time spent working on them is well invested. To develop and test your first categories, we recommend that you write a short piece to try out how easily you can use them. Some categories give rise to a number of ideas and suggest possibilites for action, whereas others remain sterile.
- It is an advantage in action research (in contrast to classical empirical research) if the teacher-researcher does the coding, so as to make use of relevant background information not accessible to non-participants in the situation. This implicit knowledge of everyday, self-evident things can, however, lead to 'blind spots'. Therefore we recommend that you talk about the categories, and how best to structure them, with a critical friend who can help you to become aware of any blinkered assumptions which stand in the way of you understanding.

M27   WRITING THEORETICAL NOTES

At any stage in the research process – e.g. when formulating questions or analysing data – ideas and theories are likely to come to mind relating to the research question: what certain data mean; how facts could be explained; how an important concept could be defined, etc. Such ideas should never be wasted, even if they are not needed at the present stage of the research, but should be recorded in the form of a theoretical note (TN).

Theoretical notes help us to move beyond the detail of events to a conceptual level, to develop theories, uncover relationships, and find significance. Writing them takes only a few minutes and is a quick way of capturing emergent ideas during the research process. Writing theoretical notes usually gives some immediate satisfaction, as they offer access to your own ideas which may have been hidden or partly hidden up to this point.

Theoretical notes should always be dated and labelled with a suitable catchword, so that they can easily be found again. It's a good idea to make a brief note of the data or event that gave rise to the ideas. This short section is intended only as a reminder. Further information on this quick and economical first form of analysis has already been given in Chapter 2.

M28 QUANTIFICATION

Teacher-researchers are concerned with the complex problems of practical action in schools and classrooms. Quantitative data are not as valuable in this context as in classical social research, as they often represent too little of the holistic structure of practice.

Nevertheless, some elements of quantification are of great importance in people's thinking. Often when we say that something is 'significant' or 'common', we have come to this judgement by counting, comparing and weighing up. Intuitive counting is often a precondition for developing categories. It is important to become aware of the close connection between our judgements and quantitative aspects of our experience, and to quantify consciously whenever it is useful and gives a good return for effort.

Quantification can be useful in the following situations:

1 *To carry out a preliminary survey and get some data quickly:* For this purpose you can make use of the fact that numbers are much easier to handle than words. Morocutti (1989) carried out research into pupils' participation in her lessons. As a preliminary survey, she counted pupils' voluntary oral contributions in class and found out that almost all came from boys. This was important information, even if the numbers did not suggest any reasons why boys talked more than girls.
2 *To reveal prejudices:* This function of quantification is important because of the key part played by intuition in action research. There are moments when you feel a sense of revelation and everything seems to fall into place. The only problem is that you can be wrong. Observations which fit your own expectations may have been given too much significance and data not fitting your theory may have been ignored. In situations like this, quantification can be helpful to check the reliability of intuition.
3 *To explore the generalisability of findings:* Sometimes results relating to only a few people (or a single case) have more general validity and this can be confirmed by quantitative methods.

M29 SHAPING METAPHORS

Metaphors transfer meaning

A metaphor transfers meaning from one field of experience (often a colourful one) to another field of experience (often an abstract one). A 'scapegoat' according to the Bible (Leviticus 21–2) was a goat sent into the desert loaded with the sins of the Jewish people. Since the eighteenth century this image has been used for a person who has to pay for other people's misdeeds. It would take a great many words to explain the multitude of associations this metaphor brings to our understanding of what it means to be an outsider.

Metaphors go back to the roots of language. Originally there were words only for things that could be perceived sensually and these had to be used to convey abstract ideas as well (see Reiners 1961: 317). For a name to be transferred from one thing to another, there must be something in common that allows a comparison. This can be seen in the example of the scapegoat. But a metaphor only becomes interesting through the ramifications of its meaning, including its emotive connotations, all of which are transferred to the new object. By this means, a metaphor provides the opportunity to see something freshly, offering a new perspective on the concept, object or event to which it is applied.

Metaphors generate meaning

A pupil who sees the teacher as a 'strict judge' will relate to him differently from another who regards him as a 'walking dictionary' or a 'fatherly friend'. We want to explain this generative character of metaphors (whereby they create new meanings, see Schön 1979) with the help of two different metaphors for learning:

Learning as the 'imprinting' of meaning

This metaphor transfers the idea that learning takes place in a manner similar to recording pictures on a film: the lens of the camera corresponds with the sensual organs; the film with the brain; the concepts are frames of similar pictures superimposed upon each other – for example, numerous imprints of different chairs build up the concept of a chair. The metaphor of 'imprinting' transfers certain attitudes from our understanding of filming to the process of teaching and learning. The pupil is seen as someone 'comprehending passively', and the teacher is seen as someone 'giving actively'. This attitude also generates norms of behaviour:

- Pupils should pay attention so as not to interrupt the flow of information coming from the teacher. Making sure that the pupils are well disciplined and receptive becomes one of the teacher's most important tasks.

- Pupils cannot be allowed to act independently, because the teacher has all the information and is therefore the only one able to decide what should happen.
- Curriculum content must be taught by repeating things several times so that they can be memorised (imprinted). The teacher's task is to prepare information so that it can be passed on in this way.
- Mistakes have to be avoided, as every mistake leaves traces that are impossible to erase. The teacher's task is to pass on to the pupils information that is guaranteed and error-free.

Learning as the 'construction' of meaning

This metaphor carries the idea that learners themselves frame their process of learning and 'construct' new knowledge, using the experience and knowledge they already have. This metaphor is similar to photosynthesis, where the plant builds organic matter from inorganic matter with the help of light and chlorophyll. The pupil is seen as an active constructor of knowledge who 'understands' facts by reconstructing them using his or her own resources. This attitude generates different norms of behaviour:

- The teacher should 'start from where the pupil is at', because the pupil's existing knowledge provides the materials for constructing further knowledge.
- The teacher should encourage pupils' independence if they want to exploit their maximum potential for learning.
- The teacher should build on pupils' interests because they will provide the energy and motivation necessary for learning.
- The teacher should offer a variety of activities to cater for the differences in pupils' prior experience.
- Mistakes, far from harming the learning process, will provide an opportunity to reflect on learning strategies and improve them. The teacher should encourage the pupils to monitor their own progress, and support them in doing so.

The metaphors of learning as 'imprinting' and learning as 'construction' call for totally different, even contradictory courses of action – for a pupil to turn to a classmate and ask a question may be seen as an unwelcome disturbance
useful part of the learning process in terms of the second one.

Metaphors enrich the research process

Looking for metaphors and analysing them can help teacher-researchers in several ways. The process widens horizons and enables a better understanding of the teacher's task. Metaphors provide alternative approaches to reality, like mirrors reflecting different facets of the same complex event. The more facets there are, the deeper the understanding of a situation can be, as each facet reflects different aspects of reality. For example, the metaphor 'learning as imprinting' emphasises the curriculum as presented to the student and disregards the processing of the curriculum by the student. The metaphor 'learning as construction' emphasises the dynamics of the students' activities and disregards the cultural and social conditions of learning.

Metaphors are good at communicating complex matters, as they carry a lot of information in a few words. They are – despite consisting of words themselves – the pictures (images) of language. The metaphor of 'imprinting' evokes a number of associations which can remain unspoken, as the reader already knows them from familiar areas of experience. On the other hand, misunderstandings can result from metaphors, as a language full of images is not very precise: differences in people's experience can conjure up different associations. This is especially true of the feelings evoked by metaphors.

Metaphors are of a heuristic (generative) character. They cannot replace the analysis of data, but they can stimulate new directions for analysis and in this way enrich the research and development process. For instance, the metaphor of 'learning as construction' has encouraged many teachers to develop a method of teaching oriented towards problem-solving (see Posch 1986b). See also Schön's interesting example of a developmental process inspired by a metaphor (Schön 1983: 184–7).

Metaphors open up new action strategies. Strategies of action often seem normal and obvious only from the point of view of the generative metaphor upon which they are based. As soon as the metaphor changes, new strategies of action become relevant. If learning follows the 'imprinting' metaphor, it seems obvious that the teacher should structure lessons down to the last detail. If, however, learning is seen as a constructive process, then this approach seems inappropriate. Understanding the generative character of metaphors can help teacher-researchers to distance themselves from the apparent obviousness of daily routines. If you know that you see reality only through the 'glasses' of metaphors (a metaphor again!) it is easier to change them – and new strategies of action become possible (see Chapter 4, p. 52).

Finding metaphors

According to Reiners (1961: 335), metaphors are valuable only if they come to mind naturally. It is no good searching for them consciously. However, Miles and Huberman (1984: 221) give some useful tips on how to assist intuition:

- *Handle data playfully*: for example, asking yourself, if I only had two words to describe this situation, which ones would they be?
- *Talk about data with colleagues*: conversation in a relaxed atmosphere may spawn new and unusual perspectives.

Metaphors usually lead to a radical reduction of data. We advise you not to use this method too early in your research as metaphors can limit your capacity to see beyond them thereafter.

CRITICAL METHODS OF DATA ANALYSIS

Again and again new understandings emerge during the analytic process: new ways of looking at what is familiar, new insights into cause and effect, the way the system functions, etc. How much can we trust our findings? How can we apply quality criteria to the research (see Chapter 5, p. 74)? How can we avoid being trapped by explanations which at first sight seem plausible, but eventually prove to be incorrect? Research involves formulating hypotheses before being sure and therefore taking the risk of being wrong; research also involves careful effort to weed out false judgements – knowing that this will never be wholly possible and that every finding can have only a tentative status.

Critical analysis should consist of two activities: checking the reliability of any evidence that substantiates a finding, and searching for any evidence *against* it. Both activities are important in testing the trustworthiness of findings. Both also contribute to their development: the first by enriching and enlarging them, the second by restricting and defining them and therefore clarifying and sharpening understanding.

It is important that the findings should be clearly formulated before this critical process begins so that they can be either confirmed or disproved by the data. This means relating interpretations to observations (e.g. using the 'ladder of inference', see M12). The reality represented in the data must have the chance to 'speak for itself' – even if the teacher-researcher's main interest is in finding supportive evidence to reduce the amount of work required, or to validate a chosen course of action. It is important to remain open to data that question your theories rather than confirm them, and which therefore encourage further reflection. In the long run, this is an important part of justifying your confidence in your own practical theory. It does not imply denying your own convictions and judgements, which is impossible for a teacher (and is only an illusion for professional researchers). But it does imply a readiness to step back from your assumptions, look at the data, and be open to any evidence that is counter to your assumptions.

The critical analysis of findings is not primarily a question of procedures. More important is intellectual integrity and the determination to be honest with yourself and others. All researchers are under pressure to be successful, especially when implementing and evaluating something new. The feeling that you have to prevail over your own insecurity and other people's scepticism can threaten your willingness to accept unexpected results. It is nevertheless an important part of learning to become a researcher.

Testing the reliability of results is essentially a never-ending process and there can be no such thing as absolute reliability. Nevertheless, the research must stop somewhere. One indication that it is time to finish is when it appears that collecting any additional data would yield nothing new in either a positive or negative sense. This situation is called *saturation*. There is, of course, also a pragmatic limit arising from a teacher's responsibility to act. Since the research is intended to be useful to practice, there is not always time to wait for saturation. In any case, the critical process is not completed with the end of data analysis, but continues as ideas are translated into actions (see Chapter 7).

M30 TESTING THE FINDINGS

Stearns *et al.* (quoted in Miles and Huberman 1984: 72) suggest a procedure for formulating and critically analysing findings:

1 Write a series of sentences on cards, each expressing one important result of the analysis (one sentence per card). The sentences are either freely based on your experience, taken from notes (e.g. your research diary), or taken from hypotheses or analytical notes developed while coding data (e.g. M11).

2 The sentences (cards) are sorted into sets according to the issues to which they refer.

3 Each set of cards is then laid out in a way that makes them easy to survey and clarifies the relationships between them.

4 Each card is checked against the available data. Any data which seem to relate to the sentence are cut out and placed beside the card (you will need to use photocopies of your data to do this – don't destroy the originals!).

5 In the light of the selected data, look again at the sentences and expand, modify and illustrate them, either by writing additional sentences and adding these to the layout of cards, or by rewriting the original cards. In this way, the sentences and data make up

the 'backbone' of a written report, and if this procedure is followed with every single sentence, the report will be rich in detail and grounded in the data.

The following example is taken from action research into the support given to students on teaching practice. Mentor teachers, university teachers and the students themselves all wrote case studies which were analysed as a group exercise during a weekend seminar. The analysis took place as follows: each participant wrote three statements from their findings on cards (step 1). The cards were arranged in an order (step 2) and relationships between cards were identified (step 3). Then, relevant arguments for and against the statements were found in the case studies and cut out (step 4). After examining and developing each statement (step 5), a report was 'put together' analysing and recommending ways of supporting students on teaching practice. The following passage was taken from one group's report:

Statement (developed from a sentence on a card):
The first few days of teaching experience in the introductory course to school practice are too soon to decide on a starting point for a case study, since students are too busy with the basic problems of their school practice.

Evidence for (+) and against (-) the statement, using extracts cut out from the data:

+ CS22/1   Students' statements:
            — 'It didn't seem to make sense to me that I had to write a case study at the beginning of the term.'
            — 'I cannot imagine what I should write about.'
            — 'What could I use as a focus for a case study? Why can't I think of anything?'
            — 'I haven't got any idea at all. I'll just invent something.'
− CS20/6   Mentor teacher's statement: '(. . .) Case studies help to make problems in teaching become visible.'
            And,
− CS20/7   'Asking students to write case studies gives structure to lesson observations, practice teaching and reflection, and has become a useful tool that enables me to get away from the arbitrary jungle of talking about lessons.'

M31 COMMUNICATIVE VALIDATION

Communicative validation is a method for checking the validity of
an interpretation through establishing a consensus view between an
interviewer and interviewee. Teachers use this method when they
tell a pupil their interpretation of what has been said. If the pupil
concurs, this is seen as an indication of the validity of the teacher's
interpretation.

Some authors interpret this method more widely, regarding it as
communicative validation if the researcher's interpretations are
compared with the experiences of those affected by the analysis in
some way, or with interpretations of other people familiar with the
issues: for example, if one or more fellow teachers are asked for their
oral or written comments on the findings.

The amount of agreement indicates the validity of the results of
the analysis. However, as in all other cases, the validity that emerges
through this communication process is fragile and temporary.
Agreement could also result from the unequal distribution of power
in communication, or from cultural prejudices shared by the interviewer and the interviewee, etc. Disagreement in interpretation on
the other hand does not in principle devalue the result, but
challenges the researcher to face the differences of opinion and
explain them (see the example in Chapter 5, p. 74).

The method of triangulation described at the end of Chapter 5 can also
be regarded as a method of critical analysis as it compares alternative
perceptions and interpretations of events with each other.

COMPLEX METHODS OF DATA ANALYSIS

Pattern analysis

What are patterns?

Patterns are 'regularities of behaviour' or 'forms of interaction which
occur over and over again'. This is a working definition (see Ireland and
Russell 1978) which we hope will be deepened and extended by the
example that follows. This is a transcript (translated) of part of a tape-
recording of a lesson on Germanic literature for 14 year old pupils in
Austria. See if you can identify some patterns as you read it.

Extract from transcript of a lesson (18 April 1986)

T: Well, first of all, here are some new worksheets (the next 4   1
     minutes cover comments on homework and exercises).
     Well ... Now we are going to do some work on literature,
     that's why I've handed out these worksheets. We've got to
     about the same place as we are at in History, which is fine.   5
     You will get these worksheets for each chapter in literature
     from now on, on the left side you can always see what
     happened in literature at a given time. I 've underlined the
     facts you should particularly try to remember – OK? That's
     work that you actually should have done yourselves. On   10
     the right-hand side I've listed things that are characteristic
     for that time. Now, I have a question: What kind of things
     are listed on the right? Who can explain to me what I've put
     there? Yes, Bernhard?
Be: Historical facts.   15
T: Well, historical facts! Is there anything else? Something
     special?
PP: (inaud.)
T: Well, not only historical facts, but cultural facts.
PP: Dates, religious events, books.   20
T: Yes, that too, there is a system! That's *one* part.
P: First of all dates.
T: First of all just historical facts.
P: Then culture ... then comes art.
T: Then art. I will present that in a similar way on each sheet   25
     from now on. Is that clear? On the left is literature, German
     literature. On the right historical events, cultural events, art,
     music and literature that is not German, if there is any. OK?
     Recently we have dealt with early Germanic history in our
     History lessons – and those Germanic peoples – you know   30
     this already, what was it they didn't have? ... in order to
     do what is normally done when we think about
     literature ... Clara?
Cl: No writing, right?
T: Right, so they had no writing. That means, that someone   35
     could say, wait a minute, if there wasn't any writing there
     couldn't have been any literature. You could say that
     theoretically, couldn't you? ... But nevertheless the ancient
     Germans had literature although they had no writing, as
     literature doesn't only refer to written documents, but to   40

	everything that is done with language; that is what literature basically is, in a broader sense. And so even the ancient Germans had their literature. Why is this Germanic literature interesting for us, if they didn't have writing? Probably . . . Walter?	45
Wa:	(no answer)	
T:	If they had no writing . . . literature that hasn't been written down normally gets lost . . . in theory . . . I could imagine? . . . Rudolf?	
Ru:	Oral tradition.	50
T:	Oral tradition, yes, that's right. This is important. Oral tradition and only later, when they were able to . . . when someone was interested in it . . . to write it down . . . only then was Germanic literature written down, right? So the notion of ancient Germanic literature, that means literature or stories, narrative poems and other things we are going to learn about a bit later . . . . So these are the things that have been handed down orally over a long period of time and were only written down much later. Remember that, they were written down in about the eighth century for the first time, but ancient Germanic literature existed even earlier. Right? This concerns the ancient Germanic literature, that had only been passed down orally before and was partially written down in the eighth century. Well, what could this ancient Germanic literature have been about?	55 60 65
PP:	About heroes, battles . . . about gods.	
T:	About heroes, battles, gods; so it deals with things that concerned the ancient Germans. So what kinds of ideas and thoughts can we find in this literature? Maria? . . . Hans? . . . Karla? . . .	70
Ka:	Well . . . culture.	
T:	Well, what about this Germanic culture, have we already learnt something about it?	
Ka:	Warlike and rural.	
T:	A warlike and rural view of the world! Good! So things like that which concerned the ancient Germans . . . wars, rural things or important events . . . good. And there are different kinds of literature, they are listed on the left, the first kind of literature is the so-called ritual verse, what could that mean, what might you understand by that? Christine? . . . Paula?	75 80
Pa:	Describing customs.	
T:	Describing customs, that would be possible, that might be possible. But what does ritual mean? Annemarie?	

An:	Well, ritual, that was in the Middle Ages. There is a group of people that has to fight or something (further murmuring, inaud.).	85
T:	Good. And what about the concept of 'ritual', doesn't it still exist today? Werner?	
We:	It's a custom.	90
T:	Yes, it is a custom – relating to what in most cases?	
P:	To gods.	
T:	To gods – or some religious activity. So a ritual is an action taking place according to certain rules. That means, normally everyone knows what he or she has to do at each stage of it, right? You might know of some rituals in everyday life today, can you think of any? Veronika . . . Sandra?	95
Sa:	Daily meals.	
T:	Yes, daily meals. How does it work, for instance? . . . There is a ritual, well, yes, that's right. Totally right!	100
Sa:	You wait until everybody has got something to eat.	
T:	First you wait until everbody has got something, and then?	
Ha:	Grace.	
T:	Yes, maybe you say grace (pupils laugh).	105
P:	Everyone says 'Mahlzeit' (Bon appetit) don't they?	
T:	And then everyone says 'Mahlzeit'. No one starts eating before that, OK? That means there is a ritual, right? First you eat the soup, then the meat, and then the salad. In other cultures it's different.	110
P:	Italians eat spaghetti first.	
T:	Yes, correct. That's a ritual, they eat the salad as a starter, there are different rituals . . . . And then Hans said before you begin there is grace, but of course he meant this as a joke . . . maybe.	115
Ha:	No.	
T:	No joke, OK. I thought it was a joke. I was wrong. Now maybe you already know what ritual verse is. Prayers or spells that were chanted in connection with the religious activities of the ancient Germans. And strictly speaking this is also literature, right? Is that clear? It might rhyme – if it does then it is at least something similar to literature and poetry. So this is this group. So the ancient Germans had, we don't really have to remember this so well, they also had a so-called ritual verse, a kind of literature or poetry that accompanied their prayers and worship. These could be little prayers and spells, they've been found on ( ) weapons and tools they had, you probably know that.	120 125

P:	(inaud.)	
T:	Yes, right, on swords there is something engraved to give it	130
	special power. So that was ritual poetry. It goes back to the	
	ancient Germans. Then a second kind of literature the	
	ancient Germans had, right, is the so-called magical poetry,	
	the magic spells. They are usually short spells – having	
	what purpose? Martha? . . . Edith? . . . Rudolf?	135
Ru:	Well, making people believe something!	
T:	I don't understand what you mean. I don't follow that.	
	What do you mean by that?	
Ru:	Magic has something to do with fortune-telling.	
T:	So this is a spell I say to make people believe that magic	140
	exists? Is that what you mean? I don't think that was the	
	purpose of the spells.	
P:	Weren't spells like that for if a sick person was cured, or	
	something like that?	
T:	Well, right. A spell with abracadabra and things like that.	145
P:	Conjuring up demons.	
T:	Right, conjuring up demons, correct! So there are spells. We	
	must remember that (inaud.). There are the so-called	
	Merseburger Spells. Next lesson I'll bring them with me	
	and we'll have a look at them.	150

(Lesson continues)

What patterns did you notice? A very simple and repeated pattern is
the sequence of alternating speech by the teacher and the pupils. Each
time the teacher speaks, this is followed by a pupil speaking, and this in
turn is followed by the teacher. This could be called the T–P–T pattern:

T:	Well, what about this Germanic culture, have we already
	learnt something about it?
Ka:	Warlike and rural.
T:	A warlike and rural view of the world! Good! (ll.72-5)

This example shows some characteristics of patterns:

1 *Patterns select data.* From the data as a whole, only the data connected
  by patterns are selected. In doing this, certain data are emphasised, and
  other data unrelated to the pattern remain in the background. Even
  selected data are only seen from a certain perspective in relation to the
  pattern.
2 *Patterns structure data.* They organise the contents of the data. The order
  is *discovered* and at the same time *constructed*. This depends on the
  content of the data but also on the prior knowledge, expectations and

ideas (theories) of the person who identifies the patterns. Patterns are segments of the dense network of interrelationships existing in the data or emerging from it.

3 *Patterns interpret data.* They are presumptions (hypotheses) about the nature of teaching and learning:

- Each pattern presupposes that there could be an underlying order upon which is a key aspect of the teaching process;
- Each pattern presupposes deeply rooted attitudes (e.g. of the pupils, of the teacher, towards their roles, etc.) which are keys to a better understanding of teaching.
- Each pattern also assumes that it has effects, that it transmits messages that have influences (e.g. on attitudes).

Looked at on a more basic level, patterns indicate what is routine and habitual. They are usually largely unconscious, controlled by tacit knowledge hidden in unspoken routines.

How is pattern analysis done?

We want now to show how pattern analysis is done, using the transcript already quoted.

Stage 1: What is a pattern?

What are the bits that make up a pattern and what relationships exist between these bits to make the pattern recognisable as a unit within the flow of events? How are patterns related to each other?

During this first stage it is useful simply to describe patterns, starting from intuitive hunches and then trying to elaborate their characteristics and relationships. Further interpretation should not begin until they have been reliably documented (see M12). One pattern has already been identified above. We called it the T–P–T-pattern. It consists of a pupil's utterance in between two utterances of the teacher. Let's have a closer look at this simple pattern:

T: So what kinds of ideas and thoughts can we find in this
         literature? Maria? . . . Hans? . . . Karla? . . .
Ka: Well . . . culture. (ll.68–71)

It is striking that the pupil answers with a catchword and that the word is complementary to the teacher's question, in the sense that it fills the gap left by his question. The teacher's question requires part of a sentence as an answer (perhaps only one word) to complete his statement. This is what the pupil supplies. Let's call this pattern the 'sentence completion pattern' (see Figure 9). There are five examples in the transcript (ll. 31f.,

43–6, 70f., 91f., 134–5). A variation is the 'listing pattern' which prompts pupils to list concepts in answer to the teacher's question.

T: Well, what could this ancient Germanic literature have been about?

P: About heroes, battles . . . about gods. (ll. 64–6)

Here too, the pupil's short answer fits the gap in the teacher's question. We can find several examples of the 'listing pattern' in the transcript as well (ll. 11f., 64f., 96f., 103). As both patterns appear frequently, it is likely that they are established routines. The following passage shows this:

T: (after explaining the layout of the worksheet): Now I have a question: What kind of things are listed on the right? Who can explain to me what I've put there? Yes, Bernhard?

B: Historical facts.

T: Well, historical facts! Is there anything else? Something special? (ll.12–17)

The teacher's question requires the pupil to explain facts on the worksheet. The pupil, however, interprets this as a request to list them.

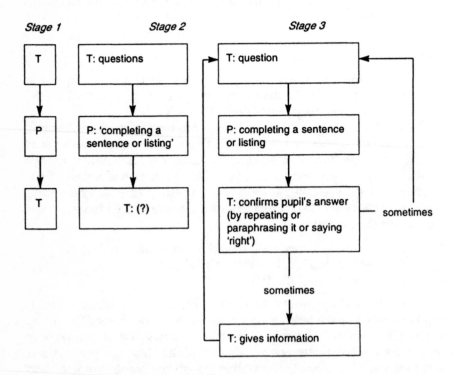

Figure 9 Development of the T–P–T pattern

The teacher accepts the pupil's interpretation with his response. In this way both patterns remain stable, even though the teacher's question originally asked for something else. In a similar way, the following question could be an invitation to begin a discussion:

T: If they had no writing . . . literature that hasn't been written down normally gets lost . . . in theory . . . I could imagine? (ll.47–9)

Nevertheless, the pupil's answer is a catchword again: 'Oral tradition'. This means that he interprets the teacher's question according to the 'sentence completion' pattern.

Let's try to differentiate the T–P–T pattern more carefully still by having a closer look at how the teacher reacts to the pupils' 'listing' or 'completion sentences'.

T: And what about the concept of 'ritual', doesn't it still exist today? Werner?
We: It's a custom.
T: Yes, it is a custom relating to what in most cases?
P: To gods.
T: To gods – or some religious activity. So a ritual is an action taking place according to certain rules. That means, normally everyone knows what he or she has to do at each stage of it, right? You might know of some rituals in everyday life today, can you think of any? Veronika . . . Sandra?
Sa: Daily meals.
T: Yes, daily meals. How does it work, for instance? . . . There is a ritual, well, yes, that's right. Totally right! (ll.88–101)

From this passage we can develop a hypothesis about the 'sentence completion' pattern:

1 A pupil's correct answer is confirmed by the teacher repeating the answer (l.91);
2 This is followed by a further question from the teacher (l.91);
3 Sometimes some information is added between confirming the pupil's answer and asking the new question in order to stimulate his or her response (ll.93–6).

This pattern can in fact be found in many other passages of the text (see Figure 9). Looking again at the transcript, we can find further evidence: the teacher does not always confirm what the pupil says by repeating it literally, but sometimes just paraphrases or says 'right, correct'. It would seem that these variations have the same confirming function. Let's continue our analysis by looking at how the teacher reacts to pupils' wrong answers. Surprisingly, there are hardly any examples of this in the text. Only two passages can be interpreted as 'not accepting the pupil's answer'. In one, the pupil does not answer at all (ll. 43–9), so that the teacher repeats the question, making it easier by adding some further explanation – and then asks another pupil. In the other, the teacher says 'I don't understand what you mean' (ll. 137–8) after a pupil has answered and asks for further explanations. So, there are not enough data to derive a further pattern for cases where pupils answer 'incorrectly'.

When teachers on a course are given this transcript, they are able to see the T–P–T after reading the first half, and are then able to predict many utterances of both the teacher and pupils in the rest of the transcript. If the pattern allows them to predict future interactions, this indicates that it is a characteristic pattern for this specific group. It is sometimes a rather unnerving experience for them to find out how easily other people's behaviour can be predicted – and what if their own behaviour can also be predicted? Who wants to be predictable? Who would be pleased to know that his or her behaviour is in some ways mechanical?

This kind of regular pattern – for both pupils and teachers – is usually the result of unconscious routines that have been established through experience. But routine behaviour should not be discounted. On the contrary, it is important to ask to what extent these routines reinforce our aims and values, and what consequences they have.

Stage 2: What is the significance of the pattern?

What does it show: for example, what assumptions, skills, intentions or fears of the teacher or pupils?

These questions assume that patterns are surface symptoms of fundamental relationships. Their significance goes beyond the data itself. What does it mean if a teacher embeds the pupils in his or her train of thought in the way expressed by the T–P–T pattern? First, it means that the teacher controls the way in which pupils respond to the subject matter. The most important control mechanisms are the questions the pupils are asked and the comments on their answers. If we look closely at the transcript, it appears that the teacher's aim is to get the students to come up with ideas that fit his own thinking: he asks the questions in such a way as to maximise the likelihood of the pupils producing answers that meet his expectations. If a pupil does not give the answer he expects, or fails to answer, the teacher ignores 'the wrong answer' and rephrases the question to another pupil. You can find examples of this in the text (ll. 31–43). Even when he appears to be asking for an everyday explanation of the concept 'ritual' he obviously expects only catchwords from his pupils: 'to gods' (l. 92), 'daily meals' (l. 99), 'grace' (l. 104).

What is the thinking that lies behind these patterns? We interviewed the teacher to try to find out and now list some of his responses. (Note: to understand what follows you need to know that, in the Austrian educational system, oral examinations take place in the course of normal lessons. Although there are also written examinations, the history of German literature is only examined orally.)

- 'I need some subject matter which I can examine.'
- 'If they are afraid of being asked a question they pay attention.'
- 'They have to know how they will be graded in the exam . . . I am finding it more and more difficult to give grades.'
- '[Because I have so few periods with them] I can't afford to waste any time in the lessons.'
- 'The pupils like it because it reduces the risk for them [of failing] . . . . If I asked questions in the exam which required interpretation of literature, I am afraid that some of them would fail.'
- 'I like to separate the things that really matter (i.e. their ability to respond to literature) from preparation for oral exams.'

(INT/S: 2)

From these statements we can infer some of the teacher's assumptions which give rise to these patterns:

- He thinks that these patterns enable him to examine the pupils' knowledge in a way that is fair and not too stressful.
- He thinks that they are good for discipline and ensure that the pupils pay attention.
- He thinks that this kind of teaching is expected of him and makes the best use of the time available.

The interpretation placed on a pattern should be plausible in the context and fit in with the analysis as a whole. This is the best way of deciding whether or not a possible pattern is of value. We recommend that you read relevant passages of a transcript several times, looking closely for emerging associations. In this way you can pick up important clues as to the pattern's meaning and importance to the teacher and the part it plays in his or her professional self-image. It is not a good idea to discount too quickly those patterns you or others do not like, because they nearly always have some significance and you rarely gain anything by ignoring them. Equally, before changing routine patterns, you should at least partially understand their meaning and the part they play in the complex system of teaching activities (see Chapter 4, p. 53).

Stage 3: What are the effects of the pattern?

Which skills and attitudes are strengthened by the pattern? What kind of evidence is there for or against our interpretations of its effects?

The transcript of this lesson does not tell us much about the effects of the patterns on the pupils. Those pupils who have taken an active part obviously accepted the pattern, were able to work with it, and even seemed to force the teacher to stick to it. However, the majority of pupils did not take part, so it is conceivable that they did not accept the pattern and as a result did not volunteer answers or reply to the teacher's questions.

The teacher interviewed three of the pupils about his way of asking questions. Here is his summary of their answers (Sorger 1989):

- The way questions are asked makes it relatively clear to the pupils what is expected of them.
- The pupils feel involved in the lesson, even if only through the 'risk of being caught out if your mind wanders'.

For the pupils, these patterns of interaction with their teacher obviously offer a clear framework in preparation for the examination, both in terms of subject matter and the format of the exam. Let's speculate on other possible consequences of the T–P–T pattern:

- What effect does it have on the atmosphere in class? Is the teacher right in his assumption that the pupils are satisfied with it? Are they all satisfied? On what does he base this belief? We can see from the transcript that at least six pupils made oral contributions and in addition there were times when several pupils were talking at once. This indicates that a number of pupils appear to be happy with this teaching method, but the data do not tell us how many. We get some indication of the general atmosphere from the number of voluntary contributions made by pupils (without being asked by name). The percentage is about 50 per cent of all contributions (although this is difficult to judge from the transcript).
- What effect does it have on learning? It is even more difficult to get clues from the transcript as to how much the pupils were learning. According to the teacher, the pupils were adequately prepared for the exam, which means that they learnt what he wanted them to know in the exam. Although we have no transcript of the oral exam, it can be assumed that the same patterns occur, so that the lessons can be seen as training for oral exams.
- What consequences does it have on teaching? Teaching which uses this pattern could be described as 'close guidance'. The teacher decides on the learning task by asking the questions; he decides on the subject matter and its organisation by the format of his questions; and he defines the quality of pupils' answers by his comments, which at the same time allow him to give additional information. A strength of close guidance of this kind is that information can be tailored to the pupils' needs (or, at least, to the needs of those who contribute). A further strength is that it helps the students to prepare for – and the teacher to plan – the exam. A weakness is that knowledge acquisition is implicitly

defined as answering set questions. This kind of teaching would be unlikely to make a significant contribution to the pupils' ability to think independently.

Any pattern will have a number of effects. The effect of a pattern depends on the situation in which it occurs and on the personality traits and abilities of those concerned. For this reason we recommend that you always look for a number of possible effects, to prevent being blinkered by the first one that comes to mind. Sometimes some effects can be identified in the transcript itself, but normally you will need to collect more data.

Stage 4: To what extent does the pattern and its probable effects correspond with what the teacher intends?

Are short-term intentions betrayed (e.g. if pupils do not react as expected)? Are long-term intentions undermined (e.g. if the effects of patterns are not in line with educational aims)?

When discussing the transcript of the lesson, the teacher said for example: 'I'm not happy with using it [the T–P–T pattern].' It seems that the teacher has teaching aims that are not in line with the pattern. What are they? Does he want his pupils to move beyond the acquisition of facts to an understanding of concepts and theories? Does it bother him that the pattern might encourage them to learn for the sake of the exam rather than out of their own interest in the subject? The teacher's case study gives some clues:

> . . . only then did my real problem begin to emerge. I have to give grades, so I must teach things I can test, and (at the same time) I want them to know what is likely to come up in the exam; but, on the other hand, the aims which are important in studying literature and the kinds of tasks which would support those aims are very different. I just submit to the pressure of circumstances.
>
> (Sorger 1989)

This shows that the teacher feels under pressure and unable to achieve the aims that he 'really' considers worthwhile (see p. 147). At this stage of the analysis it is important to consider these 'real' aims, as well as the blocks to achieving them. Reflecting about these issues can give new perspectives that help in bringing about improvements.

Stage 5: If the effects of patterns do not match intentions, what new action strategies should be developed? What are the strengths we can call on to improve teaching?

One way of developing new action strategies is to identify and develop those patterns whose effects potentially match your intentions better than others.

T: Right, so they had no writing. That means, that someone could say, wait a minute, if there wasn't any writing there couldn't have been any literature. You could say that theoretically, couldn't you? (ll. 35–8)

This question (see also l. 47f.) indicates a different strategy which is, however, resisted by the pupils because of the dominance of the 'listing' and 'sentence completion' patterns. It offers an invitation to the pupils to engage in a 'discussion pattern' with the teacher. Another example of this type of interaction comes at that point in the passage where the teacher asks a ('real') question in trying to understand a pupil's statement:

T: ... so-called magical poetry, the magic spells. They are usually short spells – having what purpose? Martha? ... Edith? ... Rudolf?
R: Well, making people believe something!
T: I don't understand what you mean. I don't follow that. What do you mean by that? (ll. 134–8)

Potentially this is another pattern, which is, however, not pursued by the teacher. We call it the 'follow-up pattern'. Both interventions show possible ways of overcoming the restrictions of the T–P–T pattern. Both put emphasis on the pupils' ideas and therefore are supportive of the teacher's wider educational aims. Further ideas on developing action strategies are given in Chapter 7.

Pattern analysis is a creative process in which a teacher begins a 'conversation' with the reality of his or her teaching from transcripts of lessons. The process of pattern analysis does not consist merely in identifying existing patterns, but is an active process of constructing personal meaning, by relating intentions to what is perceived to be happening in reality. On the other hand, this construction is not a purely personal matter, as the data (the transcripts) act as a frame of reference providing evidence of particular patterns and therefore making it possible to discuss them.

Dilemma analysis

Dilemmas for teachers

The term 'dilemma analysis' was coined by Richard Winter (1982). It is a method which can be used with any data, but it is particularly useful with interview transcripts (e.g. see PALM 1990). Dilemma analysis is based on the notion that teachers are continually faced with dilemmas that require professional decision-making. In every case these dilemmas can be expressed in the following terms: 'On the one hand . . . but, on the other hand . . . '

Here is an example of a dilemma:

On the one hand it is important to keep an overview of the classroom to ensure that every pupil is getting on with his or her work. On the other hand it is important to engage individual pupils or small groups in discussion, from time to time, so as to encourage them to think deeply about concepts and problems (which will require your full attention).

Dilemma analysis is not as difficult as the name seems to indicate. For example, we interviewed the teacher of German literature (whose lesson transcript we discussed earlier in this chapter) about his approach to teaching. Here is a short extract from this interview. As you read it, see if you notice any of the tensions and decision points. We suggest that a good way of going about it is to work with a partner: begin by reading through the data, individually, and mark any places where you note inconsistency, tentativeness or decisions; then talk over what you have found and, together, draw up a preliminary list of dilemmas.

I have just had the autumn exams.[3] This time, when I was setting the questions, a lot of things had become clearer and I thought, what shall I do now? I could move away from teaching and examining factual knowledge more or less totally, and just work on the texts, and judge the students right from the start on the quality of their responses. But this is is where my social responsibility comes in. If I did that, I could be accused of only wanting to create an elite. It would mean that those who are intelligent, who can make the links, who actually don't need me as a teacher, strictly speaking, but would learn anyway, would be favoured and the others would be neglected. I have to take these things into consideration, because the ones who need my help to widen their mental horizons are more important to me than the ones who have a wide mental horizon already. And this is the reason for my emphasis on facts and testing facts – so that they can climb this mountain. But by doing this I narrow their chances of doing anything independently.

(INT/S: 3).

Everyone is likely to find rather different dilemmas in analysing any text, because there is a tendency to pick up on points which resonate with your own experience. Compare your own outcome in the above example with our analysis. We found the following tensions emerged from the interview:

---

3 These are 're-take' examinations for pupils who failed a subject in the summer.

- On the one hand, the teacher wants to get away from teaching and examining facts and would rather just 'work on the texts'.
- On the other hand, this would imply judging the pupils on the quality of their thinking and their responses to the text and would lay him open to the accusation of 'creating an elite' and favouring those who need his help least.
- On the one hand, testing factual knowledge should help those who are unable to 'climb the mountain' when working on texts.
- On the other hand, by doing this he restricts their chances of learning to work independently.

We found plenty more examples of dilemmas in the interview as a whole (which lasted almost an hour):

- On the one hand, I want to teach my pupils to approach literature critically, to open their minds to literature – and through literature to problems of our time and society – so that they become citizens able to think and function fully in a democracy. This means that they must respond critically to authority, become more independent and self-reliant in their thinking, and develop their own ideas. That's the whole reason why we read and analyse literature.
- On the other hand, I choose the books and in doing so I restrict their independence, because it's true of me too, that I obey an authority, the authority of the curriculum and the authority of the regulations governing examinations and reporting. I have to obey these rules . . . the pupils might change schools or get another teacher who has to build on what I've taught them.
- On the one hand, I have to assess the students.
- On the other hand, I don't want to be the assessor, I should be teaching them to evaluate their own work.
- On the one hand, the lower-achieving pupils want something they can rely on.
- On the other hand, the higher-achieving pupils find this (the concentration on factual knowledge) a burden because they have achievements to be proud of but they rarely get the chance to display them in a competitive exam situation.

We also analysed an interview with three of the pupils. We found further contradictions between the teacher's views, and the pupils' views and still more contradictions between one pupil's views and another's, for example:

- On the one hand, the teacher wants to give more opportunities to the lower-achieving pupils by focusing on factual information.
- On the other hand, these very questions seem to be viewed by pupils as punishments and instruments of control, causing them problems rather than offering them opportunities.

- On the one hand, pupils say they pay more attention when the teacher asks questions because it is 'embarrassing' for them being 'caught' if they don't know something they are asked.
- On the other hand, they say that lessons are much more interesting when 'you think for yourself and find out things on your own'.

How to carry out dilemma analysis

Stage 1   Finding dilemmas

It is not difficult to find dilemmas. You will probably find there are quite a number. Here are two more examples from an extensive list given by Berlak and Berlak (1981: 135f.):

Knowledge as content versus knowledge as process

On the one hand, knowledge is regarded as content (structured information, facts, theories, generalisations).

On the other hand, knowledge is regarded as a process (critical thinking, problem solving) (ibid.: 147).

Equal allocation of resources versus differential allocation

On the one hand, all children should receive the same share of resources (teacher's time, books, use of computer, etc.).

On the other hand, some children 'need' more than others (ibid.: 159).

In carrying out dilemma analysis, data is selected, structured and interpreted so that contradictions come to light rather than commonalities. This method of analysis is easier when applied to data that interpret social reality and reveal its tensions (e.g. interview data) rather than data that focus on actions and events (e.g. observation data).

Stage 2   Formulating and exploring dilemmas

One way of formulating dilemmas is through the linguistic structure 'on the one hand – on the other hand', which has been illustrated in the above examples. Perhaps you are wondering: How can I get a lever on a dilemma so that I will be able to cope with it better in future? We think the following pragmatic approaches are helpful. They are drawn from examples taken from the interview quoted earlier in this chapter:

1 *Is the dilemma solvable?* Many dilemmas express contradictory and unavoidable aspects of situations so that they cannot be resolved by any course of action. An example is the contradiction between

autonomy (choosing your own path in learning) and structure (working within rules and structures):

- On the one hand, testing factual knowledge should help those who are unable to 'climb the mountain' when working on literature.
- On the other hand, by doing this he restricts their chances of learning to work independently.

This dilemma is not solvable as the teacher's support role is inevitably linked with a restriction in the pupil's room to manœuvre.

2 *Is the dilemma related to the complexity of the situation* which makes it difficult to see what is happening? Many dilemmas result from having to act in situations where many factors are unclear, and causes and effects are only partly understood. A teacher whose primary aim is to encourage lower-achieving pupils usually does not have sufficient knowledge about their weaknesses and what causes them. In addition, he or she will know little about the consequences of various actions intended to help these pupils (e.g. asking factual questions in exams, not working independently on books, etc.).

3 *Is the dilemma emotionally stressful?* Emotional stress often results from believing that you have to take some course of action which goes against your instinctive judgement.

- On the one hand, the teacher has to give grades because he is required to do so by law.
- On the other hand, he does not believe in giving grades because the pupils come to depend on them.

Stage 3 *Working on dilemmas*

We work on dilemmas to solve them if possible. Even if a dilemma is judged to be 'unsolvable', we can still look for an acceptable way of coping with it. Just talking about a dilemma may give rise to ideas for solutions.

In the interview already quoted (INT/S), the teacher mistrusts grades, on the one hand, because they make pupils dependent on him. On the other hand, he knows that he has to give grades. In the course of the interview, new ideas occurred to him about how he could deal with this dilemma in an acceptable way:

- defining the assessment criteria beforehand. These criteria could make it easier for pupils to work out the reasons for particular grades on their own;
- writing comments on students' written work;
- talking to pupils about the work he has assessed.

Unfortunately it is impossible to give any generalised explanation of how to deal with dilemmas. So we want to take a further passage from the data as an example of how to understand dilemmas better, explain them and derive action strategies from them.

In comparing the teacher's statements with some of the things his pupils said, an interesting contradiction emerged. On the one hand, the teacher wants the pupils to respond to literature critically and become independent in their thinking. On the other hand, the pupils said in the interview that they pay more attention when the teacher asks them questions, because it is embarrassing for them being 'caught' if they don't know something they are asked, and it is boring without questions like this. The teacher's and the pupils' aims seem to be clearly contradictory.

When we take a closer look at this dilemma, it becomes even more complicated. The teacher's statement contradicts other statements he has made: he does want the pupils to acquire knowledge of facts. The pupils' statements are also not free of contradictions: in another statement they say that lessons in which you have to think for yourself and find things out on your own are much more interesting than other lessons. Obviously there are other reasons why the pupils work, as well as wanting to avoid embarrassment (when getting caught day-dreaming).

It seems as if during lessons neither teachers nor pupils always do what they themselves consider valuable (taking a longer view). They are busy with 'content-oriented' learning, with passing on knowledge (teacher), and with remembering and reproducing knowledge (pupils) – But they also want to support independent thinking (teacher) and think for themselves and discover things (pupils) i.e. defining and working on problems.

How can these contradictions be explained? One possible explanation could be that these two kinds of teaching and learning contain different levels of risk for both pupils and teachers. Problem-oriented work ('thinking for yourself') offers less security than the acquisition of knowledge. The pupil has to go beyond the information offered by the teacher and work with it using his or her existing knowledge. So there is a danger of not coming up to the teacher's expectations.

Under what circumstances will a situation like this be seen as a risk? Probably, when the pupil regards the lessons as a form of trade (grades for effort) and when, as a result, the economic principle holds sway (maximum results for minimum effort). In these circumstances, the pupils become interested in making a good 'deal' (as good a grade as possible, with as little effort as possible) and reducing the risk of poor grades. This may also be true for teachers in a similar way. They are interested in pupils who achieve something, who take part in the lesson, and who are well behaved. They get achievements and good behaviour more easily if they restrict themselves to asking only for the knowledge they have already given the pupils. In this way, the risk of failure for teachers is also kept very low (see Doyle and Ponder 1976).

Even in a case like this where a dilemma is 'unsolvable', analysing it can help to understand it better and find an acceptable *modus vivendi*. We believe that another useful outcome of the analysis can be that you begin to accept the dilemma as something 'normal', and this reduces any frustration resulting from it (e.g. frustration in feeling 'whatever I do conflicts with something I believe to be important'). A dilemma can also be discussed with the pupils: for example, a teacher could check the extent of pupils' interest in problem-oriented work to find out how much support there would be for some work of this kind in the daily routine.

The function of dilemma analyses

Analysing and working on dilemmas may be important in these ways:

- *Valuing minority views*: Views which are taboo or which are not dis-cussed for other reasons (eg. because those holding them do not have enough power) can be expressed in the form of dilemmas. By juxta-posing different views, the common phenomenon of the 'social hierarchy of credibility' is overcome (see Chapter 5). Problems are presented in a way that is not too threatening, making it possible to discuss them and analyse them rationally. Minority views are not only a social phenomenon. Within each person's mind, there are views which are devalued and repressed, but which none the less have consequences we are not aware of. Dilemma analysis can help in pointing out our personal 'minority views', which makes it possible to have a closer look at them and deal with them.
- *Reducing stress*: Dilemma analysis is an alternative to searching for definite answers which can solve one tension only at the expense of increasing another one. If we accept that contrary perspectives can be enriching, we experience emotional relief. Our energy is freed to search for ways of dealing with dilemmas that we can accept.
- *Enabling discussion*: Winter (1982) developed dilemma analysis in order to introduce an egalitarian note to discussions between student teachers, their teacher mentors, and college supervisors. Through dilemma analysis, he was able to ascribe equal value to students' perspectives and the perspectives of those who had a higher status in the social context. His list of dilemmas enabled good discussions to take place. In a similar way, dilemmas can facilitate discussions between pupils, parents and community groups, or between teachers in the same school. The discussion is likely to be more stimulating and productive if the issues to be discussed are expressed in terms of dilemmas.

Chapter 7

Developing action strategies and putting them into practice

In this chapter we want to look particularly at developing action strategies and putting them into practice. As we have made clear in earlier chapters, in teachers' action research, the knowledge generated about school practice is used to improve learning and teaching in schools. Transforming the knowledge and insights developed through action research into practical action is also a way of testing the theories you have developed: Does my practical theory about this situation stand the test of being put into practice or do I have to develop, modify or change it? In practical terms, action researchers ask the following questions at this stage:

- How can I develop action strategies that fit my practical theories and that are likely to improve the situation?
- How can I select appropriate action strategies from the range of alternatives available?
- How can I develop and put into place the action strategies I want to try out?
- How can I monitor the effects of the action strategies and record the outcomes?

These are all questions which will be explored in some detail in this chapter.

PRACTICAL ACTION AS AN INTEGRAL PART OF RESEARCH

Example of implementation of an action strategy

In experimenting with using word processing as a tool for teaching writing, a teacher organised her class of 11 year olds into groups and asked them to write stories collaboratively. Each group was asked to write a 'long story', over a period of two weeks, and to produce drawings and maps to go with it, on paper. The teacher found that the pupils were very highly motivated by using the computer and that this had an obvious positive effect in their interest in their writing. However, it also had an unwelcome side-effect in causing increased tensions within the groups: some quarrels broke out and in two of the groups (one of boys and one of girls) there were tears. Using a range of data (an 'outsider's' observation notes, her own diary (see Chapter 2, p. 16) and a series of interviews with the pupils), she investigated these tensions. To her surprise she found that they seemed to be coming about because the group members were trying to collaborate with each other much more closely than usual: everyone wanted to take a turn writing on the computer, so it was not possible for them to 'escape' from collaboration by allocating separate tasks to each other and working individually. This led to two hypotheses: that the children might collaborate more successfully if they were shown that co-operation was valued by their teacher; and that they needed some teaching in how to collaborate – it would not happen automatically.

On this basis, she decided on an action strategy to improve group collaboration: to introduce 'collaboration' as the topic for a class discussion. During an hour, each group explained to the rest of the class the strategies they had been using to make group decisions. It became clear that one group which was using the democratic principle and allowing the wishes of the majority to override the others was experiencing a lot of tensions. An alternative suggestion, put forward by another group, was that you had to talk through each idea until everyone came to a consensus. In the process of putting this action strategy into practice (through listening to the children's discussion), the teacher realised that her two hypotheses – on their own – were too simple. Collaboration in group work is more difficult than she had thought – probably for adults as well as children. She realised that she would also need to alter the kind of writing task she was setting.

Thus, in putting this action strategy into practice, she encountered some success, but also gained a new understanding of the problem. This resulted in rethinking her 'new practical theory of the situation' (that the children needed to be taught how to collaborate and made aware that she valued collaborative work): What had been misjudged in her practical theory? Which important conditions had been neglected? What alternative action strategies would be possible? Such deliberations eventually led to a better understanding of the situation, and specifically to setting shorter written tasks for the groups working on the computer so that the pressures of time were reduced (see Somekh 1985).

Action research is research by practitioners, undertaken to improve practice. For practitioners, it is not enough to develop theories about a situation: they also want to change the situation, as a result of their new knowledge, to improve the working and learning conditions for themselves and their students. To make it worth investing time and energy in research, which after all cuts across both professional and private life, a teacher must go beyond generating knowledge and theories to making improvements in classroom practice. Developing action strategies in practice, however, means more than just making practical use of research results. It is itself a part of the research process. In planning action strategies, we formulate the outcomes of analysis as a preliminary practical theory. In developing action strategies in practice, we test the outcomes of analysis and thus, indirectly, test the preliminary practical theory (see Chapter 5, p. 77). From the success or failure (most often a mixture of the two) of our carefully planned action strategies, we can evaluate aspects of our practical theory, and find out ways in which it needs to be developed, modified or radically revised.

Action research is characterised by a close interrelationship of action and reflection (see Chapter 9, p. 207). Another way of putting this is to say that using research results to improve practice, by means of developing action strategies, is an integral part of action research. The trustworthiness of research results is not established by clever analysis based on any specific theory, or by rigorously applying a set of validation procedures, but rather by a process of interrelating research and action. By continuously putting reflection into action, and subjecting action to further reflection, both the theories developed from reflection and the stock of action strategies are extended, subjected to analysis, and improved.

Some people say that research is a 'never-ending task'. Is this also true of action research? It certainly applies to day-to-day professional reflection. Action research, however, is day-to-day reflection made more systematic and intensive. Thus, action research concentrates for a specific period of time on issues that deserve close scrutiny, but it will finish for pragmatic reasons, even if some questions are unanswered and need further investigation, for example:

- because the researcher is reasonably satisfied with the outcome;
- because he or she has to cope with another task which will consume all available energy;
- because he or she simply needs a rest from extra demands.

In comparing action research with natural or behavioural science, Elliott (1984a: 75) describes 'the implementation and evaluation of action-strategies as a form of hypotheses testing'. In the same way that some other researchers develop hypotheses as concrete propositions based on their theory, teacher-researchers design their action strategies on the basis, and as a consequence of, their practical theory. Developing action strategies in practice corresponds to the testing of hypotheses in traditional research.

In fact, trying out action strategies may be thought of as a kind of *field experiment*. The word 'experiment' does not command much respect in education. The idea of an 'educational experiment' is a contentious one. Objections to the kind of laboratory experiments conducted by experimental psychologists are sometimes extended to all experiments: they manipulate individuals, the findings have very little relevance to real-life situations outside the rigidly controlled laboratory environment, etc. However, we agree with Mollenhauer and Rittelmeyer (1977: 184) who argue that 'experimenting – in the sense of trying-out new educational strategies – is fundamental to every educational practice which is not routine'. Since teaching is characterised by complexity, ambiguity and development (see Chapter 9, p. 205), it is not possible to plan what will happen in a classroom with any certainty. As this is the case, teachers become 'researchers' when they investigate their practice to evaluate its appropriateness in terms of their educational aims (see Schön 1983).

WHAT ARE ACTION STRATEGIES?

Up to now we have used the term *action strategies* without defining it. Let us now give some examples. In the introductory example of this chapter, a teacher tried to clarify ways of 'improving group collaboration' when using a computer in teaching writing. She developed an action strategy, namely to 'introduce "collaboration" as the topic for a class discussion'.

In another case, a teacher, who had recently taken over a new class, felt irritated by the behaviour of one girl who seemed to her to be unfriendly and sullen. After a while she became aware that she was beginning to dislike her. Their relationship seemed to be moving towards open conflict when she asked an external 'critical friend' to interview the girl. This revealed that she had been having some problems in adapting to the new teacher's more informal teaching style and, generally, to the change of teachers, since she had been one of the previous teacher's favourite pupils. The conversation, however, also showed that the teacher's impression (and fear) that this pupil did not like her or her teaching was utterly unfounded. As a result of this new information, the teacher no longer had any reason to have a negative attitude to the girl, her manner in addressing her changed, and the tension went out of the situation. As the teacher put it: 'I look at Karen with different eyes now and I find it easier to approach her. I address questions directly to her if she doesn't volunteer any answers, and she is becoming noticeably more active and seems to enjoy the classwork more. She is still rather a quiet girl, but I don't interpret it as sullenness any more' (Posch 1985: 60).

In a third example, a university teacher was attempting to develop her course on 'Statistics in the Social Sciences' which she felt needed improvement (see Altrichter 1986b). A graphical reconstruction of the situation, after the first cycle of investigation, is set out in Figure 10. For the sake of clarity, we give only an excerpt (see M9 for the full reconstruction).

Whenever she introduces a new concept she begins by explaining it in words (stage 1). Then she does an example on the blackboard (stage 2), and afterwards she asks the students to do another exercise in their books (stage 3). Usually, the students have difficulty in understanding (stage 4) because the concept is difficult and too much information is being given all at once. If she feels that she is not explaining things clearly, or the students show signs of not understanding, she can feel herself becoming tense and she tries to explain again. However, this makes her teaching become jerky and even less clear. When interviewed she said: 'My behaviour is "reactive". Whenever something unexpected pops up or I pick some sign that they are not understanding, I react immediately and abandon my lesson plan. I must learn to observe these things and store them away to think about later, without being put off my track' (Altrichter 1986b).

On the basis of this interpretation of the situation, the teacher decided upon the following action strategy (and four others which, for the sake of clarity, we do not quote here) (strategy 5). *To take a deep breath*: Whenever she felt that her explanation was becoming nervous, jerky and difficult to understand, the teacher decided that she would 'take a deep breath'. In this way, she hoped to avoid these nervous reactions. In the 'breathing-space', she hoped to be able to think whether it was actually necessary to

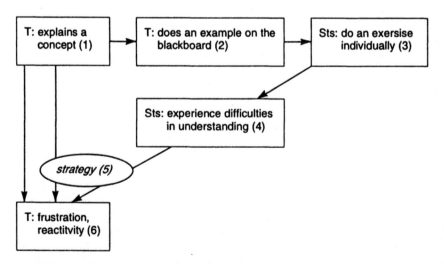

Figure 10 Excerpt from a graphical reconstruction – 'Course on statistics'

abandon her planned sequence of explanations. Through this strategy she hoped to break the vicious circle of quick and unthinking changes to her lesson plan which she was finding annoying and which she also thought were getting in the way of the students' learning. We will return later to discussing why it is not always easy to translate a 'good intention' like this into action (see later in this chapter). When an action strategy is developed from the analysis of practice, it is important to be able to relate the strategy to a specific point in the analysis. You may find it helpful to draw a diagram, such as the one shown in Figure 10, to show how it relates to the theory.

Let's use this example to explore some of the characteristics of action strategies:

- Action strategies are actions which are planned and put into practice by the teacher-researcher in order to improve the situation or its context.
- Action strategies are connected to educational aims. They are used to maintain or develop the educational quality of a situation. They are considered 'successful' if the desired effects come about without unexpected negative side-effects.
- Action strategies are typically tightly linked to theories developed from practice as a result of action research into the situation. The diagram in our last example shows this clearly: it sets out the teacher's interpretation of the situation (i.e. her practical theory); her action strategies can easily be given a specific place in this diagram. Diagrams are useful not only as a technique for developing action strategies but also as a method of looking at them carefully. Diagrams quickly show the points in the practical theory at which no action is being taken on a practical theory (which leads to questions such as: Why not? Will there be any side-effects of neglecting these aspects of the situation?) or whether action strategies are planned which do not actually arise from the practical theory. Sometimes this indicates a routine 'ad hoc strategy' which cannot be justified by the analysis of the data. More often, however, such a 'floating' action strategy points to some incompleteness in the analysis: the action strategy expresses intuitive knowledge about the situation which would not otherwise have been made explicit. Reflecting on the 'floating' action strategy helps to extend the practical theory.
- Action strategies can be thought of as preliminary answers to the researcher's questions or 'experimental' solutions to the problem he or she is investigating. In this way, they are always relevant to the theory because the process of carrying them out throws light on the practical theory of the situation.
- Action strategies may aim to make changes of very different scales: for

example, one teacher might decide to make profound changes to her whole style of teaching to give the pupils much greater autonomy in learning, whereas the university teacher in our last example has basic-ally kept her style of working but adapted it by making some slight changes in her behaviour.

- The extent to which an action strategy is new can differ widely. By using the terms 'change' or 'improvement', we may give the wrong impression that only significant and radical breaks with existing practice count as 'action strategies'. This is not true. Researching and analysing a situation may just as easily lead to corroboration of existing practice and underlying theories. In some cases, there may be no visible changes in terms of actions, although views and attitudes are greatly changed: for example, earlier in this chapter (p. 156) we des-cribed how a teacher came to 'look at her pupil with different eyes', no longer feeling antagonised by her, and therefore able to act towards her without feeling tensed up. In other cases, analysis of a problem may lead to quite new actions.

- When we speak of 'improvement' or 'solving a problem', we do not mean to imply that all the problems of schools and classrooms can be 'solved' satisfactorily. Sometimes the analysis of a problem shows that important contributory factors lie outside the teacher's sphere of influ-ence (e.g. a pupil's home background; the school timetable). 'Solving a problem' in a case like this often does not mean making it vanish, but developing a different attitude towards the problem which helps to limit personal strain. Often a change in attitude makes it possible to make a number of small changes which are helpful, but which previ-ously did not seem to be worth the effort.

- The term *action strategy* needs to be understood in terms of the following provisos:

    - Complex social situations are not changed by one single action. Usually, an action strategy will consist of a number of co-ordinated actions planned on the basis of the research.

    - Do not expect immediate solutions. Change is usually a long-term process, in the course of which several single elements of a system begin to move and action strategies have to be adapted and modified. Planning action strategically means being prepared to learn from the outcomes of the 'first wave' of a change strategy and using this to inform the 'second wave' (see Kemmis and McTaggart 1982: 24).

    - In any social situation, actions usually have unforeseen side-effects. These unexpected outcomes have to be judged in terms of our educational aims. We do not simply ask 'Did we achieve the ends we set?' but rather 'Do we like what we got?' (see Schön 1983: 141; Argyris *et al.* 1985: 218).

In what follows, we will put forward some ideas and methods for coping with the kind of practical difficulties likely to arise from developing action strategies and putting them into practice.

HOW CAN I FIND A VARIETY OF SUITABLE ACTION STRATEGIES?

Where do we look to find suitable action strategies? The most important source is our new understanding gained from analysis of the situation. Understanding an issue, by uncovering the network of interrelationships, not only leads to a new awareness of the situation, but also usually offers a wealth of ideas about possible action.

A second important source is the actual process of data collection. Simply finding out pupils' attitudes may be enough to suggest possible solutions (see the example earlier in this chapter, p. 153). Indeed, interviewing a pupil may itself be an action strategy which changes a situation.

A third important source is our own aims, objectives and values as teachers. What exactly ought to be different? How should a relationship change to make it more satisfactory for both the teacher and the pupil? How should the classroom be organised to provide students and teachers with worthwhile learning experiences? Debating what we really want is a part of the process of clarifying the issue which becomes more and more important as the research progresses. In the course of problem analysis and data collection, the teacher-researcher's aims become more practical and realistic as they are better informed by knowledge of the situation.

Fourthly, ideas and suggestions for suitable action strategies may come from external sources: for example, from conversations with colleagues, information about how other people have coped with similar situations, and ideas in books and articles. We have deliberately left this fourth source to last because it is most useful, in our experience, when used in conjunction with other sources. No advice from an experienced colleague, and no book, can replace your own analysis of the situation, an understanding of its complexities, and a clear view of what you are aiming for. But both sources may yield valuable ideas if they fall on fertile ground: if you have already developed an understanding of the situation and possible action strategies which can be broadened and modified by external suggestions. This is because such suggestions, instead of remaining discrete and separate, are integrated with your own conception of the situation.

Despite the large number of educational books available, it is not easy to find those which both provide good ideas relevant to your own specific situation and are written in understandable language. It is a great advantage for teacher-researchers to have contacts with colleagues who have fought their way through some of this literature, or with 'critical friends' in higher education institutions. Reports and case studies written by practising teachers are often particularly useful. Such case studies are indicated by an asterisk in the list of references at the end of this book.

Developing action strategies is a constructive and creative activity which is interwoven with the researcher's personality and the specific situation in which he or she lives and works. As a result, there is no one way of going about it, and we can only offer suggestions which we hope will facilitate your search for action strategies:

- Don't be content with just one idea. You need to have the opportunity of choosing between several possible strategies. In some situations this is particularly important: the more different strategies you think of, the greater the chance of unusual solutions coming to mind which may help you to escape from 'vicious circles' and dead-end situations.
- Don't worry too much about feasibility to start with. First of all, these ideas are for broadening your awareness. They provide new perspectives and create the impression that it is at least possible to think of solutions. This may be an important starting point for constructive thinking. To start with, it is more important to consider the potential opportunities offered by an action strategy than to think about possible difficulties (all solutions are bound to raise difficulties). This means that you can concentrate on your inner strengths which should inspire some confidence. Don't reject a possible action strategy too quickly just because some difficulty occurs to you.
- Don't forget to consider existing strengths. When we talk about 'improving a situation' or 'solving a problem', it is part of our culture to think in terms of mistakes and guilt. However, there is another way of looking at it. We can often bring about improvement by emphasising strengths and building on processes that are already operating in the system (see our discussion of the systemic approach in Chapter 4, pp. 54–6). It pays to reflect on questions such as: What are (my, our, the pupils', etc.) strengths in this situation and how can I create the conditions to build on them? What processes are in operation that already tend towards an 'improvement of the situation' and how can I strengthen them?
- Sometimes action strategies become obvious during the analysis of the situation, sometimes we have to search for them. When the latter is the case, a group is usually better than an individual. A group supplies a wide variety of ideas from the varied experiences of its members. In addition, collecting and discussing action strategies for a particular situation is often not only illuminating for the teacher who is looking for ideas, but also enriches the insight of other members of the group into similar situations.

Various methods can be used to identify possible action strategies. Diagrams, produced as part of the process of analysis, may also be a used to identify potential action strategies (see M9). As in the case quoted above, every element and every relationship in a diagram gives rise to questions: Can I intervene constructively here? Which action strategies could I use to bring about some positive development at this point on the diagram? Another possibility is that metaphors developed during data analysis may lead to new ideas for action strategies (see M29). Brainstorming (see M4) is another alternative, useful for collecting many different ideas from a group of people.

M32 INDIVIDUAL BRAINSTORMING

If you do not have access to a group of colleagues willing to reflect with you on your research situation, it is possible to brainstorm individually. This is a form of 'reflecting through writing' (see Chapter 2, p. 25). Set aside some time without interruption (approximately 15 minutes) and take a clean sheet of paper or a new page in your diary (you may prefer to use a word processor, but for this exercise we prefer to use paper). Then, jot down all the associations that come to mind when you think of the question 'What can I do in situation x?' It is important to 'go with' your associations and not to reject any immediately as unrealistic or trivial. Evaluation of the quality of the ideas takes place after, not during, this exercise.

HOW CAN I CHOOSE WHICH ACTION STRATEGY TO PUT INTO PRACTICE FROM THE RANGE OF AVAILABLE ALTERNATIVES?

In the process of analysing a situation and searching for action strategies, a particular alternative sometimes becomes obvious. You feel that your understanding of the situation is changed and clarified through looking at it in this way, as if this course of action had become the obvious and natural thing to do. Usually, however, the path to deciding on a specific action strategy is not paved by such intuitive clarity. Then, you need to weigh alternatives carefully, judging their feasibility with respect to the teacher, the pupils and the educational aims of the situation.

M33 CROSS-CHECKING ALTERNATIVE ACTION STRATEGIES

Deciding on an action strategy is a very individual process tailored to the specific circumstances of a situation. Subjective judgement often plays a more important role than any formal evaluation procedure. Nevertheless, the following criteria can often be helpful.

1 *Usefulness*

- How useful is this action strategy?
- Will it solve the problem? For how long?
- Might there be any additional positive effects?
- Might there be any negative side-effects?

These questions may be answered with the help of the research data you have collected or simply from your own knowledge of the situation. Sometimes, however, you will find you need additional information. This serves to show how many decisions in everyday life have to be taken on the basis of insufficient knowledge (because of sheer lack of time). But, bear in mind that it is impossible to foresee all eventualities before taking action, and that uncertainty and 'mistakes' are therefore unavoidable. Being aware of this can give you the confidence to face problems as they occur, accepting them as an expected feature of life as a teacher (or any other professional). In this way you make problems accessible for development – instead of denying and repressing them.

2 *Practicality*

- How practical and feasible is this action strategy?
- What room for manœuvre will there be when implementing this strategy?
- Can this be done alone or does it require the goodwill, support and co-operation of others?

Some ideas can appear to be very useful but simply not feasible in this particular situation. They may take too much time. They may require the co-operation of other people (e.g. colleagues, parents) who are not willing to give it. They may need financial resources which are either unavailable or out of proportion to the expected usefulness of the idea. Or it may be that the teacher does not have the necessary knowledge and expertise, or the opportunity to acquire them quickly enough to make it worthwhile. In the light of the practicality criterion, those action strategies are preferable which give the teacher most room for manœuvre and which are least dependent on other people and institutional structures. However, this does not imply that such action strategies are useful in the sense of criterion (1) or acceptable in the sense of criterion (3).

3 *Acceptability*

- Will this action strategy be acceptable to the teacher(s), pupils and others concerned?

An idea may be useful and feasible but it may not 'fit' the teacher's personality and circumstances or the pupils' situation. Personal ownership of an idea is more important than its quality by more objective criteria when it comes to many teaching problems, but particularly those relating to interactions between people. This third criterion highlights the personal nature of a decision on an action strategy. However, coping positively with classroom problems also requires the other partners – the students – to feel comfortable with the solution and be prepared to support its implementation. Generally, this is more likely if the chosen strategy gives the pupils more room for manœuvre and greater responsibility.

A group, as we have said before, can be supportive at the stage of looking for ideas, but this is seldom true when it comes to deciding which alternative should be put into practice. This is a decision which needs to be taken by those actually concerned. As a teacher-researcher, you cannot allow this burden to be shouldered by colleagues or so-called experts. Outsiders may have creative and striking ideas which shed new light on a situation you have been wrestling with for some time; but they have much less knowledge of the web of idiosyncrasies and routines – each with their history – which are so strong an influence on what happens in the classroom. In addition, outsiders don't have to live with the consequences of their suggestions and this makes it easy to give advice too lightly.

M34 NOMINAL GROUP TECHNIQUE (NGT)[4]

Summary

Nominal Group Technique (NGT) is a highly structured procedure for decision-making in groups. It ensures that all members of the group voice their ideas. It prevents discussion from getting stuck on just a few aspects of an issue, helps to bring more ideas to light, and enables quicker decision-making than many other procedures (e.g. an unstructured group discussion).
A group undertaking NGT is a group only nominally; its interactions are strictly controlled by the group leader according to the NGT rules. It may help to think of it as a development from the

4 For further discussion of this method, see Delbecq *et al.* 1975; O'Neil and Jackson 1983; Elliott 1981; McCormick and James 1983: 160f., 240; Hegarty 1977.

idea of group brainstorming (see M4): by comparison, NGT offers more participants the chance to contribute their ideas, and ensures a decision is made, or some priority decided upon, between suggested alternatives.

Procedure

The NGT process contains the following phases:

1 *Explanation of NGT and its stages (5–10 minutes)*
   The objectives of the method and its stages are explained. With most groups it is useful to project an overhead transparency indicating the various stages and their time limits.
2 *Clarification of the question (5–10 minutes)*
   The question to be considered by the group is announced. (This needs to be decided in advance, either by the group leader or by a planning group of some kind. See the section 'Occasions for use' on p. 167 for examples.) Group members are given a short time to clarify the issue. If appropriate, the question may be reformulated. Discussion at this stage must deal only with the wording of the question; substantive comments come in the later stages and must be vetoed by the group leader at this point.
3 *Individual listing (10 minutes)*
   Working individually, participants list short statements and phrases which come to mind in answer to the question. Silence is important at this stage to ensure that group members write down as many ideas as possible without being influenced by one another.
4 *Collection of statements (20–45 minutes)*
   Each participant *in turn* is asked to read out *just one* of the statements he or she has listed. The group leader writes these on a flipchart without changing the wording in any way. During this stage no evaluation, interpretation or discussion of statements is allowed. The collection of ideas continues to rotate around the group until all ideas are recorded on the flipchart. Meanwhile, completed sheets are torn off and posted on the wall or a display board. (Participants who have run out of statements or whose answers have been anticipated by other group members 'pass' in later rounds.) This highly structured procedure gives an equal voice to all the participants, in a way that seldom or never happens in normal group discussions.
5 *Clarification of statements (approx. 15 minutes)*
   Participants can ask for any necessary clarification. At this stage there is an opportunity to eliminate repetitions and to reword

statements, provided the original author is in agreement. If possible, very general statements should be avoided in favour of more specific, concrete ones. Comments and judgements should still be avoided at this stage.

6 *Individual selection (5 minutes)*
The participants are asked to study the statements on the flip-chart paper. Working individually, they then select and write down on a piece of paper the five statements that seem to them most relevant with respect to the initial question.

7 *Individual ranking (5 minutes)*
The participants then individually rank these five statements in order of importance, giving the most important statement '5', the least important '1', and so on.

8 *Collection of rankings (10–15 minutes)*
The ranking points awarded by each individual are recorded in turn on the flipchart paper beside each statement. After all the participants have given their rankings, the group leader adds up the 'marks' and identifies the six statements that have the highest scores.

9 *Discussion and interpretation of results (approx. 30 minutes)*
In this final stage, the participants discuss the results and their implications. The NGT process usually breaks a problem down into its constituent parts, with the result that the context and relationships between the parts may be lost. Therefore, it is important at this stage to re-create an understanding of the problem as a whole. The following questions may help to direct discussion:

- Which statements do participants generally agree about in their rankings, and which create the greatest divergence of view?
- What are the reasons for agreement? Are the statements so general that everybody finds it easy to agree? Do they represent generally shared prejudices?
- What are the reasons for differences of view? Do they relate to different working conditions, different styles of work, differences in attitudes or educational aims, etc.?
- Does the result suppress minority views (statements that are important to just one or two people)? How does the group want to deal with that?
- Do the winning statements deserve the weight that has been attached to them by the NGT procedure?

Afterwards the group may move on to discuss what consequences should result from the exercise.

Group size

The optimal group size for the NGT procedure is 8 to 10 people: with more, the whole exercise becomes too cumbersome, and with fewer there is increasingly less need of such a procedure. If there are many more potential participants it is possible to run two (or more) parallel NGT processes. The results of the parallel groups can be shared (possibly adapting stages 6 to 9 for the whole group).

The role of the group leader

Leading a group in NGT can be quite challenging. The leader's task is to structure the information flow and promote the development of ideas by keeping the group to the NGT rules. However, they must not do this so strictly that group members lose their interest and enjoyment in participating. The following advice may be useful for NGT leaders:

- Don't re-interpret people's ideas.
- Don't develop ideas of your own – you are not a participant.
- This is not a debate – don't allow people to challenge or attack each other.
- Give people time to think.
- Don't offer interpretations or search for 'patterns'.

Occasions for use

NGT may be helpful:

- if a group wants to decide on a collaborative project ('finding a starting point for group research'). For example, a group of teachers from the same school might begin with the question: What are the current strengths and weaknesses of our school?
- if a group wants to explore possibilities for development in a collaborative project ('clarification of the starting point'). For example, having identified 'lack of support for pupils with Special Needs' as the focus for a collaborative project, a group on an NGT exercise might address the question: What are the most important reasons for 'lack of support for pupils with Special Needs?
- if a group wants to think of a number of action strategies and select one for collaborative action (developing an action strategy and putting it into practice). For example, they might address the question: 'What actions and organisational changes would encourage pupils to become more independent learners?'

NGT is useful not only for action research but also for decision-making in all kinds of groups, e.g. in working parties with the brief to develop a course, or teaching materials.

Problems and drawbacks of NGT

- Some participants may react against the strict rules of NGT. You can guard against this to some extent by explaining the reason for the rules.
- The rules of NGT change the dynamics of a group. Sometimes 'power struggles', suppressed early on, surface later.
- As always with voting, there is a danger that minority views may be neglected. Steps should be taken to ensure that the result fairly represents the whole group, particularly if the group is intending to go on working together.
- The wording of the initial question is very important and can be difficult. If it is too narrow, the participants' thinking is unduly limited. If it is too broad, there may be the problem that different participants interpret it differently. (When in doubt, it is probably better to err towards breadth.)
- The leader's role in NGT is quite demanding. It may be difficult to see that the rules are kept without spoiling participants' enjoyment by 'policing' the procedure too tightly. Sometimes this can be a little daunting.

HOW CAN I PLAN CONCRETE STEPS TO MAKE SURE I FEEL COMFORTABLE WITH MY ACTION STRATEGY?

Earlier in this chapter (p. 157) we gave the example of a teacher deciding 'to take a deep breath' as an action strategy to be used at certain points in her teaching. What concrete form might this strategy take in the classroom?

- Whenever the teacher feels that the students are having difficulties in understanding, and she is in danger of producing a rushed explanation, she could give herself a mental order to 'stop'. This pause 'to take a breath' would give her a chance to decide whether any reaction were necessary and, if so, what kind of reaction would be appropriate. The disadvantage is that it may not be easy to keep cool and pause for reflection in the stress of the situation.
- Alternatively, the teacher could announce that she is going to pause to think, and justify this to her pupils. The disadvantage mentioned above might also apply in this case and there is the additional problem that some teaching time will be lost.
- Another possibility would be for the teacher to ask a question (or

'bounce back' a pupil's question) to keep the pupils thinking while giving herself time to think. Here, the drawbacks are that the students are deceived about the teacher's real intentions while she still cannot concentrate her full attention on thinking.

- Yet again, the teacher could interrupt the flow of work and explain what she sees as a problem: I don't think you have understood everything. Perhaps I'm not being clear. Is that true? A disadvantage of this strategy may be that the pressure to react precipitately will rise if more students say they have not understood. Also, it is often difficult and time-consuming to decide on a solution in collaboration with a large group of pupils.

This example makes it obvious that it is necessary to plan concrete steps to put an action strategy into practice, taking into account the advantages and disadvantages of different alternatives. In order to put an action strategy into practice, it is necessary to feel comfortable with the idea and have confidence that you can carry it out. (Does this action strategy suit my way of working? Can I do that? Are these actions part of my repertoire? If not, could I develop the necessary competences?) Here are some possible ways of developing confidence in action strategies:

- Imagine the situation and play it through in your mind. Mental training, similar to that used by athletes to prepare themselves for specific movements, is useful preparation for simple, relatively isolated actions. It is more difficult to use this method for complex sequences of interactions, although it can alert you to possibilities and consequences which you have not thought of before.
- Try out the action strategy in advance at home or at school. For example, a Physics teacher we worked with once carried out some key experiments, on her own, before the lesson in which they would be a particularly important part of her explanation. Such 'trial runs' could also take place with other classes where you find it easier to experiment with 'new' action strategies – e.g. where there may be fewer discipline problems.
- Visit a colleague's classroom where this action strategy is already in use and talk it over with this colleague afterwards. This may help you to develop a clearer awareness of the possibilities and limitations.
- Try to arrange an opportunity to become more familiar with certain action strategies within the school's in-service training programme (e.g. setting up a school-based short course or working group).

As a rule, it is not possible to feel completely comfortable with an action strategy until you have put it into practice. It is easier to try out something new if you normally have an experimental attitude to your teaching. Putting an action strategy into practice is a 'test' and we can't expect everything to work out well immediately. However, we can expect to learn something which will add to our professional development.

HOW CAN I CHECK THE RESULTS OF ACTION STRATEGIES AND RECORD THE EXPERIENCES I HAVE GAINED?

The most important and most interesting tests of an action strategy do not lie in cross-checking with yourself (as in M33) or in any procedures for group decision-making (as in M34) but in putting it into practice. In order to learn as much as possible from trying it out, it is important to consider in advance what data to collect and for what purpose. In general terms, all the methods of data collection and analysis which we have already described are suitable. A *time plan* may help you to think through and prepare the complex task of co-ordinating research activities with different action strategies.

M35   TIME PLAN

It is often a good idea to plan the steps of your research before you put the first action strategy into practice, so that you don't develop unrealistic expectations and find that you run out of time at the end of the school year. The following time plan was developed by a Physics teacher who was researching the issue: 'My students learn Physics by memorising facts. They do not seem to develop an understanding of the concepts and processes on which the facts are based' (see Kemmis and McTaggart 1982: 11, 30).

Step	Date	Monitoring	Comments
Finalising general plan	24.4.81– 1.5.81		Availability of tape- recorder to be finalised. X to agree to swap rooms.
First action step	4.5.81– 15.5.81 2 weeks 4 lessons	Tape-record 20 mins of Year 10B Science in the two single periods each week. Write impressions in spare period which follows (diary). Interview students (three to begin with) for impressions.	Allow two periods on Friday pm to edit tape. (Just write out questions and answers.) Collate with impressions (mine and students).
Evaluation	After vacation 1 week		Verbal report to Science faculty first Friday after vacation: 5.6.81.
Revise general plan	8.6.81– 10.6.81		
Second action step (plan) (implement)	2 weeks 10.6.81– 26.6.81*	As previously	Suspend microphone more carefully.

Figure 11 Time plan

* *Note* If you think that this Science teacher was caught out by the end of term and unable to finish his research, you are not quite right: he is Australian and June is the high noon of his school year.

If an action strategy does not bring about the expected results, there may
be several reasons:

- a problem in the way the action strategy was put into practice: you may
  not have been sufficiently comfortable with the action strategy and
  may have carried it out in a diffident manner or in a different way from
  what had been planned;
- a problem in the conceptualisation of the action strategy: for example,
  too little time may have been allowed for the action strategy to make
  an impact, or you may have misjudged how much preparation the
  pupils would need before the new approach was implemented;
- a problem in the analysis of the situation: your own prejudices may
  have seemed more convincing than the data, so that you never
  engaged in a 'reflective conversation with the situation'; or you may
  have failed to take alternative interpretations into account, or jumped
  to premature conclusions;
- a problem in the collection of data: important sources of data may have
  been overlooked;
- a problem in the problem definition: perhaps the problem you investigated was not the 'real' problem, or alternatively the problem (your
  aims or the context, or both) may have changed in the meantime.

To check the results of action strategies, you need criteria of success.
When can you say an action strategy was successful? Perhaps, if it:

1 has resulted in an (as a rule intended) 'improvement of the situation',
   in such a way
2 that it has not also caused unintended, negative side-effects which
   detracted from the main, positive effects, and
3 if the 'improvement' is not 'short-term' (vanishing after only a short
   time).

In saying this we have, however, uncovered another layer of the problem.
What teachers, students and other interested parties consider to be 'improvements' varies, depending on their objectives and the values that
guide their action. The examples in Figure 12 may shed some light on this.
How do these claimed 'improvements' differ?

- The aims and values (which are the basis for regarding something as
  an 'improvement' or 'progress') may be more or less explicitly stated.
  In case 1 (see Figure 12), the teacher makes her interests clear. 'Improvement' means: 'I get what I want'. In case 3, the teacher becomes
  aware of her interests only after a surprising discovery. 'Improvement'
  means: 'I like what I get'.
- The teacher's aims and values may change in the course of the research.
  In case 2, the teacher states an interest explicitly, at the beginning,

which recedes into the background in the course of the research, because hitherto neglected values suddenly become much more important.

- Some improvements are in terms of processes, others are products. In case 4, the teacher feels more at ease and in control of the teaching process when 'taking a deep breath'. In case 3, there is an improved 'product': a higher standard of homework and an increase in the pupils' level of interest.
- Some improvements refer primarily to the emotional well-being of teachers or pupils (cases 1 and 4), some refer to performance (case 3), and some to new or deeper insights (case 2).

Objectives/values	Research and action strategies	Improvements
1 The explicit wish of a teacher to be accepted by a particular pupil and to reduce the mutual dislike which seems to be developing (Posch 1985)	Interview with the pupil by a 'critical friend'	Insight from the interview that the pupil respects the teacher and her fears were groundless
2 At the beginning: the teacher's explicit wish to increase the level of oral participation in the class (Morocutti 1989) Later on: the result of the tape-recording makes the teacher aware of hitherto implicit values: preference for working with boys; on the other hand commitment to overcoming the lack of women's voice in society.	Tape-recording a lesson analysing the participation rates; Result: most contributions originate from boys	Insight into subconscious freedom to make a conscious decision to opt for one or other of two conflicting values
3 Teacher's interest in encouraging pupils to discuss topics in as much depth as possible (Altrichter 1985)	Setting 'open' topics for written homework which require a personal response	Teacher learns to her surprise that the students can find homework stimulating and that as a result the quality of the content and language increases
4 A university teacher wants to respond to students' problems in understanding (Altrichter 1986b)	At critical moments (i.e. when the students seem to have problems understanding) she 'takes a deep breath' to win some time for deliberation	Awareness of ways of responding in a more composed way to students' problems in understanding her teaching

Figure 12 Examples of classroom improvements

All these 'improvements' are subtle in character rather than spectacular. In our experience, classroom improvements often appear rather inconspicuous on superficial examination: teachers and/or pupils feel a little better and/or perform a little better than previously. However, in the long term this 'little' can make a difference.

What is considered to be an improvement depends also on *who* is making the judgement. What appears to be an improvement to a teacher need not be regarded as such by a pupil. What they both welcome need not conform to the values of other people (e.g. different community interest groups) or to the values of the state as embodied in laws and regulations. We want to distinguish four voices to show clearly the multiplicity of criteria which can be used to evaluate improvements.

1 The voice of the individual teacher

All the examples just provided exemplify this voice. Teachers try to improve a situation; in doing so their personal values are uppermost in defining what may be considered as improvement. In addition to the individual interests of teacher-researchers in changing unsatisfactory situations, there is also a collective, societal interest in teachers taking responsibility for the development of their own practice.

2 The voice of other people concerned

Action research assumes that effective development of social practice is only possible with the collaboration of all those concerned in this practice. There are both ethical and epistemological reasons for this. For ethical reasons, action researchers need to collaborate with others in a negotiated evaluation of the situation. Epistemological considerations lead to including all the other people concerned because the knowledge developed through action frequently depends on their willingness to co-operate (see Chapter 5, p. 77).

Who counts as a person concerned cannot be definitely and finally settled in advance, however. Certainly, all the participants in the situation that is being researched, and all those who will be affected in any way by the action strategies being implemented, must be included: in most cases this means the pupils. Other people concerned (such as parents or colleagues) are sometimes only 'discovered' in the course of the research: for example, in an interview with a pupil another teacher is mentioned and he or she then becomes a 'person concerned'. Of course, the ethical code should apply to all those concerned in the situation in even an indirect way, but another important consideration is that, in the long term, successful action strategies will depend on tapping into their knowledge and expertise.

3 The professional voice

A characteristic of professionalism is that the practice of an individual member of the profession should be open to scrutiny by professional colleagues. Evaluating practice is a matter not only for the individual teacher-researcher and those directly or indirectly concerned, but in some sense concerns all teachers as a professional group. This professional evaluation begins when teachers voice their knowledge, experience and professional values in conversations about their classrooms and schools. If such conversations go beyond the narrow circle of close colleagues, they contribute in the long term to a shared stock of knowledge and values, which connects teachers as members of a professional community and distinguishes them from other groups.

This professional dimension is evident in the recognition that teachers as a profession have taken a particular responsibility in society. This professional responsibility requires both specific expertise and a professional ethic (a reflexive understanding of educational aims, willingness to undertake what society expects of the profession in an autonomous way, and willingness to be accountable for the freedom necessary to carry out these responsibilities).

The development of such a professional community depends upon both external solidarity and continuous internal critique of professional action, knowledge and values: as a result, the tenets of the profession can be communicated to the public in good conscience.

4 The voice of the community

In the last resort, the community as a whole, including various interest groups, has a stake in the evaluation of teachers' practice, since educational institutions have been established, and are maintained, to meet society's needs. The variety of vested interests in schools is reflected, on the one hand, in legal requirements and the bureaucratic structure of the school, but also on the other hand – and in no way less obviously – in the statements and interventions of interest groups expressed most forcefully through the media.

What counts as 'improvement' is ultimately the result of a – sometimes implicit – process of negotiation between these four voices, each of which can claim some legitimacy. However, we think

- that the complexity of the teaching process necessitates freedom of action, which, in turn, requires a high degree of professional knowledge, self-critique and responsibility;
- that therefore there is a necessity for a high level of professional debate which takes into account both the interests of the learners and the interests of society more generally;

- that this dynamic process of self-reflection and continuous development must be embedded in a professional community and promoted by it.

Community interest groups and state institutions should both challenge and support this process, but they should not replace it with a multitude of restrictions. Such regulations can certainly solve some problems in the short term. In the long term, however, they will prevent schools from developing into institutions capable of coping with society's developing needs in a creative and constructive way.

Decisions about what counts as improvement, success or failure are judgements about complex situations which are shaped in a multi-faceted social process. Not least for this reason, it is only seldom possible to speak of success or failure in a strict sense. Only a more cursory inspection will suggest successes without any negative side-effects, or failures without any positive side-effects. This should be a source of confidence to us all in continuing to research and develop our professional situation (even if progress seems small), accepting discrepancies and 'problems' as natural characteristics of complex professional work; on the other hand it should remind us to be cautious and sceptical about claims of large-scale improvements.

Action research is an 'art of the possible' which does not aim for a predefined ideal state, but helps us to see the potential which is implicit in a situation, and to put into practice action strategies that correspond more closely than previously to our present values. To this end, its cyclical character is most important. The 'test' of action strategies leads to everyday practical action, to new starting points for reflection and, thus, in some cases to new research cycles. To explore a new starting point, resulting from the implementation of action strategies, the ideas in Chapter 4 are relevant. This new starting point will often include novel questions, which have only emerged because 'improvements' resulting from prior research have raised the level of aspiration – making it possible to see further potential for innovation and, thus, leading to a further spiral of professional development.

Chapter 8

Making teachers' knowledge public

The final stage of action research is when the process and outcomes are made public. In this chapter we begin by explaining why, in our view, 'going public' is an important part of action research. We will then discuss different ways of reporting your own research, and possible audiences, and end by giving some advice on the most common form of present-ation, that is, the written report.

WHY IS IT IMPORTANT TO MAKE TEACHERS' KNOWLEDGE PUBLIC?

Have you ever wondered why books on education are usually written by people who have either not taught for a long time or never taught at all? Have you noticed that on in-service courses you sometimes pick up from colleagues good ideas which you wish you had heard before?

In the teaching profession there is not a strong tradition of making teachers' professional knowledge public. Professional bodies such as subject associations and the Classroom Action Research Network regularly publish teachers' writing, and the growth of school-based in-service training has done much to break down the unspoken rule that teachers should not tell colleagues about their achievements. Nevertheless, these are all exceptions to the prevailing tradition of teacher privatism. Such a tradition is detrimental to the development of insights on professional practice, to the professional status of teachers, and in the last resort to the quality of educational practice. In this chapter we will concentrate on the reporting of knowledge resulting from action research projects. However, we believe that these arguments are equally valid for other kinds of teachers' knowledge based on experience.

Public reporting prevents teacher knowledge from being forgotten

Between the classroom and the staffroom teachers destroy their most valuable property, the knowledge borne from their experience

(adapted from Gürge 1979: 46)

This quotation from a teacher's diary is symptomatic of the low esteem in which many teachers hold their own knowledge and experience. Action research aims to rectify this by giving teachers practical methods to develop knowledge from their experience and to make a contribution to the shared knowledge of the profession. Reporting is an important final step in realising this aim: it saves knowledge and insights from being forgotten in two senses of the word: by reporting and communicating your own experience you root it more deeply within your own memory, as well as making it available to other teachers and the professional community as a whole.

The process of reporting teachers' knowledge increases the quality of reflection on practice

Preparing to report the experiences and outcomes of action research involves further reflection and analysis which sharpen initial interpretations and give rise to additional insights. In addition, in actually reporting research to colleagues, you engage in further theorising upon practice. It is as true here as in any other situation that there is no better way of learning something than having to teach it.

Reporting the outcomes of your action research is also a prerequisite for getting feedback and critique. Through reporting, you make it possible to receive comments and at the same time demonstrate your own willingness to think more deeply about your practice. It is also true to say that the publication of results is considered to be an essential part of the quality control procedures for more traditional forms of research.

Through reporting research, teachers clarify their own position and bring influence to bear on educational policy by means of rational argument

In analysing your own experiences and reporting them, you make it clearer to others where you stand and why. We do not want to over-estimate the importance of rational arguments in public debate, but we believe that teachers would strengthen their ability to shape educational policy and improve conditions in schools if their voices were more often heard presenting well-argued reports on professional matters.

By reporting their research knowledge, teachers meet the requirements of professional accountability

A teacher's professional standing depends to a large extent upon other people: on the co-operation of pupils and to some extent of their parents, on the support of governors, education advisers or inspectors and so on.

Teachers cannot afford not to care about the impression they make on others. Most of what a teacher does, particularly anything innovative, relies on the co-operation of those concerned. This, in turn, depends upon their understanding and knowledge of the teacher's aims. Communicating the outcomes of your research to those concerned has a twofold effect:

- It shows your commitment to those concerned (for example, pupils and parents) as partners in a common endeavour, and places a responsibility on them which is likely to strengthen their co-operation.
- It disseminates knowledge about classroom practices and teaching and learning conditions and, in this way, empowers those concerned to make a constructive contribution of their own.

By making their research knowledge public, teachers can play a more active role in teacher professional development and initial teacher education

Mentor teachers, who are involved in the training and induction of new teachers, and those leading in-service courses, need to have a range and depth of teaching experience, and be able to explain it and draw meaning from it when working with students. They need to open their knowledge and their practice to critical questioning and be ready to change on the basis of experience. Last but not least, they need to be open to differences in students' ideas and practice (which could imply criticism of their own teaching) and use critical questioning as the basis for their own and their students' reflection on their practice – becoming a sensitive partner and adviser in their education. In short, they need to be 'reflective practitioners', able to communicate their practical theories and classroom knowledge to their (future) professional colleagues (see Schön 1983).

By reporting their research knowledge, teachers reinforce their professional self-confidence

After a number of years in the job, many teachers feel that their professional development has come to a standstill, that their work has become routinised, and that they themselves are isolated. Taking as our sample 80 participants on an in-service course, we used the 'Nominal Group Technique' (see M35) to find out what teachers find most damaging professionally. A sense of lack of co-operation from colleagues came out top. Reporting on research can help to overcome this problem because it documents individual professional development and makes it visible. In the long term, research knowledge developed by individual teachers can build up a collective knowledge base upon which individual members of the profession can draw, and which forms a bond between them (see Elliott 1985). We think that such a knowledge base, primarily produced by teachers, is an indispensable prerequisite to strengthening the collective self-confidence of teachers and overcoming their damaging sense of isolation.

By reporting their research knowledge, teachers improve the reputation of the profession

Many teachers are aware of having a low status in society and find themselves subjected to adverse public opinion. They feel powerless victims of the media. Although it is true that teachers have been much criticised in recent years, probably in part as a result of a public crisis of confidence resulting from economic depression, in our view there is a relationship between the low self-esteem of teachers and their low profile in public debate on educational matters. As a result, they receive very little feedback on their contribution to the formation of public consciousness. They have passively to accept scandals in the media and the complaints of dissatisfied parents, because they have no voice in public educational debate. We believe that by contributing to building up a professional knowledge base on educational matters, and participating in public debate, teachers can raise the self-esteem and status of the profession.

DISSEMINATING TEACHERS' KNOWLEDGE: WHAT, HOW, TO WHOM?

If you believe that it is important to make teachers' knowledge public, you still have to decide how this should be done. When choosing the method of reporting, it is helpful to ask yourself three interrelated questions:

- *What:* What should you include (descriptions, research methods, analysis of findings, action strategies, etc.)?
- *To whom:* Who are your audiences?
- *How:* What method of reporting do you want to use?

Having already spent some time discussing the 'What', we now want to concentrate on the other two questions.

Possible audiences for action research

Usually, teachers underestimate both the degree of likely interest in their research and the size of their potential audience. In courses with an action research focus, we sometimes use the following exercise to clarify this point:

M36 POTENTIAL AUDIENCES FOR ACTION RESEARCH REPORTS

You have been studying your professional practice for some time, have collected some data, analysed it, and come up with some insights: who might be interested in this work?

. . . .

. . . .

Please compare what you have written with the list below, which was drawn up by participants in an action research course. Which potential audiences did you leave out? Was this because of the content of your research, or the plans you had already made for reporting your research, or did some of these audiences simply slip your mind? Did you have a tendency to forget particular kinds of audiences – for example, people external to the school, or pupils? Are these 'forgotten audiences ' really irrelevant or are you simply unused to addressing them?

Possible audiences for action research reports – a list drawn up by participants on an action research course

Myself, teacher colleagues in my own school, teachers in other schools in our catchment area, participants on in-service education courses, my pupils, their parents, the head, inspectors and advisers, researchers, the course evaluators, the media, the local community.

Methods of reporting

Sometimes the same research results would interest several different audiences, but different methods of reporting would be needed. For instance, you could report to the local community by writing a short article for your local newspaper or a letter to the editor. For a teacher colleague, this kind of article or letter would be too short and provide too little information. Let's look now at different methods of reporting which you could use.

Involving others in the research

If you ask other people to co-operate with you and participate in the research process, it is important to keep them informed of your research aims, methods and results so far, if you want them to make a useful contribution.

1 Involving pupils

Baker *et al.* (1986) did research on group work with 'able' and 'less able' pupils. They used a video camera to collect data and then discussed the recording with both groups of pupils. Here are some results from the teachers' point of view:

- The self-confidence of the less-able pupils increased.
- When some students found out that they did not ask any questions, they changed their behaviour.
- The teachers were made aware that as the self-confidence of the more-able pupils increased and they contributed more in discussions, they received even more attention than before, whereas less-able pupils gradually received less attention because their participation did not improve to the same extent.

The first two results probably could not have come about if the pupils had not been involved in the research process.

2 Involving a 'critical friend'

When you invite an outsider to support you in collecting data about your teaching, good communication is important. The partnership might begin with a preliminary conversation so that you can explain the starting point for the research and some of the initial insights. The next step would be to talk over ideas for the first stages of the research. This not only helps your critical friend to get a clearer picture of your concerns, but also helps you to clarify ideas by talking them through. We have found that student teachers and probationary teachers can make good critical friends if the partnership is properly established through this kind of discussion and takes place in a relaxed atmosphere.

3 Collaborative research

We use the term 'collaborative research' when several teachers (from the same school or several schools) collaborate in their research by sharing experiences and discussing outcomes, though not necessarily sharing the same focus. In the Inquiry-based Learning in Initial Teacher Education project in Austria, it became clear that teachers who shared their experience, and who discussed their findings frankly in groups of three, needed very little support from external consultants (see Altrichter 1988).

Sharing ideas and research experiences with visitors

One American study compared several methods of disseminating ideas and strategies for teaching. The most effective method was to give teachers the opportunity of visiting colleagues who were also involved in innovation in their own teaching (Glaser *et al.* 1966). No other form of dissemination (except direct collaboration in an innovation) provides such a holistic impression of a teacher's teaching methods and ideas as becoming a temporary participant in a lesson and following this up by a discussion with the teacher.

Oral reporting and seminar-style discussions

1 A group of teachers carried out action research into problems experienced by students from different ethnic groups and then presented their findings at a meeting for pupils and teachers organised by the school (Wakeman 1986a).
2 Teachers on a two-year in-service course presented their research and development work to each other and invited discussion (Posch 1986).

An oral report is the most familiar way of communicating experiences. However, from your experience of in-service courses, you may have found that this kind of reporting is not necessarily stimulating and effective. It is useful for teacher-researchers to think of different ways of sharing their experiences with other teachers, taking into account that reporting orally is a form of teaching and needs to be effective in those terms. In Wakeman's (1986a) example, the teacher-researchers decided to present their work to colleagues in a workshop format. As a useful bonus, teachers who research their own reflective practice, and who learn how to present their work to others, develop many of the skills needed to become initial teacher trainers or in-service course providers.

Graphic forms of presentation

Sometimes research can be presented graphically in the form of diagrams, tables, caricatures, etc. If you can present a surprising or thought-provoking finding in this kind of concise form (perhaps on a staffroom notice board), there is a good chance that it will attract attention and give rise to discussion.

Audiovisual presentation

Audiovisual methods of presentation have proved to be a valuable way of reporting to pupils and parents. Recently, it has also become more and more common for audiovisual material to be welcomed as part of the submission for academic qualifications, at all levels. For reporting to pupils, parents and colleagues, it does not seem to be necessary to produce finished products that stand by themselves without a commentary. It seems to be better to present clips from a video and talk about them, followed by discusson, rather than spending a lot of energy on the production of perfect videos or slide shows. For example, on one occasion we found it worked well to present experimental teaching strategies with the help of a rough-cut video without sound. This video was given a 'live' commentary by one of the project teachers, who took questions from the audience afterwards.

Exhibitions

To prepare an exhibition about your own teaching, you need to think carefully and analyse your experience so as to plan what you want to communicate, depending on your audience. To give an example of an appropriate occasion for such an exhibition, at the beginning of an in-service course, we asked teachers to present a selection of their teaching experiences and insights on posters and be ready to explain them to one another.

Exhibitions of teachers' work usually aim at a specific audience, perhaps of parents or pupils. However, they are often limited to presenting teaching 'products' in the form of students' work. It is much rarer to find notes and commentaries on the teaching process, perhaps because teachers tend to think that this will not be of any interest to the audience. This need not be the case. A description of the context in which they were developed is sometimes much more revealing than the end product.

Acting on results

One way of disseminating research experiences and outcomes is to turn them into practical action. This can mean planning and carrying out changes in your teaching as a result of your research (this is discussed more fully in Chapter 7). Another possibility is that research findings can lead to strategic or political action (with a small 'p'). If, for example, you find that organisational structures are blocking changes you want to make, it might be useful to raise this in discussions of educational policy within the school or the education authority.

Computer networks

Computer networks are beginning to be an important way of disseminating research. Once you have established a habit of using electronic mail daily, it becomes an excellent way of keeping in informal contact with a partner or critical friend and exchanging numerous queries, comments and bits of useful information. It also makes it possible to work collaboratively with teachers in other countries, by overcoming the problems of delay caused by post taking several days. Computer networks are also useful when engaging in collaborative writing with a partner at any distance, particularly if you need to go through several drafts of a document in a short period of time.

Written reports

Written reports are only one method of disseminating action research. They may not be the most useful way of communicating teachers' knowledge to other teachers, but at the moment they are the most usual and often the most visible method. Written documents can take very different sizes and forms, including letters to the editor in local or regional papers, notes on the staffroom notice board, short articles in a magazine or journal of a professional association, or longer papers in a journal such as *Educational Action Research*, to give a more comprehensive report of the research and its findings. Because written reports currently have such importance, we will deal with their writing and design in the next section. (To submit papers to *Educational Action Research: an International Journal*, write to Bridget Somekh at CARE, University of East Anglia, Norwich NR4 7TJ, UK.)

WRITING REPORTS TO DISSEMINATE TEACHERS' KNOWLEDGE

Formats for writing

Case studies are the most usual format for writing about action research. We will also describe a format which might be called a *cross-case analysis*.

Case studies

Case studies – in our wide definition of the term – are written reports in which teachers present information about one case taken from their practice: including the context and starting point, research methods, the stages of the research, findings, proposed action strategies, and emerging issues that may be the subject of further work. There are many different ways of structuring a case study and no fixed rules, but here are some suggestions:

1 Following the chronological sequence of the research

The simplest and safest way to write a case study is to communicate your experiences and findings in the step-by-step sequence in which they occurred. It helps with writing (and with reading) if you also illustrate the chronological sequence in a diagram or a list as in the example that follows.

This is an extract from a published research report. The research was commissioned by the teacher (head of Science) and undertaken by another teacher who was on a full-time advanced diploma course.

1 The initial meeting between the teacher and myself. October 16.
2 Classroom observation. October 30.
3 Classroom observation. November 6.
4 An interview with the teacher during which he commented on the transcripts of his lessons and my 'pattern analyses'. November 20.
5 An interview with three pupils from the class. November 30.
6 A second interview with the three pupils, at which they listened to the tape-recording of their first interview and commented upon it. December 14.
7 A second interview with the teacher at which he listened to the tapes of my interviews with his pupils and stopped the tape to comment whenever he wished. The tape I made on this occasion places his comments in the context of the original tape which can be heard, clearly, though slightly more faintly, in the background. January 19.
8 A joint discussion between the teacher, his three pupils and myself. February 12.

(Somekh 1983b: 32)

The chronological form of presentation is not always the best because the whole reseach process is included, irrespective of what is more or less interesting. Sometimes it is difficult to make links if the sequence of events and interpretations is chronological. In addition, the chronological order of presentation can occasionally entice the researcher to concentrate too much on description at the cost of analysis and interpretation.

2 Developing a case study from an issue

Many teacher-researchers do not report the whole of their research, but select one or more issues that appear to be of special interest to discuss in more detail. Writing the case study then becomes a continuation of the analytical process by which the central insights and their supporting data have emerged.

For example, a teacher carrying out research in a school as part of an advanced diploma course was commissioned by the head of the English Department to look at the teaching of 'language across the curriculum'. As part of her investigation she was invited by a History teacher to observe a lesson (for 'lower-ability' 13 year olds) on the change from 'strip farming' to the enclosure of land in England in the eighteenth century. Her written report begins by presenting a general issue:

The Head of English had identified 'copying' as a problem. He felt that pupils might be copying out chunks from text books without understanding what they were writing, and I felt this was an interesting line to pursue in view of some of the findings on the readability of written material used in schools.

(Somekh 1980: 47)

After two short paragraphs describing the context and events of the History lesson (20 lines approx.), the report then lists seven 'patterns' analysed from a transcript of part of the lesson (see Chapter 6, p. 134). This is followed by an analysis of 'the difficulties experienced by the pupils in doing the written task'. It emerges that the pupils have successfully 'negotiated' the task with the teacher from one that requires reading, synthesising and reconstructing information and concepts to one that requires only copying (mainly from the worksheet rather than the book). The report ends with a discussion of further evidence taken from inter- views with the History teacher and his pupils, which confirms the analysis, but also raises a new issue for another action research cycle: that this teacher's expectations have been lowered by his knowledge that this is a 'B band' or 'lower-ability' group.

Reports based on issues are particularly appropriate when reporting extensive and complex research projects. They are also well suited to the teacher-researcher's interest in development, which is usually directed at specific aspects of the situation. On the other hand, readers of this kind of case study may find it difficult to identify the teacher's 'learning path' (how understanding developed over time). If you choose this format, you should explain why certain issues were selected for close analysis.

3 Portrayal

In a portrayal, an event (for example, an episode in the playground or part of a lesson) is described vividly and in great detail without much analysis and interpretation. The idea is that the reader should be able to gain an understanding of the situation and bring his or her own judgement to bear without becoming dependent on the interpretations and value judgements of the authors. Texts of this kind can be very good at stimulating a discussion. However, they are in fact analytical, although the interpretation is not made explicit, and sometimes this can make it difficult for the reader to get a critical purchase on the situation.

4 Shedding light on a case from different perspectives

We have experimented with a form of reporting in which we present a particularly vivid scene, event or short extract from data and illuminate it from different perspectives. The scene is like a prism with its facets illuminated from different sides so as to provide different meanings. The idea is to stimulate the reader to review the significance of the scene with respect to his or her own practical experience.

In an article 'Intermissions – a discovery in higher education' (Altrichter 1984), we included just two short scenes from observation data – in which teaching was interrupted by the teacher leaving the room – and confronted these with a variety of materials that were relevant to a consideration of 'intermissions' or 'pauses': definitions from educational encyclopaedias; statements from learning theory; a written account from our own experiences in teacher educaion; and a short story by Bertolt Brecht called 'The Art of Stopping Teaching' (Brecht 1977).

One potential disadvantage of this form of reporting is that the desire to stimulate ideas may become stronger than the writer's consciousness of the importance of giving an exact account of what happened. In any case, to be successful, this kind of reporting must be clear and vivid so that it brings the reader to reflect deeply on the scene for some time.

5 Reporting action research through the use of key statements

An alternative to voluminous and elaborate reports is to condense an account into brief, carefully worded statements. Teachers, for instance, can summarise the outcomes of their research in a well-structured, written presentation of about one or two pages, short enough to be pinned on the staffroom notice board and read by colleagues (see Platten 1986: 12).

An extreme form of reduction is a list of hypotheses. Elliott (1976: 35–50) tried to reduce the most important outcomes of the Ford Teaching Project to their conceptual core and formulate them as hypotheses. For example, the following statement is the first of 43 hypotheses on 'developing self-monitoring ability':

> The less a teacher's personal identity becomes an inextricable part of his professional role in the classroom, the greater his ability to tolerate losses in self-esteem, which tend to accompany self-monitoring.
>
> (Elliott 1976: 44)

The brevity of this form of presentation has its strengths and weaknesses. On the one hand, it is not easy to condense a lengthy research process while still retaining the analytic detail. However, if it is possible to master this conceptual challenge and present the main insights gained in a brief but clear and intelligible way, this is an important achievement. Condensed forms of reporting are generally short enough to be easily read, but they are often too thin to be illuminating to the reader. In addition, supporting evidence and the implications of the research are often left out, so that the reader does not know how the statements were arrived at, and what conclusions can be drawn from them. A way of overcoming this is to follow each hypothesis with some extracts from data which provide enough of the context to enable the reader to understand it. This could be done, for example, by following the suggestion in M30.

Cross-case analyses

If a team of teachers, or members of a project team, want to report similarities and differences of outcomes from several cases, other approaches are necessary. The following procedure is one way of going about it (see Elliott 1984a).

M37 PRODUCING CROSS-CASE ANALYSES AS A TEAM

Context

After 18 months of research on the 'Teacher–pupil Interaction and the Quality of Learning Project (TIQL)', the project teachers had produced about 30 case studies. They then faced the task of pre-paring an analytical summary reporting the main points of agree-ment and any differences in their outcomes.

Procedure

1 The project teachers in each school brainstormed a list of the most important issues that had arisen in their research.
2 The project co-ordinator read all the case studies and from these, and the teachers' lists, developed a list of issues. One issue, for example, was: 'The effects and implications of pupils' anxiety, self-confidence, interest and motivation on the quality of learning' (Ebbutt n.d.: 17).
3 Then a three-day workshop was held, attended by all the project teachers and central team members.
4 After a discussion of the list of issues, in which some where eliminated and others were combined, the teachers worked in groups, each focusing on one issue of their choice.
5 Each of the groups read those case studies that appeared to be relevant to the issue.
6 Based on their notes from reading, each group produced brief analytical notes including the following:

- hypotheses, summarising in one sentence the main points of agreement and any differences arising from the case studies;
- comments, explaining each hypothesis, and references to illustrative material in the case studies.

7 At the end of the workshop, some of the teachers used these brief analytical notes as the basis for writing analytical summaries on each issue, as a means of reporting the knowledge developed from the case studies. These cross-case analyses were then collected and published as chapters in a book (Ebbutt and Elliott 1985).

The book and its related hypotheses represent the project teachers' contribution to the development of a common stock of professional knowledge about the practice of teaching. It is hoped that it will function as a source of insights and strategies for other teachers to explore when reflecting about their classroom practices.

(Elliott 1984a: 77)

Criteria to use in writing reports

Let us assume that you are about to produce a written report. You have thought carefully about its contents and possible audience, and you now have to decide what criteria to use in writing your study.

Unfortunately, there are as many answers as there are possible people to consult. There are some commonly agreed criteria, but not enough to make the decisions unproblematic. It can be particularly difficult for students on accredited courses whose writing will be assessed by different people and who may have to address different audiences in different papers.

The criteria listed below are ones that we use ourselves. We can give good reasons for them but that does not necessarily make them any more valid than a different list which someone else might put forward. If you are not dependent on other people to assess your written reports, we recommend that you develop a personal style that suits you and is accessible to the reader. It may be helpful if you begin by defining the criteria which you yourself use in judging written texts, for example, by asking questions such as:

- What kind of texts do I enjoy reading?
- Thinking back to the last two texts I have read, what did I like and what didn't I like about them?

However, comparing your ideas with other people's may prove useful. Here are some of ours:

Is the writing supported by data so that a reader can easily visualise what happened?

Are the points made sufficiently clearly to be understood by readers who have no direct experience of the case described? Do you give supportive arguments for your claims and credible evidence from the data? Later in this chapter we give some practical suggestions for writing. When you are thinking about answers to these questions, see in particular (pp. 196–9): (6) The 'backbone' of the writing, (7) the introduction, (8) the conclusion, (10) substantiating arguments with data, (13) techniques for structuring a report.

Are conflicting evidence and alternative interpretations considered?

Do you present arguments and data only in support of your own opinions? Or are conflicting data and other possible interpretations made available to the reader? Do you discuss any potential sources of error? Are comparisons drawn with colleagues' experiences or with findings reported in the research literature? Is the study more generative (inviting the reader to reflect on his or her own practice) or more definitive (presenting results as final and unquestioned)?

When writing a research study, we all hope to be able to present clear-cut results, and in trying out action strategies, we hope to be able to report success. These expectations are shared by teacher-researchers and academic researchers alike. Teachers often feel under pressure to take action and be successful – especially if they are involved in innovations. This may sometimes mean there is an even stronger tendency for them to want to come up with definite findings and demonstrate success than for researchers who enter the situation from outside.

There is a real danger of cheating oneself and others by definitive success stories. Reporting research knowledge *does* serve to increase a teacher's personal profile and that of the teaching profession; however this should not be its primary and dominant function. The main aim of writing reports of action research should be to enable more reflection on teaching and in so doing to improve professional practice. For this purpose, discrepancies in the data, contradictions and inconclusive ideas have their value in reports. They provide much better starting points for both the writer's and the reader's further learning than clear-cut success stories. (see Chapter 3, p. 33)

Is the context of the research made clear?

Are the specific characteristics of the situation and the research context put forward? Are your judgements of the conditions and likely validity of your insights presented? Are your own preconceptions made clear?

Action research findings are not directly transferable to other situations. They can only have the status of hypotheses, which may serve to stimulate thinking about other situations. (See Stenhouse's (1985: 42) telling phrase: 'Using research means doing research'. To be able to reflect on other people's experiences in his or her own context, the reader must have an understanding of both the general context and specific features of the case described.

Is the text written in a way that is understandable, vivid and interesting?

Do the linguistic and formal characteristics of the text make reading enjoyable or does the reader have to fight his or her way through the text? Does it arouse emotions? (see point (14) on p. 199). Are there striking and interesting passages? Are examples and metaphors used (see M29)? Are stimulating ideas put forward? Unfortunately, too many authors write their research reports in a boring and long-winded manner. When writing action research reports for an audience of other teachers, it is important to take the trouble to make them readable and linguistically attractive.

Is the report ethically defensible?

Did you negotiate with all those concerned what would be put into the report and tell them that you intended to publish it? Was their feedback incorporated in the report? Have you respected the confidential nature of some of the information? We have already addressed ethical issues in Chapter 5 (p. 77). They are part of the whole research process but are of special importance when it comes to producing written reports of the insights gained through the research.

Does the presentation include analyses or is it primarily descriptive?

Is there interpretation and explanation of the events as well as description? Are links established between points? Does the report draw conclusions for subsequent action and provide open questions for further investigation?

There is a tendency, especially the first time you write a report, to offer very few analytical points and interpretations in order to reduce the risk of getting it wrong. We want to challenge this view. The main aim of action research is to gain a better understanding of professional practice and this is not possible without developing specific explanations and practical theories. You should take the risk of giving interpretations and of drawing conclusions if they appear to be plausible and relevant for developing new strategies. Luckily, the risk of being wrong often goes with the opportunity to learn something new.

FURTHER IDEAS ABOUT WRITING

Why is writing so difficult?

Two further constraints on teachers researching were, firstly, the difficulties of writing about one's own practice, and secondly, the reservations that teachers have about whether they have anything worthwhile to say. Many teachers have not written at length since college days and need reassurance about their ability. Teachers seem to be very sceptical of their colleagues' ability to say things of importance about the profession.

(Wakeman 1986b: 90)

Teachers who have found the process of research well worth the effort often shy away from writing about the experience because they cannot see much sense in it. We want to put forward some possible reasons for the resistance to writing which we all experience, and use these as a starting point for putting forward some arguments in favour of writing as an important part of action research.

1   Writing is difficult. It is often hard to put ideas down on paper, even if they seemed clear and logical when thinking or talking about them beforehand. There are gaps in your argument and you find that some concepts are too vague, as new connections and implications come to mind. These difficulties spring from the fact that writing is not just about communicating the definitive outcomes of analysis but is in itself a form of analysis. It is a continuation of the process of analysis under narrower constraints, because our inner thoughts have to be given shape and form. Although we may see them as provisional, they become our 'product' in a material sense, and can be examined by other people. These very difficulties are a symptom of the fact that writing offers a new kind of depth to our reflection and research.

2   As the above quotation from Wakeman makes clear, the sense of alienation which many teacher-researchers experience in relation to writing is an expression of the low esteem in which they hold their own practical knowledge, and a symptom of low individual and collective professional self-confidence. Many of us believe that our everyday experiences and the knowledge acquired from practice cannot be useful to anybody except ourselves. Teachers are often pleasantly surprised when their work arouses the interest of other teachers in action research projects or at conferences. Action research places a premium upon the dissemination of teacher knowledge – including written reports – because one of the aims of the movement is to strengthen the professional self-confidence of teachers. The aim is to

prevent teacher education, and research into teaching, from being completely surrendered to experts who are external to the field.

3 Teachers' difficulties with writing are also, in part, a result of the fact that – surprising as it may seem – they do not need to write at any length in the course of their professional work, and therefore have no chance to practise it. In terms of their career, it is irrelevant whether or not teachers investigate their teaching and/or publish written reports about it. Furthermore, their work does not usually allow the space or time to reflect deeply on their experience and write about it. Staffrooms are often more like distracting waiting rooms than places for concentrated work. Stenhouse (1975) and Schön (1983) suggest that the ability to reflect upon and develop practice, and to present this for public scrutiny, is what distinguishes a professional. If they are right, teachers' organisations should strive to ensure that these professional qualities are taken into account in training and promotion, and that suitable working conditions are provided to promote them (for example, by creating time for reflection and opportunities for debate with colleagues during the working day). Action research projects try to provide teachers with a better context for reflection (for example, by establishing small groups to discuss experiences, providing the guidance and facilitation of 'critical friends', and suggesting practical research methods).

4 Part of teachers' antipathy to writing may spring from their perception that it is the traditional form of academic communication, but not the most meaningful method of disseminating knowledge within the profession. We agree with this to some extent, but believe that teacher-researchers should master this form of communication until better alternatives are found.

All of this suggests that it is important to develop better writing skills and find ways of simplifying the difficult job of writing.

An introduction to writing

If there is time available in projects or (in-service) courses, the following questions and exercises can provide a good starting point:

M38 WHAT DOES WRITING MEAN TO YOU?

1 *Individual work (15 minutes):* Each person writes a short piece covering the following questions:

- From all the written texts you have ever produced, which piece are you most proud of? Why?

- What was your last piece of writing? What kind of writing have you done most often during the past year?
- What causes you problems in writing? What is fun?
- On the basis of your answers so far, try to respond to the following question, if possible in a single sentence: What does writing mean to you?

2 *Pair work (20 minutes):* Partners exchange their writing, read each other's, and discuss any differences, similarities or surprises.
3 *Plenary (20–30 minutes):* Anything interesting or controversial which emerged in the pair work is reported to the group. At this stage it usually becomes clear that in one way or another everybody has to cope with writing difficulties. It can be helpful if the facilitator (course tutor) joins in by presenting his or her own experiences and difficulties with writing.

M39 LEARNING TO BE FLEXIBLE IN WRITING

Many writers experience the block of not being able to give up 'dead ends'. The following exercise (based on an idea of Gibbs (n.d.): 54) can produce the right mental state for flexibility by showing from experience that there is always more than one way to describe something.

1 *Individual work:* Participants are asked to write a description of an event which is part of the shared experience of the group. (An alternative is to watch a short extract from a video together and then describe it individually.)
2 After about 10 minutes, the facilitator interrupts this work and asks the participants to write a second description of the same event but in a completely different style.
3 *Pair work:* Partners exchange their writing, read each other's and discuss the differences in their approach.
4 *Plenary:* Partners report back on this experience in a plenary session and the group as a whole discusses whether it is possible to identify typical strategies.

You might also like to look again at M3, which can be a useful exercise to help develop facility in writing.

ASSORTED TOOL-BOX FOR PRODUCING WRITTEN REPORTS

If you are writing a report of your research and its outcomes, the following may prove helpful.

1 Take it step by step

Try not to think of the writing task as a huge enterprise, in the future, but as a continuous process, to be built up step by step. You have already taken the first steps: the records in your research diary, the data summaries, analytical memos, hypotheses, etc.

2 Don't aim for immediate perfection

Don't expect to produce a finished manuscript straight off, ready to be printed. Give yourself the right to begin by producing a draft which you will be able to revise later. This attitude helps to reduce the stress when writing.

3 Try to get feedback

Whenever it is possible, give your draft writing to a critical friend (perhaps a colleague) and ask him or her to read it and comment on it. This feedback may be more relevant if you suggest some questions to guide the comments. When you are given feedback it is best not to defend yourself or to correct 'wrong interpretations' (after all, you may not have written what you intended to say!). Try instead to get as much as possible out of your critical friend. Then spend an hour or so quietly reflecting on it and deciding which points you can use to develop your document and generally improve your writing. Most people find it stressful at first receiving comments on writing (probably because writing is such a personal process) but it is ultimately very reassuring to go through this stage before publishing a report more widely.

4 Getting the right conditions

A relaxed atmosphere and a place where you cannot easily be disturbed provide the best context for developing your ideas and expressing them on paper. For many people who can type, a word processor also helps to produce the right conditions for writing. At the end of some action research projects, a writing weekend is scheduled, to provide time and quiet in a pleasant atmosphere for writing and consulting with colleagues and external facilitators (see Pickover 1986: 32).

5 Resources and materials

Before you begin to write, all the resources and materials you may need should be laid out near where you intend to work, especially:

- all the data which you have collected, such as diary, observation notes, analytic memos, lists of action strategies, diagrams and quotations, etc.;
- apparently obvious things such as paper, correcting fluid, scissors and glue (if you want to cut and glue sections of data into your manuscript, it's best to photocopy the original so that you can still go back to it in its original form), and, if you are using a word processor, computer discs (including a spare for a backup), printer paper, etc.;
- books and other resources that you may need to refer to (for example, a dictionary, a relevant policy document or report, the case study a colleague has written on the same issue, a book that has been important in your thinking during the research).

6 The 'backbone' of the writing

Before you put a word on paper, it is important to think about the shape of your argument and how this shape can best be expressed in the structure of your written report. For this purpose, it is useful to think about the 'starting point' of your research and to reread your data analysis. It is often helpful to make a plan or diagram of your argument: Which are the main points and what will be the best order in which to present them? The 'Clusters' exercises outlined in M3 can help you to start.

Above all, the purpose of this preparatory work is to get a mental vision of the thread of the argument which will form the backbone of the writing, and which the reader will be able to follow (you hope with enjoyment). What form the backbone of the writing takes will depend on the theme of your study, your chosen form of presentation, and the nature of the results. It might be a chronology of events, a step-by-step exploration of an intriguing issue, or a telling metaphor used to establish connections between different areas, etc.

7 The introduction

The introduction to a written report should tune the reader into the text and prepare him or her for what is to follow. The following suggestions may prove helpful:

- What question will be investigated in the report? (It may also be useful to limit the scope by saying which aspects of the question will *not* be dealt with.)

- What was the context of the study? What background information is needed to understand it? What research methods did you use?
- Why is this question important to you? What importance might it have for other teachers?
- What will be the structure of the report?

When planning the report, you should try to give yourself provisional answers to these questions. However, some of the answers will change or develop during the process of writing. Therefore it is probably best:

- to jot down a few catchwords for the introduction while working on the plan of the report and make a note of other ideas while writing the report, and
- to write the introduction after the report is finished.

8 The conclusion

If you want to be nice to your reader, spend time on the final part of the report, because it summarises the main arguments. The conclusion is an opportunity for you, as the author, to emphasise once again the points that you believe to be important.

The following should help in deciding what to include in the summary:

- What were the main findings of the study?
- What ideas for practical action emerged? Which of them were tried out and with what success?
- Which questions remained unanswered or arose as a result of the study?
- In what larger context could the issue(s) discussed be subsumed?

9 Defining central concepts

Most written reports contain a limited number of central concepts, which appear prominently in hypotheses, working theories and diagrams and which recur throughout the report. In working on an action research project, you will have pursued an issue for a long time and become very familiar with its central concepts. They are likely to have a very specific meaning which will be clear to you but not necessarily to the reader. It is therefore well worth the effort to decide which of these central concepts need to be explicitly defined. Diagrams are sometimes useful to illustrate the relationship between different concepts.

10 Substantiating arguments with data

As a teacher-researcher, when you come to the end of the action research process, you can look back to a large number of experiences and a quantity of data which assisted you in developing insights. When you write the report, these experiences and data should be used again and again to provide evidence for your main arguments and to illustrate them – by literal quotation, paraphrasing them, or referring to them.

Sometimes teacher-researchers use quotations from their data in the written report without noting their source. It appears from talking to them that this is not so much the result of carelessness as a failure to recognise that their data are important. This is unhelpful modesty because it is important to reference quotations properly to the data. An easy way of cross-referencing your report to the data is to list the data in an annex, or as a table in a section on research methods, and give each item an abbreviated code and number which can then be used in references. You can see how we use the code reference INT/S in quoting from an interview transcript in Chapter 6 (p. 143).

11 Procedures for quotations and references

When writing a report, you will refer to your own data, and sometimes also to other people's ideas taken from published books and papers: quoting is an established tradition. Quotations must be formally referenced to allow readers to cross-check with data and to follow up ideas in the literature. The reference can also be helpful for you, as author, if you need to go back to an original source to make corrections or wish to refer to it again in a subsequent report.

There are several different traditions for setting out quotations and referencing them to their source. What is important is that

- the method used is consistent throughout the report;
- the source can be quickly identified by the reader without having to use detective skills.

12 Unrecorded data

While writing the report, ideas and experiences sometimes come to mind which support or modify the argument, but which are not available as recorded data. It is useful to 'quote' these kinds of experiences, by describing the event which produced the idea, for example: 'This assumption is not borne out by my experience in a role play with class 1c, when the following happened . . . '

13 Techniques for providing structure

The inner structure of the writer's ideas, the logic and thread of the argument, should be clear in the design and presentation of the text. Here are some ideas:

Using linguistic patterns which imply structure

- on the one hand . . . on the other hand . . .
- both . . . and . . .
- at first . . . then . . . finally . . .
- first . . . second . . . third . . .

Highlighting passages

- underline
- capitalise
- italicise
- use bold type
- use large type

Employing structuring devices

- divide into paragraphs
- indent to show new paragraphs or quotations
- use single- and double-line spacing (e.g. present quotations from data in single-spacing and the rest of the text in double-spacing).
- use subheadings
- use stars, bullets, numbered points, etc.

Including passages of text that indicate the structure of the argument

- introductions that introduce the reader to the flow of the argument and provide necessary background information:
- passages that summarise the most significant points so far (either at the end of a section or as a conclusion to the whole piece);
- explicit transitions from point to point (e.g. 'Now I come to my third point');
- diagrams showing the structure of particular arguments or concepts.

14 Giving examples

Examples drawn from personal experience are particularly important in writing that is addressed to an audience of teachers. In everyday conversation, we use examples if we are not able to explain something on a more abstract level. When we sense that we are not being understood, we take a step back, so to speak, and draw on a concrete example (see M12).

Doyle and Ponder (1976) put forward the notion of teachers as 'pragmatic sceptics' who judge new ideas and proposals for change first on the basis of a 'practicality ethic'. Elliott stresses that this should be taken into account when presenting teachers with educational innovations:

If change proposals are to stand a chance of getting implemented under normal conditions of decision-making in schools they should:

1 Specify concrete procedures for accomplishing change.
2 Provide examples of how these procedures might be implemented in typical classroom environments.
3 Specify ways in which procedures can be legitimately adapted and modified by teachers in the light of their own assessments of particular situations.
4 Provide examples of the sort of benefits teachers can expect in return for the effort they are expected to put into the implementation process.

(Elliott 1984b: 159)

This does not mean that teachers have no interest in the ethical and theoretical justifications for teaching strategies. It simply means that new ideas must show themselves to be practicable, before they are given detailed consideration. It follows that it is important to include examples in written reports, to illustrate the practicability of educational theories and their likely consequences.

M40   FROM INTERVIEW TO TEXTUAL COLLAGE

If you are finding it very difficult to start writing a case study, this idea may prove helpful (modified after Prideaux and Bannister (n.d.)):

1 Ask a colleague or a critical friend to interview you about your research and tape-record the interview. It is often easier to talk about experiences than to write them down, especially if your partner shows interest and prompts you with requests for detailed descriptions and explanations.
2 Transcribe the interview or parts of it (see M21).
3 Mark those passages that contain important statements referring to your research question, the research situation and its context, or your methodology. Cut these passages out, spread them on the floor, and try to arrange them in a sensible sequence.
4 Construct the case study from these passages. In some places it will be necessary to write intermediate passages to link the quotations from the interview. Such intermediate texts are generally much easier to write than the main text.

Chapter 9

Behind the scenes:

a theoretical foundation for action research

At the end of this book, which is filled with practical examples of action research and suggested methods for carrying it out, we invite you to have a look at the theoretical backstage of this approach to research.

Action research is primarily concerned with change, being grounded in the idea that development and innovation are an essential part of professional practice. At the heart of teaching lies the complexity of social interactions (usually involving large groups), in which there is always opportunity for improvement. In this context, the natural tendency of human beings to reduce complexity by establishing routine practices has the advantage of freeing us to handle a large number of decisions and actions at the same time, but inhibits our ability to understand our own motivation and the consequences of our practice. Action research rejects the idea that changes and improvements are needed because there is some deficiency or failure on the part of teachers, and sees change instead as an inevitable and important part of being a professional. Moreover, as Lawrence Stenhouse recognised (1975), curriculum development has little chance of success unless it involves teachers in exploring the implications of the changes for their own educational values, and finding out how to make any necessary alterations to the routines of their practice. This approach to change presupposes a reflective view of professionalism, which is very different from the commonly held, technical rational view.

Technical rationality, as a way of conceptualising political and administrative intervention in educational systems, follows these three basic assumptions (Schön, 1983):

- There are general solutions to practical problems.
- These solutions can be developed outside practical situations (in research or administrative centres).
- The solutions can be translated into teachers' actions by means of publications, training, administrative orders, etc.

Technical rationality is operationalised in the classical Research–Development–Dissemination (RDD) model of innovation. Researchers produce the theoretical background for an educational innovation. In the development phase, the theoretical framework is applied to solve a practical problem in general terms. The result is a product for a specific group of consumers (a curriculum, teaching and learning materials, etc.). It is tested, and directions for use are developed. The product is then disseminated to teachers. Strategies are applied to reach, train, and stimulate or pressurise them to accept the innovation and use it in a prescribed way (information booklets, training courses, administrative incentives and pressures, etc.).

The result is a hierarchy of credibility. It implies that a person is the more credible, the higher (s)he is in the institutional power structure, i.e. the closer (s)he is to those who develop theories and make policy. The teacher is considered more credible than the pupils, the head of department more credible than the teacher, the principal more credible than the head of department, etc. This hierarchy of credibility expresses a genuine mistrust of practitioners. Within the conceptual framework of technical rationality, they are working on a low level of theoretical knowledge and are merely applying what has been predefined in the academic and administrative power-structure above them. Improvements of school practice are in this view primarily a result of improved general and applied theories and norms transmitted to the teacher (and of incentives and control mechanisms used to ensure their correct application).

Reflective rationality, in contrast, follows these three very different assumptions:

- Complex practical problems demand specific solutions.
- These solutions can be developed only inside the context in which the problem arises and in which the practitioner is a crucial and determining element
- The solutions cannot be successfully applied to other contexts but they can be made accessible to other practitioners as hypotheses to be tested.

These assumptions are the basis of the action research, or teacher as researcher, movement. They are in line with the concept of professionality which was succinctly described by Lawrence Stenhouse as:

> A capacity for autonomous professional self-development through systematic self-study, through the study of the work of other teachers and through the testing of ideas by classroom research procedures.
>
> (Stenhouse 1975: 144)

They imply the development of new types of communication among teachers – dynamic networks of relationships to assist them in taking responsible action in the face of complexity and uncertainty. This kind of collaboration implies exchange processes among teachers or between teachers and other groups in which there is a symmetry, rather than a hierarchy of power; it is often teacher initiated and not bound to any prespecified procedures.

Reflective rationality depends upon the development of a more dynamic learning culture, based on the understanding that local initiatives exist already, and that their growth process should be supported rather than being ruptured and thwarted by imposed change. If specific innovations are forced upon schools, this tends to reduce their coping power and problem-solving capacity and to increase their dependence – because their existing potential for innovation is not encouraged but ignored and thus, in the long run, damaged.

This concept of reflective rationality is supported even by the findings of Peters and Waterman (1982), who studied the principles underlying some of the most successful American commercial enterprises. They found the following characteristics:

- Problems are defined and tackled co-operatively. Contributions to problem definition are valued even more highly than contributions to problem solution.
- Control comes after the event. The expectation is: 'Try it and we'll see' and not: 'Ask for permission before you do anything'.
- Customer satisfaction is valued highly – employees are encouraged to listen to customers and get to know their needs.
- To try is the essential thing. Employees are expected to take risks. Failure is seen as part of the learning process.
- Informal networking in small teams is highly valued and seen as an important stimulus for the spread of ideas.
- The management assumes that people have an interest in doing a good job and trusts them.
- Achievements are rewarded in various non-spectacular ways. It is assumed that people need to feel successful if they are to work well.

To understand professional change in terms of reflective rationality, we need an adequate description of complex professional action. Donald Schön's (1983) account of 'reflective practice' is based on an analysis of practice in a number of different professions. He formulates different relationships between professional knowledge and professional action. We want now to discuss these with respect to the principles of action research.

ACTION TYPE 1: TACIT KNOWING-IN-ACTION

When professional practice flows smoothly and appears simple to an onlooker, action is based on 'tacit knowing-in-action'. This type of professional action has these characteristics:

- thinking and acting are not separate (skilful, practical activities take place without being planned and prepared intellectually in advance);
- the professional is frequently unaware of the sources of his or her practical knowledge or how it was learnt;
- the professional will usually not be able to give a straightforward verbal description of this practical knowledge.

Nevertheless, these actions could not have resulted without knowledge. Their skilfulness, their situational appropriateness and their flexibility indicate a knowledge base which is 'tacit' for the time being: we know more than we can tell.

The most important example of tacit knowing-in-action are 'routines'. Routines are actions or mind-sets' which have been built up through frequent repetition; which are carried out comparatively quickly; and which are executed largely unconsciously. Routines in education have frequently been considered inferior to conscious, planned and creative actions. It has been suggested that we should increase the proportion of the latter and reduce our reliance on routine. This view is certainly too simple because routines also have positive effects. They contribute a certain stability to teaching which gives pupils the chance to anticipate what's coming and to gauge their actions accordingly. Routines are also essential in allowing us to do more than one thing at a time, which is one of the typical requirements of teaching (e.g. the teacher explains something, notes overall pupil involvement, and keeps a special eye on a particularly 'difficult' pupil).

The strongest argument for a re-evaluation of the relevance of routines comes from research on expert knowledge (see Bromme 1985: 185–9), in which it was found, for example, that less successful teachers take more information into account when they decide to deviate from the lesson plan than do more successful ones. In other professional areas, 'experts' were found to need fewer words to define and solve a problem than less experienced or less successful colleagues. Bromme argues that these results may be explained by the prominent role of routines in 'expert action'. Routines do not indicate 'lack of knowledge but rather a specific quality of knowledge organisation . . . a condensation of task related knowledge . . . which embraces concepts for problem perception, information on the conditions of problem solution and steps of problem solution.'

We assume that tacit knowing-in-action cannot sensibly be excluded from the concept of *professional action*. Routinised flowing action drawing on implicit knowledge is the basis for competent teacher action in simple, or made-simple-by-experience, situations.

ACTION TYPE 2: REFLECTION-IN-ACTION

However, whenever new and complex situations have to be dealt with, or disturbances and problems disrupt the smooth flow of routinised action, another type of action is additionally necessary: reflection-in-action.

> When someone reflects-in-action, he becomes a researcher in the practice context. He is not dependent on the categories of established theory and technique, but constructs a new theory of the unique case. His inquiry is not limited to a deliberation about means which depends on a prior agreement about ends. He does not keep means and ends separate, but defines them interactively as he frames a problematic situation. He does not separate thinking from doing, ratiocinating his way to a decision which he must later convert to action. Because his experimenting is a kind of action, implementation is built into his inquiry.
>
> (Schön 1983: 68f.)

This 'research in the practice context' need not be translated into words: it may take place in the course of action in an unverbalised form, in graphical form as sketches on notepads, or partly verbalised in a process of 'demonstration, imitation, comment, and joint experimentation' which is frequently used in the training of practical competencies (Schön 1987). Reflection-in-action resembles, as Schön says, a 'reflective conversation with the situation'.

The notion of reflection-in-action is compatible with the findings of some research on problem-solving in complex situations. For example, Dörner (1983) summarises his findings by sketching two main competencies which individuals need for autonomous orientation in complex environments:

- the competency for 'self-reflexive transformation of one's own thinking' (through reflection on one's own problem-solving actions, different strategies are compared and scrutinised for common elements; misleading stereotypes are eliminated);
- the 'competency to 'import' knowledge from one context to another, using analogues, to evaluate this knowledge, and to develop it on the basis of the evaluation.

ACTION TYPE 3: REFLECTION-ON-ACTION

To summarise: 'tacit knowing-in-action' draws on accumulated practical knowledge under simple or routine circumstances. 'Reflection-in-action' begins whenever practitioners find themselves in more complex situations that cannot be coped with by routine: such reflection occurs within action; it is not at all rare and need not be verbalised to be useful in problem-solving (see Argyris and Schön 1974: 14). The third action type, reflection-on-action, is an important feature of professional action: it occurs when it is necessary to formulate knowledge explicitly and verbally, to distance ourselves from action for some time and to reflect *on* it:

- It improves our ability to analyse and reorganise knowledge: consciously reflecting on action slows it down and disturbs our smoothly running routines, but, it also facilitates careful analysis and allows us to plan changes (see Cranach 1983: 71);
- It makes knowledge communicable: the knowledge underlying professional action can be made visible and communicated to others, such as colleagues, clients and interest groups.

In reflection-on-action, reflection distances itself from the flow of activities, interrupts it, and concentrates upon data that represent the action in an *objectified* form. This ability is a constituent part of professional competency because it is the basis for fulfilling three requirements placed on today's professionals:

- We have to cope constructively with serious problems or complex new situations. By distancing ourselves from the flow of activities, we have a better chance of dealing with the problems that entangle us; redefining them and reorganising our response. For example, when we understand that there is some discrepancy between our expectations and what has actually happened, it is possible to become aware of the 'tacit knowledge' embedded in our routine actions, to search consciously for mistaken assumptions, and to reformulate our thinking. Many exercises included in this book aim at activating this 'tacit knowledge' (see Chapter 4, p. 48, in particular).
- We need to take responsibility for the education and induction of novices into the profession and for passing on professional experience to the next generation. To do this, we need to express in a verbal and organised way the knowledge underlying our practice.
- We must be able to communicate our knowledge and our professional action to colleagues and clients (pupils, parents and others), putting forward rational arguments for them and inviting critical discussion. This too requires the ability to put our professional knowledge into words. To sum up, professionals need to be competent in all three action types. Our professional action builds on reflection-in-action. To be efficient in the run-of-the-mill situations of everyday practice, we have to rely on routines. To cope with difficult and complex problems, take control of our practice so that we can change it if we so wish, and fulfil our responsibilities to society, we have to involve reflection-on-action.

THE IMPORTANCE OF TEACHERS' ACTION RESEARCH

Action research is based on the theory of reflective rationality and sees the construction of (research) knowledge as integral with the development of action. In this sense, we can understand the process of action research in terms of Schön's analysis of the relationship between professional knowledge and professional action outlined in the previous section.

The close connections between reflective and operative elements of action are shown in the circle of reflection and action (see Figure 13). Through reflecting on our own action, the underlying practical theory may be revealed and developed. Elliott (1985: 240) uses the term 'practical theory' to denote the knowledge base practitioners use for concrete practical actions.

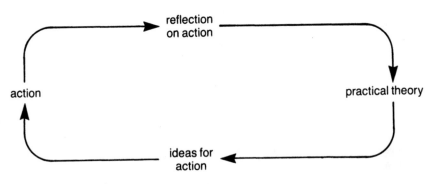

Figure 13 The circle of action and reflection

Action research makes an important contribution to:

1 the professional development of individual teachers who improve their practical theories and competence in action through reflection and action;
2 curriculum development and improvements in the practical situation under research by developing the quality of teaching and learning through new and successful action strategies;
3 the collective development of the profession by means of opening up individual practice to scrutiny and discussion and thus broadening the knowledge base of the profession;
4 the advancement of educational research.

Action research is not merely a practical model for the professional development of practitioners; it also makes an essential contribution to the further development of educational theory (see Elliott 1991: Ch. 4). It democratises research by bringing those who are usually 'subjects' of research to a position where they have equal rights and responsibilities. In so doing, it ensures the practical relevance of educational theory, overcoming one of the most fundamental problems of traditional educational research: that it progresses too quickly to abstract categories, whose relevance cannot be understood by practitioners and which, in any case, may be short-lived in the ever-changing context of practical action.

Teachers, of course, have a disadvantage as researchers in that they cannot dedicate very much time, energy and money to elaborate research designs and methods. However, teacher-researchers also have an important advantage. All forms of educational research rely upon testing ideas in practice as a means of establishing their validity. Traditionally, this takes place as a separate step, and although this has some advantages, it has the disadvantage of discontinuity and is often carried out in a relatively limited way – or not at all.

In teachers' action research, there is no separation between stages of knowledge construction (reflection) and testing (action). Reflection takes place partly *in* action, and even reflection-on-action is not limited to particular research stages. Practitioners give their research findings a practical form in action strategies, which have to stand the test of adequacy in the everyday conditions of the classroom. If they find new discrepancies between their expectations (derived from their practical theories) and what actually happens, this will be a starting point for another cycle of development of their theories and practice. In this sense, a practitioner's practice tests the validity of his or her previous research. Although it may be less focused, this test is more continuous and more long term than is possible in other forms of research. Action researchers continuously examine the expected and unexpected consequences of their action.

The rigour of action research is that practitioner-researchers must live with the mistakes of their theorising, feeling them in a very existential way as the situation 'talks back'. This is not a simple process. The results of reflection are continuously transformed into practice, and practice continuously throws up reasons for reflection and development of these practical theories. The term for this characteristic feature of action research is *reflexivity*. Through constant movement between action and reflection (in the 'circle of action and reflection,' see Figure 13), weaknesses in the practical theories are gradually detected and useful action strategies are explored and extended. Through reflexivity, the reflective practitioner's action gains quality and the research process is rigorously tested.

We too must live with the consequences of our theorising. The practical exercises in this book have been developed and tested in practice, and, through a reflexive process over a number of years, we have shaped and reshaped the ideas about action research which it contains. But the book itself needs to be developed and tested by the thinking and actions of its readers.

This is what the reader will be reading last, closing the book and leaning back in a chair. What impressions will linger in the mind? What ideas will come after the book is finished? These are the wistful thoughts of the authors sitting in front of the last pages of their manuscript. There cannot be a definitive statement on action research, because it must always be context-specific and responsive to the values and practices of the participants in the situation. This is as far as the authors were able to go in presenting a method of research which, for them, has spilled over into being a way of life. The book is not finished. There is an important chapter still to be written by you, the reader – on extending and redefining your own practice and, through this means, further developing educational theory.

References

All those items marked * contain accounts of action research undertaken by teachers.

Adelman, C. (1980) 'Self-Evaluation', pp. 88–91 in J. Elliott and D. Whitehead (eds) *The Theory and Practice of Educational Action Research. CARN-Bulletin*, no. 4, Cambridge: Cambridge Institute of Education.

* Altrichter, H. (1984) 'Pausen – Eine hochschuldidaktische "Entdekung"', *Zeitschrift für Hochschuldidaktik*, 8, 4: 527–38.

* —— (1985): 'Lehrerfortbildung durch Erforschung eigenen Unterrichts: Das Beispiel eines "Action Research"-Prozesses', pp. 170–7 in F. Buchberger and H. Seel (eds) *Lehrerbildung für die Schulreform – Österreichische Beiträge*, Brüssel/Linz: ATEE.

—— (1986a) 'Visiting two worlds: an excursion into the methodological jungle including an optional evening's entertainment at the Rigour Club', *Cambridge Journal of Education* 16, 2: 131–43.

* —— (1986b) 'Professional development in higher education by means of action-research into one's own teaching', in P. Holly and D. Whitehead (eds) *Collaborative Action Research. CARN-Bulletin*, no. 7, pp. 73–85, Cambridge: Cambridge Institute of Education.

—— (1986c) 'The Austrian INSET-Project "PFL": establishing a framework for self-directed learning', *British Journal of In-Service Education* 12, 3: 170–7.

—— (1988) 'Enquiry-based Learning in Initial Teacher Education', pp. 121–34, in J. Nias and S. Groundwater-Smith (eds) *The Enquiring Teacher: Supporting and Sustaining Teacher Research*, Lewes: Falmer Press.

—— (1990) *Ist das noch Wissenschaft? Darstellung und wissenschaftstheoretische Diskussion einer von Lehrern betriebenen Aktionsforschung*, München: Profil.

—— (1991) 'Do we need an alternative methodology for doing alternative research? Recollections of a summer day at the Victorian coast as giving rise to some deliberations concerning the methodology of action research and the unity of science (Neuauflage von 78)', pp 79–92 in O. Zuber-Skerritt (ed.) *Action Research for Change and Development*, Aldershot / Brookfield: Avebury.

Altrichter, H. and Gstettner, P. (1992) 'Action research: A closed chapter in the history of German social science?' in R. McTaggart (ed.) *Action Research: Contexts and Consequences*, London: Falmer Press.

Altrichter, H., Kemmis, S., McTaggart, R. and Zuber-Skerritt, O. (1991) 'Defining, confining or refining action research?' pp. 3–9 in O. Zuber-Skerritt (ed.) *Action Research for Change and Development*, Aldershot/Brookfield: Avebury.

* Altrichter, H., Wilhelmer, H., Sorger, H. and Morocutti, I. (eds) (1989) *Schule*

gestalten: Lehrer als Forscher. Fallstudien aus dem Projekt 'Forschendes Lernen in der Lehrerausbildung', Klagenfurt: Hermagoras.

Argyris, C. (1972) 'Unerwartete Folgen "strenger" Forschung', *Gruppendynamik* 3, 1: 5–22.

Argyris, C. and Schön, D.A. (1974) *Theory in Practice: Increasing Professional Effectiveness*, San Francisco: Jossey-Bass.

Argyris, C., Putnam, R. and McLain Smith, D. (1985) *Action Science. Concepts, Methods, and Skills for Research and Intervention*, San Francisco: Jossey-Bass.

* Armstrong, Michael (1980) *Closely Observed Children*, London: Writers and Readers in association with Chameleon.

* Baker, P. , Cook, L. and Repper, J. (1986) 'From self-evaluation to staff development: beginnings', pp. 252–65 in P. Holly and D. Whitehead (eds) *Collaborative Action Research. CARN-Bulletin*, no. 7, Cambridge: Cambridge Institute of Education.

* Bergk, M. (1987) 'Lernen aus Pausen für den Unterricht', in O. Ludwig, B. Priebe and R.Winkel (eds) *Jahresheft V 'Unterrichtsstörungen'*, Friedrich: Seelze (zit. nach dem Ms.).

Berlak, A. and Berlak, H. (1981) *Dilemmas of Schooling. Teaching and Social Change*, London: Methuen.

* Biott, C. and Storey, J. (eds) (1986) *The Inside Story. Initiating and Sustaining Action Research in Schools with External Support*, Cambridge: Cambridge Institute of Education.

Bogdan, R.C. and Biklen, S.K. (1982) *Qualitative Research for Education*, Boston: Allwyn and Bacon.

Brecht, B. (1977) *Me-ti*, Buch der Wendungen. Frankfurt/M: Suhrkamp.

Brennan, M. (1982) *Using Files*, mimeo, Victoria: Education Department.

Bromme, R. (1985) 'Was sind Routinen im Lehrerhandeln?' in *Unterrichtswissenschaft*, 2: 182–92.

Brown, L., Henry, C., Henry, J.A. and McTaggart, R. (1982) 'Action research: notes on the national seminar', pp. 1–16 in J. Elliott and D. Whitehead, *Action-Research for Professional Development and the Improvement of Schooling*, *CARN-Bulletin*, no. 5. Cambridge: Cambridge Institute of Education

Burgess, R.G. (1981) 'Keeping a research diary', *Cambridge Journal of Education* 11, 1: 75–83.

Canetti, E. (1981) 'Dialog mit dem grausamen Partner' pp. 54–71 in: *ders.: Das Gewissen der Worte*, Frankfurt/M: Fischer.

Carr, W. and Kemmis, S. (1986) *Becoming Critical: knowing through action research*, London: Falmer.

Cranach, M.V. (1983) 'Gber die bewußte Representation handlungsbezogener Kog- nitionen', pp. 64–76 in: L. Montada (ed.) *Kognition und Handeln*, Stuttgart: Klett-Cotta.

Cressey, P.G. (1932) *The Taxi-Dance Hall: a Sociological Study in Commercial Recreation and City Life*, Chicago: Univ. of Chicago Press.

Cronbach, L.J. (1975) 'Beyond the two disciplines of scientific psychology', *American Psychologist* 30: 116–27.

Dadds, M. (1985) 'What is action research?' Paper given during the Workshop 'Schulentwicklung an der Basis' at Klagenfurt University, Austria, 16–20 December.

Day, C. (1984a) 'Teachers' thinking – intentions and practice: An action research perspective' pp. 73–84 in R. Halkes and J.Olson (eds): *Teacher Thinking*, Lisse: Swets & Zeitlinger.

* Day, C. (1984b) 'Sharing practice through consultancy: individual and whole school staff development in a primary school', mimeo, University of Nottingham.

DeCharms, R. (1973) 'Ein schulisches Trainingsprogramm zum Erleben eigener Verursachung', pp. 60–78 in W. Edelstein and C. Hopf (eds) *Bedingungen des Bildungsprozesses*, Stuttgart: Klett.

Delbecq, A.L., Van De Ven, A.H. and Gustafson, D.H. (1975) *Group Techniques for Program Planning: a guide to nominal and delphi processes*, Glenview, Ill.: Scott, Foresman.

Developing Teaching: Focus on Teaching (1984): INSET pack. Edinburgh: Moray House College of Education.

DeVore, I. (1970) *Selections from Field Notes*, 1959 March–August. Washington, DC: Curriculum Development Associates.

Dörner, D. (1983) 'Empirische Psychologie und Alltagsrelevanz', pp. 13–29 in Jüttemann (ed.) *Psychologie in der Veränderung*, Weinheim: Beltz.

Doyle, W. (1979) 'Classroom tasks and students' abilities', in P. L. Peterson and H.J. Walberg, *Research on Teaching: concepts, findings and implications*, National Society for the Study of Education, McCutchan, USA.

Doyle, W. and Ponder, G.A. (1976) 'The practicality ethic in teacher decision making', mimeo, Denton, Tex.: North Texas State University.

Ebbutt, D. (n.d.) 'The "Teacher–Pupil Interaction and Quality of Learning" Project (TIQL): A Portrayal', in J. Elliott and D. Ebbutt (eds) *Facilitating Action-Research*, Cambridge: Cambridge Institute of Education.

* Ebbutt, D. and Elliott, J. (eds) (1985) *Issues in Teaching for Understanding*, York: SCDC-Longman.

Elliott, J. (1976) *Developing Hypotheses about Classrooms from Teachers' Practical Constructs*, North Dakota Study Group on Evaluation-series, Grand Forks: University of North Dakota.

—— (1978) 'The self-assessment of teacher performance', pp. 18–20 in *CARN Bulletin, no. 2*, Cambridge: Cambridge Institute of Education.

—— (1981) 'Using nominal group procedures as a basis for co-operative action-research in schools', TIQL-Working Paper No. 6, Cambridge: Cambridge Institute of Education.

—— (1983) 'A curriculum for the study of human affairs: the contribution of Lawrence Stenhouse', *Journal of Curriculum Studies* 15, 2: 105–23.

—— (1984a) 'Improving the quality of teaching through action research', *Forum* 26, 3: 74–7.

—— (1984b) 'Some key concepts underlying teachers' evaluations of innovation', pp. 142–61 in P. Tamir (ed.) *The Role of Evaluators in Curriculum Development*, Beckenham: Croom Helm.

—— (1985) 'Educational action-research', pp. 231–50 in J. Nisbet *et al.* (eds) *World Yearbook of Education: Research, Policy and Practice*, London: Kogan Page.

—— (1991) *Action Research for Educational Change*, Milton Keynes and Philadelphia: Open University Press.

Elliott, J. and Adelman, C. (n.d.) *Classroom Action Research*, Ford Teaching Project, Cambridge: Cambridge Institute of Education.

* Elliott, J. and Ebbutt, D. (eds) (1986) *Case Studies in Teaching for Understanding*, Cambridge: Cambridge Institute of Education.

* Fuller, D. (1990) *Committed to Excellence: a study of child learning using desktop publishing programs*, PALM Project publications, CARE, University of East Anglia, Norwich, UK.

Gibbs, G. (n.d.) *Learning to Study: A Guide to Running Group Sessions*, Milton Keynes: Open University Press.

Glaser, B. and Strauss, A. (1967) *The Discovery of Grounded Theory*, Chicago: Aldine Publ. Co.

Glaser, R. *et al.*(1966) 'Organizations for Research and Development in Education', Proceedings of a conference sponsored by the AERA und Phi Delta Kappa: Pittsburgh.

Grell, J. and Grell, M. (1979) *Unterrichtsrezepte*, München: Urban and Schwarzenberg.

* Griffin, E. (1990) *By Hook or by Crook: putting IT into the curriculum*, PALM Publications, CARE, University of East Anglia, Norwich, UK.

Gürge, F. (1979): quoted in *Päd.Extra*, 7, 46.

Hegarty, E.H. (1977) 'The problem identification phase of curriculum deliberation', *Journal of Curriculum Studies* 9, 1: 31–41.

* Holly, M.L. (1989) *Writing to Grow: keeping a personal-professional journal*, Portsmouth, New Hampshire: Heinemann.

Hook, C. (1981) *Studying Classrooms*, Victoria, Aus: Deakin University Press.

Hron, A. (1982) Interview in G. Huber and H. Mendl (eds) *Verbale Daten*, Beltz: Weinheim, 119–40.

* Hull, C., Rudduck, J., Sigsworth, A. and Daymond, G. (eds) (1985) *A Room Full of Children Thinking*, York: SCDC/Longman.

* Hustler, D., Cassidy, A. and Cuff, E.C. (1986) *Action Research in Classrooms and Schools*, London: Allen & Unwin.

Ireland, D. and Russell, T. (1978) 'Pattern analysis', in *CARN-Bulletin* 2: 21–5, Cambridge: Cambridge Institute of Education.

Isaacs, J. (ed.) (1980): *Australian Dreaming: 40,000 Years of Aboriginal History*, Sydney: Lansdowne Press.

Jackson, P. W. (1968) *Life in Classrooms*, New York: Holt, Rinehart & Winston.

Johnson, D. (1984) 'Planning small-scale research', pp. 5–26 in J. Bell, T. Bush, A. Fox, J. Goodey and S. Golding (eds) *Conducting Small-Scale Investigations in Educational Management*, London: Harper and Row.

* Kaser, H. (1985) *Eine 'schwierige Klasse'*, mimeo, Klagenfurt University, Austria.

* Jones, C. (1986) 'Classroom research with seven to nine year-olds,' in J. Elliott and D. Ebbutt, *Case Studies in Teaching for Understanding*, Cambridge: Cambridge Institute of Education.

Kemmis, S. and McTaggart, R. (1982) *The Action Research Planner* (2nd edition), Geelong, Vic.: Deakin University Press.

Kintner, D. (1986) 'The first two activities of action research', pp. 8–11 in B. Hutchinson and P. Whitehouse, (eds) *Teacher Research and INSET*, Jordanstown: Univ. of Ulster, UK.

MacDonald, B. and Sanger, J. (1982): 'Just for the record? Notes towards a theory of interviewing in evaluation', paper given at the AERA-conference, New York.

Malinowski, B. (1982) 'The diary of an anthropologist', pp. 200–5 in R.G. Burgess (ed.) *Field Research: a Sourcebook and Field Manual*, London: George Allen and Unwin.

* Marshall, E.C. (1986) 'Problems of revision and how it enables pupils to further the understanding of what goes on in the classroom', pp. 254–73. in J.Elliott and D. Ebbutt (eds) *Case Studies in Teaching for Understanding*, Cambridge: Cambridge Institute of Education.

McCormick, R. and James, M. (1983) *Curriculum Evaluation in Schools*, London: Croom Helm.

Miles, M.B. and Huberman, A.M. (1984) *Qualitative Data Analysis*, Beverly Hills, Ca.: Sage.

Mollenhauer, K. and Rittelmeyer, Ch. (1977) *Methoden der Erziehungswissenschaft*, München: Juventa.

* Morocutti, I. (1989) 'Mündliches Arbeiten im Englischunterricht (Oder:

Zwischen Lustprinzip und feministischem Anspruch)', pp. 72–86 in H. Altrichter, H. Wilhelmer, H. Sorger and I. Morocutti (eds) *Schule gestalten: Lehrer als Forscher. Fallstudien aus dem Projekt 'Forschendes Lernen in der Lehrerausbildung'*, Klagenfurt, Austria: Hermagoras.

* Moon, V. (1990) *Making the News*, Teachers' Voices series, PALM Publications, CARE, University of East Anglia, UK.

Nuffield (1971) *Teacher's Handbook, Nuffield 'A' Level Physics*, London: Penguin.

OECD/CERI (1991) *Environment, Schools and Active Learning*, Paris: OECD/CERI.

O'Neil, M.J. and Jackson, L. (1983) 'Nominal Group Technique: A process for initiating curriculum development in higher education', *Studies in Higher Education* 8, 2: 129–38.

* Ourtilbour, B. (1991) 'Concept keyboard with bilingual, year 1 and 2 children', PALM Project unpublished working paper: CARE, University of East Anglia, Norwich, UK.

* PALM (1990) *Supporting Teacher Development Through Action Research: a 'PALM' resource for advisory teachers*, PALM Publications, CARE, University of East Anglia, Norwich, UK.

* —— (1990–1), *Teachers' Voices: a Series of 36 Case Studies*, written by teachers in the Pupil Autonomy in Learning with Microcomputers Project, CARE, University of East Anglia, Norwich, U.K.

Peters, T.J. and Waterman, R.H. (1982) *In Search of Excellence: Lessons from America's Best-Run Companies*, New York: Harper Row.

* Pickover, D. (1986) 'Working with interested partners to meet individual needs in an infants school, pp. 28–38 in C. Biott and J. Storey (eds) *The Inside Story*, Cambridge: Cambridge Institute of Education.

* Platten, D. (1986) 'Institutional self review and development', pp. 8–27 in C. Biott and J. Storey (eds) *The Inside Story*, Cambridge: Cambridge Institute of Education.

* Pols, R. (n.d.) 'The questionnaire', pp.16–19 in B. Bowen *et al.* (eds) *Ways of Doing Research in One's Own Classroom*, Ford Teaching Project, Cambridge: Cambridge Institute of Education.

Posch, P. (1985) *Beziehungen zwischen Lehrern und Schülern*, Klagenfurt, Austria: Interuniversitäres Forschungsinstitut für Fernstudien.

—— (1986b) 'University support for independent learning – a new development in the in-service education of teachers', Cambridge: *Cambridge Journal of Education* 16, 1: 46–50.

—— (1990) *The Project 'Environment and School Initiatives'*, Vienna: ARGE Umwelterziehung ESI-Series No. 10.

* Prideaux, D. and Bannister, P. (n.d.) 'What to do with my data: Reporting Action-Research', in J. Elliott and D. Ebbutt (eds) *Facilitating Action-Research in Schools*, Cambridge: Cambridge Institute of Education.

* Prymak, Andrea (1989) 'Report from a mentor teacher in Winnipeg', in B. Somekh, J. Powney and C. Burge (eds) *Collaborative Enquiry and School Improvement*, CARN Bulletin, no. 9A, CARE, University of East Anglia, UK.

Reiners, L. (1961) *Stilkunst*, München: Beck'sche Verlagsbuchhandlung.

Rico, G.L. (1984) *Garantiert schreiben lernen*, Reinbek: Rowohlt.

* Robinson, M. (1984): 'A Shadow Study', paper presented at the CARN Conference, Cambridge.

Rumpf, H. (1986) *Mit fremden Blick – Stücke gegen die Verbiederung der Welt*, Weinheim: Beltz.

Schatzman, L. and Strauss, A.L. (1973) *Field Research*, Englewood Cliffs, NJ: Prentice-Hall.

* Schindler, G. (1990) 'The conflict', *Environment and Schools Initiative (ENSI) series*, no. 6, Vienna: ARGE Umwelterisehung.

Schön, D.A. (1979) 'Generative metaphor: A perspective on problem setting in social policy', pp. 254–83 in A. Ortonyi (ed.) *Metaphor and Thought*, Cambridge: Cambridge University Press, England.

—— (1983) *The Reflective Practitioner*, London: Temple Smith.

—— (1987) *Educating the Reflective Practitioner: Toward a New Design for Teaching and Learning in the Professions*, San Francisco: Jossey-Bass.

Selvini-Palazzoli, M. et al. (1978) *Der entzauberte Magier. Zur paradoxen Situation des Schulpsychologen*, Stuttgart: Klett.

Smith, L.M. and Geoffrey, W. (1968) *The Complexities of an Urban Classroom*, New York: Holt, Rinehart and Winston.

* Somekh, B. (1980) 'An examination of pupils' use of reading material in a classroom situation', pp. 47–55 in J. Elliott and D. Whitehead (eds) *The Theory and Practice of Educational Action Research*, CARN Bulletin, no. 4, Cambridge: Cambridge Institute of Education.

* —— (1983a), 'Teaching CSE: a self-study', MA assignment, University of East Anglia, UK.

* —— (1983b) 'Triangulation methods in action: A practical example', Cambridge: *Cambridge Journal of Education* 13, 2: 31–7.

* —— (1985) 'An Enquiry into the use of Quinkeys for word processing in secondary English teaching', MA dissertation, University of East Anglia, UK.

* —— (1986) 'Teaching poetry for understanding within the constraints of the Cambridge "Plain Texts" Literature syllabus', pp. 237–53, in J. Elliott and D. Ebbutt (eds), *Case Studies in Teaching for Understanding*, Cambridge: Cambridge Institute of Education.

* —— (1987) 'The eyes of a fly', pp. 169–78 in B. Somekh, A. Norman, B. Shannon and G. Abbott *Action Research in Development*, CARN Bulletin, no. 8, Cambridge: Cambridge Institute of Education.

—— (1991a) 'Collaborative action research: working together towards professional development', in C. Biott (ed.), *Semi-detached Teachers: Building Support and Advisory Relationships in Classrooms*, London: Falmer Press.

—— (1991b) 'Pupil Autonomy in Learning with Microcomputers: rhetoric or reality? An action research study', *Cambridge Journal of Education*, 21, 1: 47–64.

—— (1992) 'The experience of innovation', paper presented at the conference of the British Educational Research Association at Stirling, 26–9 August, 1992.

Somekh, B. and Davies, R. (1991) 'Towards a pedagogy for information technology', *The Curriculum Journal*, 2, 2: 153–70.

* Sorger, H. (1989) 'Fragen im Unterricht', pp. 95–105 in H. Altrichter, H. Wilhelmer, H. Sorger and I. Morocutti (eds) *Schule gestalten: Lehrer als Forscher*, Fallstudien aus dem Projekt 'Forschendes Lernen in der Lehrerausbildung', Klagenfurt: Hermagoras.

Stenhouse, L. (1975) *An Introduction to Curriculum Research and Development*, London: Heinemann.

—— (1985) 'How teachers can use research – an example', in J. Rudduck and D. Hopkins (eds) *Research as a Basis for Teaching*, London: Heinemann. Reprinted from 'Using research means doing research', in H. Dahl et al. (eds) (1979) *Spotlight on Educational Problems: Festskrift for Johannes Sandven*, Oslo: Oslo University Press.

* Wakeman, B. (1986a) 'Action research for staff development', pp. 229–61, in C. Day and R. Moore (eds), *Secondary School Management: promoting staff development*, London: Croom Helm.

* —— (1986b) 'Jottings from a co-ordinator's journal', pp. 84–94 in C. Biott and J. Storey (eds) *The Inside Story*, Cambridge: Cambridge Institute of Education.

* Wakeman, B., Alexander, M., Bannister, P. , Nolan, E. and Aspray, S. (1985) 'The TIQL Project at Rotherham High School', in D. Ebbutt and J. Elliott, *Issues in Teaching for Understanding*, York: Longman/SCDC.

Walker, R. (1985) *Doing Research*, London: Methuen.

Walker, R. and Adelman, C. (1975) *A Guide to Classroom Observation*, London: Methuen.

Watzlawick, P. , Beavin, J. and Jackson, D.D. (1980) *Menschliche Kommunikation*, Bern: Huber.

Werder, L.V. (1986) . . . *triffst Du nur das Zauberwort. Eine Einführung in die Schreib- und Poesietherapie*, München/Weinheim: Psychologie Verlags Union/Urban & Schwarzenberg.

Whyte, W.F. (1955) *Street Corner Society*, Chicago: University of Chicago Press.

* Williams, B. (1990) *The Bury Project*, PALM Project publications, CARE, University of East Anglia, UK.

* Winter, R. (1982) '"Dilemma Analysis": A contribution to methodology for action research', *Cambridge Journal of Education*, 12, 3: 161–74.

Winter, R. (1989) *Learning from Experience*, London, New York and Philadelphia: Falmer Press.

Zamorski, B. (1987) 'Case study of an invisible child', pp. 12–22, in B. Somekh *et al.* (eds) *Action Research in Development*, CARN Bulletin, no. 8, Cambridge: Cambridge Institute of Education.

Index